Policing beyond Mac

Policing beyond Macpherson

Issues in policing, race and society

**Edited by
Michael Rowe**

WILLAN
PUBLISHING

Published by

Willan Publishing
Culmcott House
Mill Street, Uffculme
Cullompton, Devon
EX15 3AT, UK
Tel: +44(0)1884 840337
Fax: +44(0)1884 840251
e-mail: info@willanpublishing.co.uk
website: www.willanpublishing.co.uk

Published simultaneously in the USA and Canada by

Willan Publishing
c/o ISBS, 920 NE 58th Ave, Suite 300
Portland, Oregon 97213-3786, USA
Tel: +001(0)503 287 3093
Fax: +001(0)503 280 8832
e-mail: info@isbs.com
website: www.isbs.com

First published 2007

Paperback
ISBN: 978 1 84392 212 4

British Library Cataloguing-in-Publication Data

A catalogue record for this book is available from the British Library

Project management by Deer Park Productions, Tavistock, Devon
Typeset by GCS, Leighton Buzzard, Beds
Printed and bound by T.J. International, Padstow, Cornwall

Contents

Notes on contributors

Jennifer Brown is Professor of Forensic Psychology and Head of Department at the University of Surrey. She has a special interest in police occupational culture and application of psychological theories and principles to the investigation of rape and murder. She has written a number of research papers on these topics and is currently compiling a handbook of forensic psychology with Dr Elizabeth Campbell to be published by Cambridge University Press.

Neil Chakraborti is a Lecturer in Criminology at the Department of Criminology, University of Leicester. He has published widely on issues of rural racism, ethnicity and victimisation, with a particular interest in racist and religious hate crime, fear of crime among minority ethnic communities, community safety, and anti-racism. He is co-editor (with Jon Garland) of *Rural Racism* (Willan Publishing, 2004).

Jon Garland is a Lecturer in Criminology at the Department of Criminology, University of Leicester. He has researched and published widely on issues of racism, anti-racism, ethnicity and identity, policing diversity, community safety and football-related disorder. His books include *Racism and Anti-Racism in Football* with Michael Rowe (Palgrave, 2001), *The Future of Football,* edited with Michael Rowe and Dominic Malcolm (Frank Cass, 2000) and *Rural Racism,* edited with Neil Chakraborti (Willan Publishing, 2004). In the last three years he has been conducting extensive research into issues of rural racism with Neil Chakraborti.

Simon Holdaway is Professor of Criminology and Sociology and Director of the School of Law at the University of Sheffield. A former police officer, he has for many years researched and published about many aspects of policing, particularly aspects of police race relations. His specialism is race relations within the police and he has completed research about the recruitment into and the retention of ethnic minorities within constabularies. His latest project was a two-year study of Black Police Associations in UK constabularies.

Brian Holland has worked in the 'equalities' field – including the Commission for Racial Equality – for over 25 years. At the time of writing this article, Dr Holland was an Assistant Director with Greater Manchester Police as Head of Policy and Development within the HQ Diversity Command unit. He has since semi-retired and now combines work as a freelance equalities consultant, tutor at Stockport College and is currently researching 'gun crime' in south Manchester with Manchester Metropolitan University.

Martin Innes is Professor and Director of the Universities Police Science Institute at Cardiff University. He is the author of the books *Investigating Murder* (Clarendon Press, 2003) and *Understanding Social Control* (Open University Press, 2003), as well as a number of articles, reports and book chapters. He is the editor of the journal *Policing and Society* published by Routledge. Innes is currently conducting research on reassurance policing and the manufacture of social order, as well as continuing his work in the area of major crime investigation.

Eugene McLaughlin is Professor of Criminology at City University London. He has written extensively on policing, race and community relations and race and the newsmedia. He is currently researching shifting philosophies of security and safety in multicultural polities and newsmedia reporting of homicides. His most recent publications include *The Sage Dictionary of Criminology* (2nd edn, Sage, 2005) and *The New Policing* (Sage, 2007). He is also co-editor of *Theoretical Criminology: an International Journal.*

Megan O'Neill is a Lecturer in Criminology at the University of Salford. Her research interests centre on police and policing studies and include the policing of football, Black Police Associations, and police occupational culture generally.

Michael Rowe is Associate Professor in Criminology at Victoria University, Wellington. His research interests have focused on policing and minority ethnic communities, and on the broader implications of diversity for the police service. Recently he has conducted an ethnographic study of policing and examined officer narratives about police work and the implications that these are likely to have for neighbourhood policing. He has published widely on all of these topics, most notably *Policing, Race and Racism* (Willan Publishing, 2004).

Mark Roycroft is a Detective Chief Inspector in the Metropolitan Police with 24 years' experience who has worked on major enquires including a period as a senior investigating officer. He received a Fulbright scholarship to the USA to research major enquiries, especially low volume homicides such as contract killings. Mark was a member of the National Crime Faculty and has assisted nationally with 'hard to solve' murder investigations. His Masters thesis examined the use of analysis within the UK police force and he is a trained analyst. Mark has attended courses at Europol and the FBI academy on analysis and behavioural analysis.

Anna Souhami is a Research Fellow in the Department of Social Policy, London School of Economics. She has recently completed a major two-year Home Office study (with Tim Newburn and Janet Foster at LSE) examining the impact of the Stephen Lawrence Inquiry on policing in England and Wales (Home Office 2005). Her current research explores the governance of youth crime in England and Wales. She is the author of *Transforming Youth Justice: Occupational Identity and Cultural Change* (Willan Publishing, 2007) which explores questions of occupational culture and identity among youth justice professionals following the Crime and Disorder Act 1998.

Kevin Stenson is Professor of Criminology and Co-director of the Crime and Conflict Research Centre, Middlesex University, London. His publications include (edited with R.R. Sullivan), *Crime Risk and Justice*, 2001, and 'Sovereignty, Biopolitics and the Local Government of Crime' (*Theoretical Criminology*, 9 (3), 2005).

P.A.J. Waddington is Professor of Social Policy at the Policy Research Institute, the University of Wolverhampton. He is the author of several books on policing, including *Policing Citizens* (UCL Press, 1999) and numerous articles including (with Kevin Stenson and David Don) 'In Proportion: Race, and Police Stop and Search' (*British Journal of Criminology*, 44, 2004). In 1992 he led an international inquiry into the policing of a massacre in the South African township of Boipatong that threatened to derail the peace process. He also writes a regular column for *Police Review*, widely read among members of the British police service.

James Whitfield, a former Metropolitan Police Inspector, is Visiting Research Fellow at the Open University. He experienced at first hand difficulties in relations between London's minority ethnic communities and the police during the disturbances at the Notting Hill Carnival in the 1970s, and at Brixton and Southall in 1981. His book, *Unhappy Dialogue: The Metropolitan Police and Black Londoners in Post-war Britain* (Willan Publishing, 2004), charts the history of relations between London's Caribbean community, its children and the Metropolitan Police from 1945. His most recently published article is 'Policing the Windrush Generation', which appears in the September 2006 edition of *History and Policy*.

Policing and racism in the limelight – the politics and context of the Lawrence Report

Michael Rowe

Among the few critical voices raised in response to the publication in 1999 of Sir William Macpherson's report into the racist murder of Stephen Lawrence were those that argued that the detailed analysis and extensive recommendations revealed little or nothing that many activists had not been saying for years. Why, it was asked, had it taken the authority of an establishment figure such as Sir William to force onto the political agenda issues relating to police racism that had been campaigned about from the margins for so long?

Although the Lawrence Report[1] provided a comprehensive and authoritative analysis, many of the problems identified had been well known among minority ethnic communities, political activists, and analysts for several decades. That many of the issues the Macpherson Inquiry highlighted had considerable historical resonance was evident from the initial parliamentary debate on the Report in February 1999 when Labour and Conservative MPs referred back to the 1981 Scarman Report into the Brixton riots; the New Cross fire of the same year that had resulted in the deaths of 13 young black people; and demands from the same period that an independent police complaints system be established. Speaking in the House of Commons, the Conservative Home Affairs spokesman, Sir Norman Fowler noted that he had been a member of a select committee 25 years earlier that had recommended efforts to increase the number of minority ethnic police recruits. The MP for Tottenham, Bernie Grant, suggested that the challenge was stark since 'we have been here before … This is a last chance for British society to tackle racism and to push for racial

equality. The black community is giving British society a last chance'
(Hansard 1999).

Acknowledging that previous efforts to improve relations between
the police service and Britain's minority ethnic communities had, to put
it at its best, a chequered history, Home Secretary Jack Straw promised
that the Lawrence Report would be different since the proposals
endorsed by the government would be driven forward and subject
to continued monitoring and review. Whereas the police response to
the Scarman Report had often been defensive, senior officers seemed
keen to embrace the central findings of the Lawrence Inquiry. Often
this involved them arguing that critical voices ought to avoid rushing
to judge the service on the basis of past inadequacies and instead
should recognise the strength of their current commitment to root and
branch reform. In some respects the basis of this collection go back to
those demands that judgement of the police service's commitment to
confront racism be made on the basis of post-Lawrence Report efforts
rather than the long legacy of failure and neglect that dominated much
of the preceding three decades. More than eight years have elapsed
since the report was published; time enough to make some assessment
of the extent of progress.

In many respects pledges that the Lawrence Report would lead
to reform have been kept. There has been a prolonged and wide-
ranging programme covering issues generally relevant to everyday
police work and specifically associated with the policing of racist
violence and relations with minority ethnic communities. A little over
a month after the report was published the *Home Secretary's Action Plan*
outlined a detailed response to each of the seventy recommendations
contained in the Lawrence Report, and noted that 'we know that
we must deliver real practical change. New policies or procedures
will not be enough unless they are turned into action which will
build trust and confidence, and help to provide a better service'
(Home Office 1999: 1). The Plan also noted the establishment of the
Lawrence Steering Group, to be chaired by the Home Secretary and
include members of groups such as the Black Police Association, the
Police Federation and the Association of Police Authorities. The Plan
announced that the steering group would publish an annual report
detailing the progress made in addressing each of Macpherson's
recommendations. These reports, of which four were produced until
the Lawrence Steering Group was disbanded in September 2005,
detail a plethora of policy developments and initiatives undertaken
in direct response to the recommendations of the Macpherson Report.
A review produced by the Racist and Violent Crime Taskforce of

the Metropolitan Police outlined more than 100 separate initiatives instigated in that force during the year that followed publication of the Lawrence Report (Metropolitan Police 2000). Outside the capital, the emphasis on dynamic reform of the police service was mirrored in the title of Greater Manchester Police's programme Operation Catalyst, as Holland outlines in his contribution to this collection. More widely the various chapters contained here provide detailed testimony of the impact that the Lawrence Inquiry and Report have had upon the police service, both in terms of internal organisational issues and external community relations. This volume tends to confirm the findings of the Home Office-sponsored study of the response to the report, which suggested that it had instigated significant reform within the police service, most of which was regarded by the police as positive (Foster *et al.* 2005). Measured in terms of internal reform, policy development and organisational change within the police service it appears that the Lawrence Report has proved significant, although, as several of the chapters in this volume indicate, this impact has not always translated into reform at the level of police practice.

Furthermore, it is less clear that there has been a transformation of police relations with the public, particularly those of a minority ethnic background, since publication of the report. While the Lawrence Report provides a detailed framework of reform based around 70 recommendations – many of which are reviewed in this book – these were organised beneath a more general 'ministerial priority' that the Home Secretary should seek to increase 'the trust and confidence in policing amongst minority ethnic communities' (Macpherson 1999: 327). Certain high-profile issues might have had an impact on the image of the police service among minority ethnic communities and it is clear that these relations are determined by a social context somewhat beyond the control of the police service. Among the controversies that have influenced the profile of policing and racism have been several related to the Lawrence case itself. While the Lawrence Steering Group might have overseen considerable developments in the period from 1999, reaction to the disestablishment of the group, in September 2005, led to public criticism from Doreen Lawrence who argued that this demonstrated that tackling racism within the police service was no longer a political priority (*Observer* 2005). The racist murder of Anthony Walker in Liverpool in 2005 drew a number of parallels with the Lawrence case and the police service suggested that the convictions of two men demonstrated that lessons had been learnt from the Macpherson Report. On the other hand, the police investigation into the death of Errol McGowan in Telford in 2002 was subject to criticism that officers made assumptions about the cause of his death and had ignored his concerns that he had been threatened by a gang of racists (*Guardian* 2003). An investigation by the Independent Police Complaints Commission (IPCC) into the death of Christopher Alder in Hull police station in April 1998 came to the conclusion that 'the fact that he was black stacked the odds more heavily against him' (IPCC 2006: 29). The precise impact that such events have had upon minority ethnic communities' trust and confidence in the police service is difficult to gauge, just as the more general influence of media coverage on public attitudes towards crime and policing is hard to discern (Innes 2003; Jewkes 2004). It is difficult to imagine, however, that such episodes have no impact on perceptions of the police service.

Clearly the issue of racism has featured heavily in public debates about policing throughout much of the period since the Lawrence Report appeared. Representation of the racist police officer has become a staple of media coverage as TV and press have exposed a litany of malpractice and unacceptable attitudes that, collectively, have replaced the image of the corrupt officer as the epitome of police deviance. While the establishment of the folk demon of the racist police officer may have helped to keep the issues reviewed in this book on the political agenda, this has served to marginalise institutional dimensions of racism by focusing upon individual malfeasance. In previous eras, as Whitfield's contribution to this collection illustrates, senior officers or representatives of the Police Federation often sought to deny there was a problem of officer racism or to suggest that the police service was a microcosm of society and so, inevitably, a small proportion of officers would be racist. It is a success of anti-racism that these complacent defences are no longer offered but a consensus around broader structural or institutional dimensions of racism has not yet emerged. Whether this is due to a failure to adequately conceptualise institutional racism is a question addressed by several contributors to this collection.

Changes in cultural, media and political discourses about racism cannot be attributed to a single report or public inquiry but the impact of the Lawrence Report has extended far beyond the police service and the criminal justice system. Consideration of the reaction to the type of high-profile incidents mentioned above (and many more could also be noted) does provide one measure of the nature of developments in terms of general relations between the police and minority ethnic communities. They do not provide a coherent or definitive basis, however, to judge the general state of relations between minority ethnic communities and the police service or the impact that the Lawrence Report has had. Another source of evidence is the survey data collected by the British Crime Survey, but this too provides a mixed picture. Partly this is due to a general deterioration in public esteem for the police, which makes it difficult to interpret the state of relations over time. British Crime Survey (BCS) data shows that 64 per cent of the public felt that the police were doing a 'good or excellent job' in 1996 and that this figure fell to 48 per cent by 2002–03 (Pepper *et al.* 2004: 6). Against this background it might seem unlikely that the trust and confidence of minority ethnic communities would have improved. However, the picture is less clear-cut when these data are broken down by ethnicity, as Table 1 indicates. While the percentage of all ethnic groups giving a positive estimation of the police has decreased sharply from pre- to post-Lawrence Report eras, the earlier sweep of the BCS suggested that minorities were somewhat less satisfied with the police than whites, a disparity that is reversed in the 2004–05 results.

Other findings from the 2004–05 BCS survey suggest, conversely, that minorities who have reported crime to the police are marginally less satisfied with the police response than were whites. In 58 per cent of incidents reported by whites, respondents to the BCS stated that they were satisfied with the police response. The comparable figure was 63 per cent in relation to incidents reported by those of mixed ethnicity, 47 per cent for Asians, 53 per cent for blacks, and 61 per cent for those of Chinese or other ethnic origin (Allen *et al.* 2006: 37).

Table 1   Positive estimation of police, by ethnicity

Ethnic groups	1996[1]	2004–05[2]
White	81	48
Mixed	–	50
Asian	76	53
Black	78	56
Chinese or other	–	60

[1]Percentage saying police do very/fairly good job.
[2]Percentage saying police do an excellent/good job locally.

Source: Mirrless-Black and Dodd (1997: 2); Allen *et al.* (2006: 29)

Efforts to reach a definitive judgement about the impact of the Lawrence Report on the British police service are not easily rewarded by the qualitative or the quantitative data, as the brief discussion in the previous paragraphs makes clear. Inevitably meaningful evaluation of the Macpherson Report requires careful interpretation of a range of topics and the taking into account of the broader context against which the report's recommendations have been implemented. It is to such considerations that the chapters contained here contribute, since they not only explore issues central to the post-Lawrence Report era but also place these in their wider context. The topics covered in the chapters that follow have been selected so that a broad range of issues analysed in the report are covered. Inevitably certain important areas have had to be omitted. The inability of the officers who first arrived at the scene of the attack on Stephen Lawrence to provide appropriate first aid led the Macpherson Report to make recommendations on this topic, and the police service response to this is not discussed in this collection. Similarly consideration of the work of Family Liaison Officers, a police role that has expanded considerably and been professionalised in the aftermath of the report, has not been possible in this volume.

The contributions are not intended to provide a final assessment of the impact that the Macpherson Report has had on British policing. Clearly the Lawrence Inquiry has led to a huge programme of reform that has had affected policing in ways that are sometimes obvious and sometimes more difficult to identify. A number of contributors to this book refer to the impact that a BBC TV documentary, *The Secret Policeman*, had when it exposed, in 2003, extreme and violent racist attitudes among a small number of police trainees. More recently, in April 2006, another documentary, the *Dispatches* film 'Undercover Copper', revealed that indolence, sexism and pornography continued to be features of the modern police service. Such broadcasts, with their grainy, poorly lit images of behaviour usually carefully hidden from the public gaze have become a staple of contemporary media and it is ironic, in this context, that among the first such films to appear in Britain was the secretly filmed footage of the five men accused of killing Stephen Lawrence. The film shown in 2006 revealed something of the progress that has been made in the 13 years since the Lawrence murder, but also a lot of what remains to be done. The police officer-cum-investigative journalist who made the 'Undercover Copper' film noted that while the film had raised many issues of concern about, for example, attitudes toward victims of rape, 'I did not uncover racism in my time at Leicester, which I hope will provide some reassurance for the people of Leicester' (*Leicester Mercury* 2006). This slender consolation suggests that while police officers might have stopped being overtly racist, a more widespread understanding of diversity has not been embedded within the service. Suspicion remains that the continuing problems of sexism, homophobia and a host of other prejudices might suggest that the reconstruction of the police as an anti-racist service has not been the fundamental transformation required to develop a modern professional service for a diverse society.

Outline of the book

The collection of chapters that follows is not intended to provide a definitive overview of the impact of the Macpherson Report; although it is hoped that they will be a useful contribution to such reviews. Neither do they share a single perspective. It is intended, though, that the collection will offer useful reflection on some of the key controversies that have developed as the recommendations of the Lawrence Inquiry have, or have not, been implemented. Whitfield's contribution opens the collection by placing the issues relating to the Lawrence case in their historical context. His analysis of police minority relations from the 1950s until the 1970s not only demonstrates that current problems have an even longer pedigree than is often thought but also constitute a further rebuttal to those who continue to see the post-war period as a 'golden age' of police community relations. However, this historical perspective demonstrates important breaks with the past as well as enduring continuities. Whitfield demonstrates that the police services' barely concealed resistance to engaging with minority ethnic communities reflected a broader tendency to eschew engagement with the public. For a host of reasons, the police service had become less isolationist by the time of the Lawrence Inquiry, and the Macpherson Report has contributed – along with the 1998 Crime and Disorder Act – to the further acceleration of engagement with other agencies and the public, or sections of it, more generally. The broader context of policing and the political environment in which the Lawrence Inquiry was established and the report subsequently published was markedly different from that into which the Scarman Report had been born in 1981.

The broader social, political and policing background against which the recommendations of the Macpherson Report have been implemented is reviewed in McLaughlin's chapter, which argues that many of the developments have compounded, rather than alleviated, race-related problems in the police service. He shows that the BBC TV documentary *The Secret Policeman* perpetuated an established stereotype of the unreconstructed violent racist police officer. Incongruously, though, many of the investigations and inquiries that followed the broadcast concluded that the problems of racism within the service were largely attributable to the failure of leaders to properly comprehend or challenge racism and police culture, and could not simply be blamed upon a minority of recruits. Holland's chapter later in the volume reviews at some length the impact of the documentary on the police service. McLaughlin argues that the continuing pervasiveness of sexism and homophobia, as well as racism, within the service indicates that police culture – particularly the subcultural pressure to close ranks – has not been adequately challenged and that to do so remains the compelling challenge of contemporary policing.

The emphasis that McLaughlin suggests has been placed on training as a solution to police 'race problems' is further considered in Rowe and Garland's chapter, which is based upon a study of police 'community and race relations' training, instigated in response to a series of Macpherson's recommendations. Rowe and Garland review the history of police training on diversity and argue that police officers and civilian staff have tended to respond positively to the training that they have been required to take in recent years, and that this response often ran contrary to their expectations. However, there is little evidence that the training has made very much impact on the delivery of policing or the behaviour of staff. It is suggested that there are a number of reasons for this, including the difficulty of delivering training on institutional racism given the hugely controversial, if misunderstood, nature of the concept. Rowe and Garland also argue that the impact of the training was lessened because the co-delivery of programmes to police officers and civilian staff was often not properly planned. Similarly, the involvement of community representatives in the delivery of training has often not been well considered. Fundamentally, though, it is argued that the experience of diversity training reflects a broader temptation for the police service to regard training as the panacea for problems that are complex and deeply rooted, and endure in ways that are beyond the scope of training to resolve.

That the concept of institutional racism has been poorly understood is the central concern of Souhami's contribution, which makes use of research that she and colleagues did to gauge the response of the police service to the Lawrence Report (Foster *et al.* 2005). In particular Souhami focuses on the conundrum that while the inquiry took care to differentiate between institutional and individual racism, this distinction was not recognised or understood by many within the police service. Officers have tended to believe that the Lawrence Inquiry's findings relating to institutional racism means that they have personally been labelled as racist, even though the report specifically states that this is not what is claimed. Souhami seeks to explain this conundrum and argues that while this misconception might partly be the fault of misleading media coverage it has also arisen because of ambiguities in the conceptualisation of institutional racism in the inquiry report and its application in the particular case of the investigation into Stephen Lawrence's murder.

In part, confusion appears to have resulted from the manner in which the focus of the Inquiry shifted between questions of individual conduct in a specific murder investigation and organisational processes more broadly. Officers could not understand why the actions of a particular group of officers were evidence of institutional racism rather than individual incompetence, particularly when they behaved in a manner in which their colleagues did not. For example, it is clear that not all officers' party to the murder investigation failed to recognise the racist motivation of the attack. That some did is taken as evidence of institutional racism, but Macpherson does not explain why other officers – part of the same institution – reacted differently. Furthermore, the boundary between individual action and institutional discrimination is blurred in the concept itself, particularly in the 'cultural' processes prioritised by the Inquiry. It is not clear from the Inquiry Report at what point these cumulative decisions or attitudes are transformed into a collective property that might be identified as institutional racism.

Souhami argues that some of this misunderstanding reflects conceptual confusion in the Inquiry Report, which does not maintain a rigorous distinction between the three forms of racism it identifies: that which is deliberate and overt; that which is 'unwitting' or 'unconscious'; and that which is systemic or collective. These are used interchangeably within the Report, Souhami argues, and are even elided within the definition itself. For example, evidence relating to officers use of inappropriate language, or that the circumstances of the murder were understood in stereotypical terms are at times taken as proof of overt racism, at others as indicative of unwitting racism. As a result, the Inquiry Report not only failed to clarify the meaning of the term but inadvertently replicated its central ambiguities. In conclusion, Souhami argues that the term 'institutional racism' might have been powerful and instigated reform, but the lack of clarity over what the term actually means has failed to address organisational dynamics of racism.

Holdaway and O'Neill argue that the Black Police Association (BPA) has become increasingly influential in police services in the aftermath of the Lawrence Report and that this has been part of a process whereby 'race' had come to be a subject to be managed by senior officers. The political clout of BPAs and their concern to present a 'united front' are key reasons, Holdaway and O'Neill suggest, why many associations have been reluctant to adopt a name that might be more inclusive of minority ethnic officers who do not regard themselves as 'black'. The inevitable essentialism that this entails, Holdaway and O'Neill argue, is at variance with much contemporary conceptualisation of identity and seems to be counter-productive and BPA relations with the growing number of staff associations based around cultural, ethnic, religious and sexual identities seem likely to be difficult. Holdaway and O'Neill's research also reveals fascinating insight into the ways in which BPA members have responded to Macpherson's identification of institutionalised racism within the police service. It seems that BPA chairs have understood institutional racism as synonymous with covert racism and are highly conscious of the hidden assumptions and cultural exclusiveness of a police service that is normatively white. Often their claims to have identified racism among colleagues is based upon their personal perception and the belief that they can inherently identify individuals who are covertly racist. The implications that this has for police service efforts to confront racist officers, which rely upon collecting evidence and developing prosecutable cases against alleged racists, are significant and it is not clear that the service can convince those who interpret the problem on the basis of subjective experience that racism is being tackled.

The increasing diversification of minority ethnic interests within the police service has been mirrored in external police community relations, particularly, as Chakraborti demonstrates, because security has come to dominate the policing agenda in the light of perceived threats of terrorism. One implication of this is that discussion of police relations with minority ethnic communities now tends to relate to the Muslim community rather than the African Caribbean community, which has been at the centre of debates for much of the post-war period. Controversies over the shooting of Jean Charles de Menezes at Stockwell tube station in July 2005 and the raids on a Muslim household in Forest Gate in June 2006 have raised questions about police intelligence gathering systems and community relations more generally. Charkraborti shows how there has been a parallel, sometimes contradictory, process in recent years whereby efforts to provide greater protection through the development of laws against religiously aggravated crimes have accompanied anti-terrorist provisions such as stop and search powers that have had significant impact on the Asian community. While statistical evidence on the position of the Muslim population is sparse, since statistics are collected only on the basis of ethnicity, Charkraborti argues that the Muslim community feels increasingly over-policed and under-protected; although this might be related to broader processes of Islamophobia and suggestions that Islamic and British values inevitably conflict.

That data on race, ethnicity and the criminal justice system is not collected in ways that shed light on emerging issues of concern is further illustrated by Stenson and Waddington's chapter, which examines the impact that official statistics on race and stop and search have had on debates about policing and minority ethnic communities. Stenson and Waddington argue that the continuing use of a threefold classification – black, Asian, and white – reflects the dominance of a certain political narrative relating to policing and race that emerged in the aftermath of the Scarman Report. Not only does this three-way categorisation fail to capture what Stenson and Waddington describe as the 'awesome demographic complexity' of ethnic relations in contemporary urban contexts, it also fails to acknowledge the relevance of other variables, such as gender and class, that might also explain the differentials in police contacts with the public. They argue that the spatial components of stop and search need to be considered to a much greater extent and that the continuing reliance on out-moded ethnic classification and residential population does not provide meaningful insight into police practices in this respect.

While much of the discussion of the impact of the Macpherson Report focuses on police relations with minority ethnic communities, the chapter by Roycroft, Brown and Innes provides a reminder that many of the findings and recommendations related more generally to the conduct of police murder investigations. They argue that by their very nature inquiries into particular examples of police investigative failure tend to examine specific cases in isolation, and so fail to grasp the longer-term recurring difficulties that face investigations more generally. By exploring previous failures identified in the investigation, among others of the Yorkshire Ripper case in the 1970s, Roycroft, Brown and Innes show how problems with aspects of murder inquiries, for example the processing of information, pre-dated the Lawrence case and have subsequently recurred in relation to the deaths of Holly Wells and Jessica Chapman, and Victoria Climbié. Furthermore they argue that public inquiries into perceived police failures need to be understood in their broader social context. While the Lawrence murder was horrific, racist murders were not unprecedented: indeed, there had been a number of similar murders in the vicinity in the previous few years. One reason why the Lawrence case achieved such a high profile was that it resonated with broader social concerns about the ability of the police to provide public protection, and benefited from the campaigning of Stephen's mother, Doreen Lawrence, who was able to harness the power and interest of mass media, which provided her advocacy with amplified political power. Roycroft, Brown and Innes propose a dialectical model that explains how foreground attributes of particular cases relate to broader contextual features resulting in a formal inquiry into investigative failings. In other cases, possibly where equally serious failings have occurred, such a dialectical process does not emerge.

In the final chapter Holland provides a fascinating account of how the post-Macpherson agenda played out within Greater Manchester Police, where he was head of policy in the diversity command unit. He argues that analysis of the difficulties of reforming the police service often overlook a crucial and problematic aspect of police culture, which is a short-term emphasis on emergency response. The service, Holland argues, is relatively good at providing a quick and effective reaction to identified problems, which is often an appropriate approach for an emergency service. This style of response, however, is less appropriate when it comes to inculcating fundamental change in the service such as those required by the Macpherson agenda, and is one reason, Holland argues, that police community and race relations have been fraught for so long. One of the institutional problems of the police service, as Holland describes it, is that the emergency response model provides for only a short-term agenda whereby problems are identified and then 'fixed' by a project management team that develops policy, introduces training, and so on. As other problems emerge, in this particular case the need to respond to the 2001 'mill town' riots and the community cohesion agenda that followed from it, the original issue is eclipsed by the need to respond to the latest 'crisis'. Towards the end of his chapter

Holland returns to *The Secret Policeman* documentary discussed by many contributors, and provides an incisive analysis of the impact the programme had on Greater Manchester Police.

Certain themes recur in various of the chapters included here. The problematic conceptualisation of 'institutional racism', which was perhaps the key finding of the Lawrence Inquiry, is noted by several of the contributors. The ways in which police subculture is often used in simplistic terms to account for the limited impact of policy reform is also mentioned by several authors. With luck each reader will notice points of similarity and tension amid the offerings included here. Clearly there is no way in which the huge scope of issues relating to policing, diversity, ethnicity, race and racism can be properly reviewed within the scope of one edited collection. A number of the issues considered here, such as stop and search, training, and the conduct of murder investigations are central concerns of the Macpherson Report itself. Others, such as the policing of Muslim communities, are not directly reviewed in that document but have come to occupy central positions in general debates about the need to improve the trust and confidence of minority ethnic communities in the police service. It is hoped that, collectively, these chapters provide the basis for careful and considered reflection on debates that often seem to be subject to more heat than light.

Note

1   The terms Lawrence Report and Macpherson Report are used synonymously throughout this book.

References

Allen, J., Edmonds, S., Patterson, A. and Smith, D. (2006) *Policing and the Criminal Justice System – Public Confidence and Perceptions: Findings from the 2004/05 British Crime Survey*, Online Report 07/06, London: Home Office.

Foster, J., Newburn, T. and Souhami, A. (2005) *Assessing the Impact of the Stephen Lawrence Inquiry*, HORS 294, London: Home Office.

Guardian (2003) 'Momentum in Fight against Racism "Wanes"', 19 April, p. 9.

Hansard (1999) *Parliamentary Debates*, 24 February, col. 399.

Home Office (1999) Stephen Lawrence Inquiry: Home Secretary's Action Plan, London: Home Office.

Independent Police Complaints Commission (2006) *Report of the Review into the Events Leading up to and Following the Death of Christopher Alder on 1st April 1998*, London: The Stationery Office.

Innes, M. (2003) ' "Signal Crimes": Detective Work, Mass Media and Constructing Collective Memory', in P. Mason (ed.) *Criminal Visions: Media Representations of Crime and Justice*, Cullompton: Willan Publishing, pp. 51–69.

Jewkes, Y. (2004) *Media and Crime*, London: Sage Publications.

Leicester Mercury (2006) 'Police in the Dock' 24 April, p. 2.

Macpherson, Sir W. (1999) *The Stephen Lawrence Inquiry: Report of an Inquiry by Sir William Macpherson of Cluny*, CM 4262-1, London: HMSO.

Metropolitan Police (2000) *Operation Athena: Action Plan Update*, London: Metropolitan Police.

Mirrlees-Black, C. and Budd, T. (1997) *Policing and the Public: Findings from the 1996 British Crime Survey*, Research Findings No. 60, London: Home Office.

Observer (2005) 'Lawrence: You Have Let My Son Down', 16 October, p. 9.

Pepper, S., Lovbakke, J. and Upson, A. (2004) 'Confidence and the Criminal Justice System', in S. Nicholas and A. Walker (eds) *Crime, Disorder and the Criminal Justice System – Public Attitudes and Perceptions*, London: Home Office.

Chapter 1

The historical context: policing and black people in post-war Britain

James Whitfield

In this country at least, racial discrimination is not a field in which Government action can make much difference.

(Whitfield 2006: 1)

The social and ethnic fabric of British society changed for ever as a result of the Second World War. Though many in the ruling establishment concurred in the delusion that Britain remained a major power on the world stage, the truth was that from a starting point of near bankruptcy the nation's post-war economic recovery was only possible with the aid of a massive loan injection of overseas capital (Booth 1989: 145). There was a pressing need to kick-start the economy by increasing exports; industry cried out for investment; and, with Britain still heavily engaged in military commitments across the globe, the country desperately needed additional labour to supplement its own workforce if production targets were to be met.

At the end of the war, European Voluntary Workers (EVWs) were selectively recruited on a contract basis with the blessing of the Attlee government, directed into difficult-to-fill jobs and provided with accommodation (Paul 1997: 81). It was not long before pioneer Commonwealth citizens answered Britain's call for workers, initially from the West Indies and later from Africa, India and Pakistan. The austerity that typified much of life in Britain at the time was reflected in the chronic post-war housing shortages in London and the other large cities where many of the newcomers chose to live and work. Viewed from the perspective of a British public that was largely ill -informed, their arrival was considered to be generally unwelcome.

As a result, black and Asian immigrants frequently found suitable employment hard to come by, and faced particular difficulties in the search for housing. That many were to encounter such problems was due in no small part to the prejudicial mindset of a significant number of the indigenous population, people from all social classes, who regarded dark skin tone as a sign of inferiority.

The police service also needed workers after the war. All regular police recruitment ended abruptly in 1939 (Emsley 2004). With the outbreak of hostilities younger police officers joined the fighting services and towards the end of the war police officers under 30 years of age were called up. Older police officers, men who had been eligible to retire on full pensions between 1939 and 1945, were required to remain in the police until the beginning of 1946, when the majority retired (Hansard 1948). Thus, when police recruiting began again at the end of 1945 the service included an abnormally high number of middle-to-late-service officers, and in the largest urban areas was often considerably under strength. The situation was so bad in Liverpool, for example, that the Chief Constable informed the Home Office that 50 per cent of his officers would be eligible to retire, on a pension, on or before 1 January 1946. The Metropolitan Police (the Met) had 18,700 male officers in 1939, but by 1945 its effective strength had been reduced to 13,400 male officers and it was 6,000 men short of its authorised establishment (Whitfield 2006: 2).

From 1945, the police service targeted men in the armed forces and those who had served in colonial police forces as its primary source of post-war recruits (Whitfield 2006: 2). By and large, the upbringings and prejudices of these men were those of a society that showed no interest in learning of the habits and cultures of new arrivals from the former Empire: above all, a society having little desire to participate in or encourage the development of a multi-ethnic Britain (Whitfield 2004: 40–1). As such, a largely young and inexperienced police force, led by senior officers who themselves were generally unacquainted with immigrant cultures and lifestyles, faced difficult new challenges when enforcing the law, particularly when dealing with allegations of colour prejudice and racially motivated crime.

In this chapter we will consider racial prejudice as an issue in police–immigrant relations from the early post-war years to the end of the 1960s, a period when the focus of government attention moved away from immigrants and towards what were perceived to be the potential problems that their British-born children were likely to encounter. Overt colour prejudice was a fact of life for many people from the Caribbean, Africa and South Asia during the 1950s, and while it was a source of bitter resentment for them, it went largely unchallenged among the host community. Prejudice often gave birth to mutual hostility and resentment, and on occasions to confrontation. In such circumstances the police service, charged with the task of maintaining law and order, inevitably became involved. The manner of the police response led, in time, to feelings among members of the immigrant communities that the police service was itself racist. While this may have been a generalisation, there can be little doubt, given the nature of British society at the time, that the country's exclusively white police service was tainted to some degree by such distasteful attitudes. Though racist views existed among all ranks of the police service there were many officers who worked hard to develop good relations with immigrants. Unfortunately, as Hall observed, their efforts were not always recognised or appreciated by peers and senior colleagues:

> There were many good police officers and what was sad, and this went on for twenty years, police managers would always talk about a particular police officer by name, often of a constable or sergeant – seldom an inspector – who was known to be 'good with them', 'he gets on well with them', 'he's almost one of them'. That would be a put-down. (cited in Whitfield 2003: 241)

Many of the police's problems with immigrants were, as with society at large, the result of an inability, perhaps an unwillingness, to understand immigrant cultures. Additionally, the police service's traditional priorities – the prevention and detection of crime, the maintenance of good order and tranquillity and the prosecution of offenders – had remained virtually unchanged for well over a century. In the period under consideration, 'community relations' were very much the poor relation of the police service. For their part, the majority of Commonwealth immigrants arrived in Britain ignorant of the English legal system, police powers and procedures. As many were to discover, policing in Britain was difficult to comprehend for those brought up under a colonial system of policing. As will be seen, it was in matters of a non-criminal nature, issues that had traditionally been dealt with by the police by way of referral to what was commonly called 'civil remedy', that early confusion led to later difficulties and mistrust.

This potential for conflict leads us to the two questions that are considered in this chapter. First, to what extent was racial prejudice an issue in the policing of black and Asian immigrants in the early decades of large-scale immigration, and second, did the actions and attitudes of some members of the immigrant communities contribute to the difficulties in their relationship with police during the period?

The early post-war years

In 1998, the fiftieth anniversary of the arrival of the S.S. *Empire Windrush*, with its passenger list of West Indians keen to start a new life in Britain, was commemorated as a seminal moment in the history of British community relations. This was a far cry from the response of the British government 50 years earlier. On 18 February 1949, some six months after the arrival of the *Windrush*, the Labour government organised an Inter-Departmental Conference at the Home Office to consider what were referred to as problems arising from 'coloured immigration' (Whitfield 2004: 13). Although no statistical data was available on the numbers living in Britain, it was argued that those 'coloured' immigrants already in the country had tended to settle in the poorer areas of the largest cities, and the subsequent arrival of fellow-countrymen to join them had only exacerbated problems of overcrowding and host community discontent.

The following day, 19 February 1949, an internal Home Office memorandum (HO45/23227/45) raised the issue of recruitment of men who had served in the Indian Colonial Police Service as a possible means of alleviating continuing manpower shortages in home police forces. It pointed out: 'Some [of the men] are ex-regulars who later joined the Indian Police Service, others are Anglo-Indians and some of these are, in the words of Sir George Pearce, Commonwealth Relations Officer attached to the Appointments Department at the Ministry of Labour, "rather dark".' The memo continued:

> I have discussed these men with Colonel Sorley, the head of the recruiting department at Scotland Yard. He assures me that no suitable man who had served in the Indian Police and was only a year or two over the age of 30 would be turned down without an interview. He felt, however, that the recruiting board would be most reluctant to accept any man who was dark in colour ...

These early examples demonstrate the British government's

acknowledgement that within a few months of the arrival of small numbers of black immigrants their presence was already considered to be problematic. They also show that, whatever qualifications or personal qualities an applicant for the police service possessed at the time, neither the Home Office nor the Metropolitan Police were prepared to consider the possibility of recruiting an applicant of dark skin tone for appointment as a constable in the most chronically undermanned police force in the country.

Throughout the 1950s successive British governments faced what appeared to be an insoluble problem: how were they to maintain harmonious and beneficial relations with other Commonwealth governments without giving the game away that – for the sole reason of racial prejudice – their intention was to deprive Commonwealth citizens who were black or Asian from exercising their then legal right to live and work in Britain? (Butler 2002: 104, 149; Whitfield 2004: 16–18). Much of the evidence governments relied upon to make a case against the increase in Britain's non-white immigrant population was provided by police forces up and down the country.

In 1953, and again in 1955 and 1957, the Home Office called for information from local police forces on the degree to which black assimilation was taking place. Police reports were unequivocal in their assertion that it was black and Asian people who were responsible for problems between the communities. Reports spoke of 'their [immigrants'] below-par mentality and underlying suspicion of the white race'; and of immigrants' 'lack of education, social intercourse and cultural knowledge.' At the same time, the reports glossed over the fact that white people in the research areas operated a 'social colour bar', and that 'white inhabitants, by a vast majority, will not tolerate the coloured people'. At a more general level, the reports consistently depicted black men as having a fondness for white women of the prostitute type, of lacking a sense of social responsibility, and of being overly sensitive to racial prejudice (Whitfield 2004: 41). Such stereotypical images, in which black men were associated with 'sordid sexuality' prompted Gilroy (1987: 80) to note the way in which during this period sexual relations between black men and white women 'emerged ahead of crime as a theme in the popular politics of immigration control'.

Policing immigrant grievances

Detailed reports in files at the National Archives suggest that in the

1950s there was little reluctance on the part of the police to prosecute those who committed criminal acts against black and Asian victims (Whitfield 2006: 5). Crime, however, was only one aspect of host community prejudice. At least as important was the discrimination black and Asian people faced in the fields of employment, housing, and in restrictions placed upon their access to and use of places of public resort, such as hotels, pubs and clubs. These non-criminal issues were, if anything, more serious than breaches of the criminal law simply because of their potential to adversely prejudice all members of ethnic minorities. Added to this was the fact that, unlike those who were victims of crime, there was – prior to the Race Relations Act of 1965 – no legal remedy for acts of racial discrimination. In such circumstances black and Asian victims invariably sought help and guidance from the agency traditionally associated with resolving civil disputes: the police.

For many years police officers had drawn an operational distinction between criminal matters – those for which they had the full backing of the law to enforce – and civil matters, which usually comprised a variety of incidents that included husband-and-wife disputes, neighbour disputes, landlord-and-tenant disputes and common assaults: matters in respect of which police either had no direct powers, or their powers were limited (Whitfield 2006: 5) It was common practice for police officers to refer the parties to civil conflicts and disputes to what was known as their 'civil remedy'; in effect, this meant telling the participants that if they wished to take the matter further they should seek advice from a solicitor or the Clerk at the local magistrates' court. In this way, police maintained, their actions were seen to be fair and equitable to all parties.

Unfortunately, the policy had a disastrous impact on the trust and confidence of ethnic minority communities when it was applied to cases in which an element of racial discrimination was alleged. Victims, not unnaturally, interpreted the steering by police of a neutral course in such circumstances as merely condoning the act of discrimination. Confirming that the procedure had become a problem for police, Sir John Waldron, then Deputy Commissioner of the Metropolitan Police, advised the Commissioner, Sir Joseph Simpson:

> I can well understand that many coloured people when they bring their troubles to a police station desk or to an officer in the street think that they are being treated in an offhand manner or with lack of interest or sympathy if they are merely referred to a magistrate or a Citizen's Advice Bureau. Police in the colonies

are not liked but they are feared and respected, and when they give an on-the-spot decision in a civil dispute, provided the officer is of some rank or experience, it is generally accepted and obeyed. This is, of course, in direct contrast to the instruction we give our constables but it might be worth considering in a predominantly coloured area whether or not we should take a more definite line in these civil disputes. (Whitfield 2004: 80)

The policy by which governments sought to put off would-be black and Asian immigrants from coming to Britain might well have limited the willingness of police to develop constructive links with ethnic minority communities. As the Institute of Race Relations observed regarding Home Office policy on immigrants, 'Confining of the police to a purely regulatory role may well have had something to do with the deterioration of relationships, which began to be noticeable in the early-1960s' (Rose and Deakin 1969: 335). However, this does not absolve the police service from criticism for its failure to comprehend the aggravating dimension of race in criminal and civil matters involving black and Asian citizens, and its apparent unwillingness to learn more of the customs and lifestyles of immigrant communities, particularly those who by the mid-1950s it regarded as the most problematic: the West Indian community.

The disturbances of 1958 and their aftermath

Racial disturbances in Nottingham's St Ann's district and London's Notting Hill in August 1958, followed in May 1959 by the racially motivated murder of Kelso Cochrane, were important for several reasons. First, they exposed the lie that racial intolerance was a problem that only occurred beyond home shores; second, and from a policing perspective just as significant, the incidents provoked a dialogue between immigrants and police that revealed stark differences between ethnic minority representatives and senior police officers on the purpose of community relations.

Following the Cochrane murder, a meeting was held at the Home Office involving leaders of the West Indian community in Notting Hill and the Metropolitan Police Commissioner, Sir Joseph Simpson. Community leaders expressed their desire to develop good relations with the police and suggested that one way to reduce racial tensions in the area would be for suitable people of all ethnic groups to enrol as special constables in order to assist the regular police. The

Commissioner opposed the appointment of special constables in the area and added that he did not feel it desirable to appoint 'coloured' policemen (Whitfield 2004: 116).

Undeterred by the Commissioner's negative response to their offer of help, representatives of the West Indies Federation (WIF) met with Simpson the following day and renewed an earlier offer to provide information on Caribbean customs and lifestyles as one element of police training. Again, the offer was declined. The significance of these rebuffs becomes clear when one considers police tactics to combat racial tension in the Brixton area in 1960. Although the local chief superintendent believed that there was a low risk of racial tension and that the 'coloured' population of the area was 'fairly well behaved', police decided to introduce targeted patrols of black areas – including the use of police dogs – as well as a policy of dispersing all groups of black or white people from the streets (Whitfield 2004: 145). The moving along of law-abiding groups of black men from districts where they lived was a recipe for resentment. Had police accepted the WIF's offer to provide background information on life in the Caribbean they would undoubtedly have had a better understanding of West Indian street culture, a point endorsed by former Metropolitan Police Commissioner, Sir Peter Imbert (Whitfield 2004: 147):

> It's often been said that the young Caribbean youth had a street culture whereas the indigenous youth didn't have a street culture in quite the same way. I think that we in the police didn't understand that. When we saw black youth hanging around street corners we couldn't understand why. We automatically thought – quite wrongly, of course – on every occasion that they were up to no good. But that was because of a lack of understanding of their culture and their way of life.

The dialogue that began following the Cochrane murder had the potential to set in motion a process whereby immigrant communities and police could develop better trust and understanding. That this did not occur was due primarily to the differing objectives of those involved. While community leaders and representatives of Commonwealth governments sought to increase co-operation and mutual respect, the Metropolitan Police Commissioner's rationale for taking part was largely to protect his force from criticism and to nip in the bud grievances and complaints (Whitfield 2004: 65–6). The Commissioner's understanding of community involvement's *raison d'être*, an understanding based exclusively on self-interest, was – and continued for many years to be – widely shared by high-ranking police officers.

One sees a good example of this in the directive issued to members of the Lancashire Constabulary in May 1966, when the Unit Beat System of policing was about to be launched in the county (Whitfield 2004: 100–1). The newly established body of resident beat officers were encouraged to liaise with the public; not, as one might expect, to ascertain how policing might be geared to meeting the needs of local communities, but purely to enable the police to achieve two of their primary objectives: the detection of crime and the prosecution of offenders. Officers were advised to 'cultivate at least one informant in every street … someone who is inquisitive enough to find out what is going on'. In this regard, priority was to be given to 'the woman who is always peeping behind the curtain, the window cleaner, and the retired man who keeps his eyes open' (Whitfield 2004: 101). In short, from a policing perspective, community involvement was simply the means by which members of the public could help police with their enquiries.

Developments in the 1960s

In 1959 the Prime Minister, Harold Macmillan, appointed a Royal Commission on the Police to consider problems of police accountability and the service's inability to attract and retain sufficient officers of high standard. The main points of the Commission's final report were incorporated into the Police Act of 1964.

The Act introduced a national standard for dealing with complaints against the police and established a number of rights for complainants, including the rights to attend discipline hearings and to be informed of the outcome of the hearings. However, the Act failed to alter the much maligned procedure whereby police forces investigated complaints against their own officers. As statistics showed, and as ethnic minority complainants knew only too well, the chances of a successful outcome when making a complaint were remote. For example, in the Metropolitan Police District, of 127 complaints made by black or Asian people between 1 April 1961 and 31 March 1962, six were substantiated; and of 41 allegations of racial discrimination made against Metropolitan officers in 1969, none were substantiated (Whitfield 2004: 157).

Increasing pressure was brought in the 1960s by organisations such as the Campaign Against Racial Discrimination (CARD) and the West Indian Standing Conference (WISC) for the introduction of legislation to tackle the problem of racial discrimination. At the same time, the question began to be asked why, with a black and Asian population that was approaching one million, there were as yet no black or Asian police officers? In 1964, Harold Wilson's Labour Government introduced the Race Relations Bill, legislation that would make racial discrimination in places of public resort illegal (although it failed to deal with the key issues of discrimination in housing and employment) (Whitfield 2004: 96). A copy of the Bill was submitted to the Metropolitan Police for consideration and comment.

The observations of senior police officers revealed a lack of empathy with those most affected by racial discrimination; a failure to comprehend the need for anti-discrimination legislation; and the presence of what could only be described as racist attitudes in the service, none more so than the views expressed by the Commander of the Metropolitan Police's Number One Area:

> The ordinary white citizen generally accepts his place in society and makes no attempt to gatecrash places where he would not only feel out of place but is clearly unwelcome. Coloured people do not have the ability to do this and for the most part they are hypersensitive over colour ... It must be concluded that coloured people are more conscious of their rights than their obligations and any kind of legislation on the lines suggested will result in an avalanche of complaints. (Whitfield 2004: 75)

The Metropolitan Police Deputy Commissioner, Sir John Waldron, believed that the proposed legislation was the product of Labour's 'intellectual left wing', and added that the government would be 'happy to see it played down, for they realise only too well that working Labour is as intolerant of colour as any other class' (Whitfield 2004: 75).

While the Police Act made chief constables accountable in some respects to the Home Secretary and to police authorities, it also gave legal recognition to the long-standing convention by which chief officers of police were not subject to orders or directions from either. In effect, chief constables were thereby legally empowered to determine how their areas would be policed (Whitfield 2004: 108). This included the power to appoint or reject applicants for the police service. When Labour came to power in 1964 there were no black or Asian police officers in England and Wales.

The Metropolitan Police Commissioner, Sir Joseph Simpson, had made no secret of his opposition to the appointment of black police officers. The Metropolitan Police's position on black recruitment was set out by the Assistant Commissioner 'D' Department (which at the time covered training and recruitment), on 10 December 1963:

> The truth is, of course, that we are not yet prepared to recruit any coloured men, although the time may not be too far distant when we shall be unable to turn down well-qualified men who have been born and educated in this country ... In a predominantly white population, coloured police officers would be at a serious disadvantage and it would be unreasonable to expect them to perform the specialised duties of a policeman effectively ... It is our belief in Recruiting Branch that the West Indians and other coloured people are well aware that we do not recruit coloured men but that an occasional one is encouraged to apply by various societies as a kind of sighting shot. (Whitfield 2004: 118)

The position appears to have been no better nationally. On 14 April 1965, a meeting of civil servants and a representative group of chief constables was held at the Home Office to consider the recruitment of black and Asian police officers. Each of the chief constables had received applications for appointment to the police service from ethnic minority applicants, all of whom had been rejected. The general feeling of chief constables as expressed at the meeting was that although they were not opposed in principle to the appointment of black and Asian police officers, it was the British public, they suggested, who were not yet ready to accept them. Sir Robert Mark, then chief constable of Leicester, was a lone voice in pointing out that the real reason why ethnic minority applicants were not applying for appointment to the police in greater numbers was because they believed they would not be welcome (Whitfield 2004: 119).

Between November 1969 and March 1970, the Metropolitan Police carried out an internal assessment of its community relations policies. It was found that there was a recurring misconception among police and public that the detection of crime should take precedence over its prevention. Attitudes had developed within the force that failed to recognise the value, or even the necessity, of police involvement in community affairs in order to prevent crime. The authors of the report found that a majority of police officers believed that difficulties with black people arose as a result of their 'tendency to behave awkwardly and aggressively when approached [by police]'. The report alleged that the concept of community relations was poorly understood by many officers; a problem that was compounded by lack of knowledge, a reluctance to change, a blinkered view in which the police role was seen purely in terms of law enforcement, and a reluctance to see any benefit in what were regarded as social work matters, such as community relations (Whitfield 2004: 161–2).

Immigrant perspectives and policing problems

The police faced difficult and unique challenges when large numbers of black and Asian immigrants arrived in Britain from the late 1940s. Many, particularly those from the Caribbean, came with preconceived ideas of what life would be like in the 'mother country'. McLeod noted the way immigrant writers such as V.S. Naipaul had encountered 'a post-war London that upset received notions of English identity and civility, ideas that had been nurtured from afar' (McLeod 2004: 19; Naipaul 1963). The demise of colonial rule in the 1950s accentuated the pace of decolonisation. It also hastened the downfall of a system of policing in the colonies that, as the Colonial Police Force Commissioner's Conference noted in 1954, had bred a 'traditional feeling of resentment towards the police as being the strong arm of the imperial power' (Whitfield 2004: 43). It would have been surprising, therefore, if the attitude of some immigrants towards the British police had not been adversely influenced by their experience of policing in their homelands. Different immigrant communities posed different problems for the police service. As Table 1.1 shows, the early predominance of West Indian immigrants was eclipsed by new arrivals from India and Pakistan once the Commonwealth Immigrants Act of 1962 became law.

Table 1.1 Immigration from India, Pakistan and the Caribbean: 1955–67 (Rose and Deakin 1969: 83)

	India	Pakistan	Jamaica	Rest of Caribbean	Total
1955–60	33,070	17,120	96,180	65,270	211,640
1961–30.6.62	42,000	50,170	62,450	35,640	190,260
1.7.62–1967	95,850	64,340	31,380	27,780	219,350
Total	171,720	131,630	190,010	128,690	622,050

Police reports in the 1950s suggested that it was immigrants from the Caribbean, those who felt themselves to be British, who were most problematic (Whitfield 2003: 38). This would undoubtedly have stemmed from their generally outgoing nature, and a desire to work and play with the indigenous community at a time when colour prejudice was commonplace. In effect, they were the ones who met racism head-on. Asian immigrants were viewed differently in the early years. The inability of many to converse in English tended to ensure that they socialised with other members of their immigrant communities (Whitfield 2004: 26).

The Working Party on Police Training in Race Relations (HO287/1457) observed that 'one of the significant features of our present-day society is that it contains concentrations of coloured people in twilight areas of 19th century housing.' They also noted the way in which resulting social tensions involving police tended towards a degree of friction that 'would be unlikely to arise if both groups were of the same colour'. Touching on the negative aspects of colonial policing referred to previously, they added:

> Police officers sometimes, through inadequate training and because of stories they have heard, fail to understand the attitude of minority communities. Whatever the reason, there is a risk that the policeman and the coloured citizen will approach each other with expectations that the encounter may be a difficult one. (Whitfield 2006: 10)

Policing – prejudice in perspective

Successive governments from the late 1940s viewed black and Asian immigration in negative terms for well over a decade. As a result, no measures to tackle long-standing problems of racial discrimination were put in place prior to the limited reforms introduced in the Race Relations Act of 1965 (Holmes 1988: 256). Had legislation been introduced earlier, problems between immigrants and police may have been reduced. The absence of legal powers rendered the police virtually impotent when called, for example, to deal with a complaint that a West Indian had been refused service in a pub. Incidents such as this would have adversely affected relations between immigrants and police in two significant ways. First, the complainant would probably have concluded that summoning police assistance in such circumstances was a pointless and ultimately self-defeating exercise.

Second, and equally important, it would almost certainly have led police officers to deduce that such incidents were problematic, as they were placed in a situation they had no means of resolving. Stories of such negative encounters invariably filtered back on both sides and added to perceptions of police as unsupportive and of immigrant complainants as problems to be avoided.

Policing itself was undergoing change during the period. The service's failure to recruit and retain sufficient officers to meet demands necessitated the introduction of new methods of policing: principally, the increased use of motorised patrols (by 100 per cent in some forces between 1950 and 1970). At the same time, slum clearance programmes in cities throughout the country heralded the emergence of multi-storey dwellings (the infamous 'tower blocks') that further curtailed opportunities for police contact with the community. The combination of insufficient police officers, increased use of car patrols and high-rise housing made it all the more likely that response policing and law enforcement would take precedence over community involvement.

The Home Office, representative organisations and even the police recognised that the service was blighted by a conservative outlook, a reluctance to embrace new ideas and an unwillingness to accept external criticism (Whitfield 2004). This made it almost impossible for organisations such as the WIF and the WISC to persuade the Metropolitan Police in the aftermath of the racist disturbances of 1958 and the 1959 Cochrane murder, that the introduction of a racial awareness element in police training would be advantageous. The result was that, as Imbert observed, policing of black and Asian immigrant communities was and continued to be, characterised by ignorance and misunderstanding.

Attitudes to policing in the colonies may well have led a number of immigrants to view police in Britain with suspicion and mistrust. Prior to the Commonwealth Immigrants Act 1962, Asian and Caribbean immigrants had an unrestricted right to enter and remain in the United Kingdom. It is likely, therefore, that some criminals took advantage of the opportunity to further their unlawful activities once in Britain. Although statistics showed that they were a small minority, the combined effect of the discriminatory nature of British society, an alarmist media, and a police service that tended to stereotype those with whom it came into contact, ensured that the sins of the few became the problem of the many.

As has been noted, throughout the period under consideration racial discrimination was a fact of life in Britain. The observations of some senior police officers of the time, the Metropolitan Police Commissioner Sir Joseph Simpson being one example, would suggest that such views were to be found within the ranks of the police service. The concept of community relations was viewed negatively by police officers raised on a philosophy that prized above all else the detection of crime, the prosecution of criminals and the maintenance of law and order, a point well made by one former chief constable:

> Police officers like helping people. There's no problem about that
> ... But we actually joined the job as nineteen or twenty-year-olds
> to get in fast cars, and have blue lights, and get into a bit of a
> scrum, and nick a few people, and get into the excitement of
> police work and the excitement of investigation. Social workers
> joined the social services ... (Whitfield 2004: 186)

While the views of Simpson and others would unquestionably be considered nowadays to be racist, one cannot ignore the fact that at the time they reflected the beliefs of a majority of the British people: beliefs that owed much to government failures to educate and inform. A conservative, inward-looking, largely inexperienced post-war police service, whose priorities lay elsewhere than in the field of community relations, was tasked with policing the nation's transition to an ethnically and culturally diverse society without the legislative support to ensure its success. In such circumstances, it was perhaps inevitable that the transition would be painful for those most directly involved.

Unpublished sources: The National Archives

CAB124/1191	Proposal to restrict the right of British subjects from overseas territories to enter and remain in the UK: 1954
CO318/427/11	Trinidad and Barbados riots 1937: West Indian repercussions
CO1037/2	Position of police forces in the later stages of constitutional development
	Conference of Commissioners of Colonial Police Forces – 14 July 1954
CP1037/2	Working party on the position of police in the later stages of constitutional development: 1953–4
	Home Office Circular 170/1964, Section 5 (21)
HO45/19741	Police Recruitment: conditions of service and pay: 1941–1945

HO45/23227/45	Post-war recruitment of police from overseas territories
HO45/25144	Juvenile Delinquency in Liverpool
HO287/25	Metropolitan Police: relationship with Home Secretary
HO287/250	Operational control of colonial police forces policy: 1956
HO287/1453	Home Office view on whether it should urge police forces to recruit from ethnic minorities: 1965–69
HO287/1455	Police and colour training
HO287/1457	Report of the working party on police training in race relations: 1970
HO287/1458	Recruitment of coloured policemen policy
HO325/9	Racial Disturbances Notting Hill: 1959–61
HO344/11	Immigration of British subjects into the United Kingdom 1950–52
HO344/18	Requests for official inquiries: Royal Commission into status of ethnic minorities within British society
HO344/100	Coloured people from British Colonial territories 1950
HO344/106	Chief constables' replies to questionnaires on conduct of coloured people: 1953
HO344/107	Information from chief constables: 1953–56
MEPO2/9563	Racial disturbances in London
MEPO2/9730	Training methods concerning problems of immigrant communities: 1965
MEPO2/9854	Police liaison with West Indian community in London: 1959–68
MEPO2/9992	Disturbances involving coloured persons in London: 1960–61
MEPO2/10489	Race Relations Act 1965: Commissioner's and Solicitor's observations
MEPO2/10596	Mobile Unit Policing (Accrington Scheme) implementation in the Metropolitan Police District: 1966
MEPO2/10791	Complaints against the Metropolitan Police in selected categories: 1969
MEPO28/9	Community relations survey, Metropolitan Police: 1969–70

References

Parliamentary Debates (Commons), 8 July 1965, col. 149.

Booth, A. (1989) *British Economic Policy: 1939–49*, London: Harvester Wheatsheaf.

Butler, L. J. (2002) *Britain and Empire: Adjusting to a Post-Imperial World*, London: I.B. Taurus.

Emsley, C. (2004) 'The Second World War and the Police in England and Wales' in C. Fijnaut (ed.) *The Impact of World War II on Policing in North-West Europe*, Leuven: Leuven University Press, pp. 151–72.

Gilroy, P. (1987) *There Ain't No Black in the Union Jack*, London: Hutchinson.

Hansard (1948) *Parliamentary Debates (Lords)*, 11 February, cols. 994–1034.

Holmes, C. (1988) *John Bull's Island*, Basingstoke: Macmillan.

McLeod, J. (2004) *Postcolonial London: Rewriting the Metropolis*, London: Routledge.

Naipaul, V. S. (1963) *Mr Stone and the Knights Companion*, London: André Deutsch.

Paul, K. (1997) *Whitewashing Britain: Race and Citizenship in the Postwar Era*, New York: Cornell University Press.

Rose, E. J. B. and Deakin, N. (1969) *Colour and Citizenship: A Report on British Race Relations*, Oxford: Oxford University Press.

Whitfield, J. (2003) 'The Metropolitan Police and London's West Indian Immigrants 1950–1970', PhD thesis, University of London.

Whitfield, J. (2004) *Unhappy Dialogue: The Metropolitan Police and Black Londoners in Post-war Britain*, Cullompton: Willan Publishing.

Whitfield, J. (2006) *'Community, Colonials and the Law: Policing and the Emergence of Multi-ethnic Britain'*, paper presented at conference on Crime, Ethnicity and Migration, Maison des Sciences de l'Homme, Paris.

Chapter 2

Diversity or anarchy? The post-Macpherson blues

Eugene McLaughlin

Introduction

The aim of this chapter is to offer a critical analysis of how and why the construction and reproduction of racialised relations within policing continues to threaten the core conceptualisation of the police. This is, of course, within an overall context of seismic transformations to the macro-policing landscape. The chapter begins with a brief reconsideration of the attempted 'Scarmanisation' of the police to prepare it for the challenges of policing a multicultural polity. The second part assesses the origins and effects of the cultural wars unleashed within the police by the 'institutional racism' finding of the Macpherson Inquiry. I then analyse the contents of *The Secret Policeman* documentary (BBC 2003), which sent shockwaves through the police and reignited the debate about the extent, nature and causes of rank-and-file police racism. Finally, I discuss the latest round of 'quick time' regulatory reforms to decontaminate police culture of what has been defined as 'covert' or 'stealth racism'. The critical issue to consider is the extent to which we are witnessing the painful birthing of a balkanized police culture.

Pre-institutional racism

It is unnecessary to provide a detailed overview of the post 1981 riots reform initiatives that were intended to neutralise the impact of race on policework (for an overview see Scarman 1981; Southgate

1988; Oakley 1988, 1989, 1992; Holdaway 1996; HMIC 1997, 1999, 2000; Hall *et al.* 1998; Bowling and Phillips 2002). First, forces in areas where there was a substantial ethnic minority population launched outreach initiatives and recruitment drives to produce a workforce whose demographics matched those of the community. Second, US-sourced racism awareness training courses were introduced to ensure that officers treated all members of the public in an equitable, fair, 'race blind' manner (see Southgate 1984; Tendler 1991; Council of Europe 1992; HMIC 2000). Finally, there was a broader reform programme to develop professional standards of conduct and the formulation of a 'force to service' paradigm. The overall aim was to ensure that the force could provide a quality of service, which met the different needs, priorities and expectations of the public. At a *Fairness, Community, Justice* conference in February 1993, which examined the relationship between the Metropolitan Police's internal equal opportunities policies and quality of service issues, Sir Paul Condon, the newly appointed Commissioner of the Metropolitan Police, stated:

> We must be equally intolerant of our own colleagues who fail to reach the required standards. We demand exemplary conduct from those we employ. We hold a position of trust in society and it has the right to expect the very best conduct from us ... We have a moral duty to the communities we serve, not only in the way we police them, but also in the way we conduct our own affairs. How will the public expect us to treat them if we cannot even treat each other fairly? (*Independent* 2 February 1993)

However, countering these initiatives were indications that racialisation remained central to police culture. A new generation of officers was socialised into a resentful anti-Scarman police culture that insisted there was a relationship between race and criminality and advocated a tough policing response to what was perceived as the increasing lawlessness of black neighbourhoods. This, of course, fed into and was fuelled by the 1985 riots and periodic 'mugging' panics. Despite officers being trained in specialist community and race relations courses, there were suggestions of a tacitly condoned casualised racism. Equally significantly, there were also indications that ethnic minority officers, as the classic 'outsiders-now-enemy-within', were encountering significant levels of prejudice, disadvantage and discrimination within certain police forces (Smith and Gray

1984). In the early 1990s, the inability to integrate ethnic minority and female officers into the ranks generated a series of high-profile cases of institutionalised racism and sexism. At the same moment as the police were having to defend themselves against a record number of complaints of malpractice and corruption, the fabled 'blue shield' was breached from within. What was revealed was a claustrophobic workplace culture, which presumed conformity to a hegemonic white, male, heterosexual culture and condoned vituperative sexist and racist attitudes and behaviour. Unacceptable attitudes and behaviour were going unchallenged and ethnic minority, female and gay officers were tokenised, isolated and extremely vulnerable (see Holdaway 1997). These cases produced two significant outcomes in the mid-1990s.

First, ethnic minority officers established a Black Police Association (BPA) in 1993–94, claiming that the Police Federation was unwilling and unable to promote racial equality in the workplace. The BPA replicated their US counterparts in focusing on complaints arising out of the conflictual racial dynamics within police forces and poor relationships between the police and black communities. Holdaway (1996: 195) pointed to the radical implications of this development arguing that the formation of the BPA would 'strengthen the racialized identity of its members'.

The establishment of the BPA disrupted traditional authority relationships within police forces and provided the newsmedia with a distinctive subcultural voice on policing issues. It also set the equally important precedent for other marginalised officers to set up their own representative bodies.

Second, two years later, the Association of Chief Police Officers (ACPO) sought the help of the Commission for Racial Equality (CRE) to produce an 'action plan' on race and equality issues. This plan was premised on the base line benefits of mainstreaming equal opportunities at all points of the employment cycle: enhanced corporate 'brand reputation', improved operational effectiveness, deepened public trust, and eased conflict between police officers and the public. It also spelt out the long term consequences for the police of having to fight further race-related discrimination cases: more financially costly industrial tribunals, extremely negative publicity, damaged community relations, staff demoralisation and poor performance, absenteeism and high wastage rates. So long as the police remained overwhelmingly white and male, it would be extremely vulnerable to charges of racism and sexism. The result would be that it would be extremely difficult to recruit or retain high-calibre ethnic minority, female and gay staff (CRE 1996).

Institutional racism: insidious and pervasive

The publication on 24 February 1999 of the Macpherson Report into the racist murder of Stephen Lawrence generated global newsmedia coverage and passionate public commentary. The hardest hitting official statement on race and policing ever published in the UK catapulted race relations into the forefront of the nation's consciousness (Hall 1999; McLaughlin 1999; McLaughlin and Murji 1999; Cathcart 2000; Lea 2000; Kundnani 2000; Marlow and Loveday 2000; Bourne 2001). Almost 20 years after Scarman's report, Macpherson concluded that the end result of decades of over-policing and under-protection was an acute lack of ethnic minority trust and confidence in the police. The report was a devastating indictment of the Metropolitan Police force. Individual officers of all ranks were 'named and shamed' for their mishandling of a murder investigation that was marred by 'a combination of professional incompetence, institutional racism and a failure of leadership by senior officers' (Macpherson 1999: 46.1). In the course of the inquiry it became clear that the much-lauded post-Scarman 'colour blind' policing initiatives had had little discernible affirmative impact on the police. This was most obviously evident in the inability of officers of all ranks who gave evidence to understand how 'race' might be embedded in, and constitutive of, police work. In his evidence, Sir Paul Condon, the Commissioner, conceded that the force would need to overhaul how it responded to racially motivated crime, the disproportionate application of police powers to particular ethnic minority groups, and racist behaviour by police officers. However, he refused to publicly accept that the force was 'institutionally racist'. This stood in stark contrast to the evidence submitted by the Metropolitan Black Police Association.

The Macpherson Report concluded, however, that key parts of the unsuccessful police investigation of the Stephen Lawrence murder could be accounted for by the presence not of overt racism but 'institutional racism', defined as

> the collective failure of an organisation to provide an appropriate and professional service to people because of their colour, culture or ethnic origin. It can be seen or detected in processes, attitudes and behaviour, which amount to discrimination through unwitting prejudice, ignorance, thoughtlessness, and racist stereotyping which disadvantage minority ethnic people. It persists because of the failure of the organisation openly and adequately to recognise and address its existence and causes by

policy, example and leadership. Without recognition and action to eliminate such racism it can prevail as part of the ethos or culture of the organisation. It is a corrosive disease. (Macpherson 1999: 6.34)

The 70 'disinfectant' recommendations had repercussions for every aspect of policing. The report insisted on: new procedures for the reporting, recording and investigation of racist crime; rule-tightening of discretionary stop and search powers; targets for recruitment, progression and retention of ethnic minority officers; and making racism a disciplinary offence punishable by dismissal from the police force. Proposals were presented for revising race awareness training to make certain that all police personnel were educated to not just understand but positively value cultural diversity, to recognise the connection between the cultivation of good community relations and effective policing, and to hammer home that 'a racist officer is an incompetent officer' (Macpherson 1999: 332). It was also recommended that the Race Relations Act should be amended to apply to the police and that an independent police complaints system be established.

Following publication of the report, Jack Straw, the then Home Secretary, set out an action plan for implementation of the recommendations referred to above (Home Office 1999). A Lawrence Steering Group (LSG) was established in the Home Office consisting of independent representatives from ethnic minority communities, the police and other statutory agencies. In addition to ensuring that the Macpherson recommendations were being actioned, the LSG was expected to monitor the impact of the report on the public's experiences and perceptions of the police, the way policing was being delivered, and the relationship between the police and ethnic minority communities. It also had a role in advising on the implementation of the Race Relations (Amendment) Act 2000, which came into force in April 2001. This gave public institutions a statutory duty to promote race equality in all their functions by eliminating unlawful discrimination, promoting equality of opportunity, and furthering good relations between different racial groups. Individual officers could not discriminate directly or indirectly, or victimise one another in discharging their public functions. Chief police officers were made vicariously liable for all aspects of discrimination carried out by an officer in the exercise of his or her public duty unless it could be demonstrated that all reasonable steps were taken to prevent the discrimination. The Commission for Racial Equality was given responsibility for ensuring compliance with the plethora of legislative requirements.

Post-institutional racism

The Metropolitan Police's 'Policing Diversity: Protect and Respect' strategy was intended to signify the movement from a 'colour blind' to an 'anti-racist' policing philosophy (see Metropolitan Police 1998, 1999a, 1999b, 2000; Ghaffur 2004). Constructing what was defined as the world's first anti-racist police force would require three interrelated practical adjustments regarding: recruitment, retention and career development; cultural diversity training; and the 'diversity proofing' of operational practices. The overall intention was to generate an exemplary performance culture. Despite the Metropolitan Police's efforts to re-legitimise itself through its ambitious diversity agenda, internal reactions to the Macpherson Report revealed an extremely volatile, litigious workplace racked with confusion and anger, criss-crossed with competing power networks and replete with highly racialised schisms and micro-conflicts. These anarchic subcultural conflicts were played out in the full glare of the newsmedia.

First, a radicalised Black Police Association (BPA) was extremely vocal in its criticism of what it viewed as the glaring gap between, on the one hand, the 'hand-on-heart' speeches of chief officers and the glossy official publications that extolled the rhetoric of 'institutionalising diversity' and on the other, the reality for ethnic minority officers confronting a groundswell of resentment to Macpherson's reform agenda (see Cashmore 2001, 2002). The overall intention of what was defined as an orchestrated racist backlash was to decapitate the BPA leadership, destroy its reputation and sabotage core recommendations of the Macpherson Report. Second, the sensitivities of white Metropolitan Police officers' were at an all-time high, provoking protests that the finding of 'institutional racism' was an affront to their professionalism. Concern was also expressed about the implications of the Black Police Association being effectively sponsored by ACPO and the Home Office. What might be defined as a dissident white 'reverse racism' perspective received prominent coverage and support in conservative sections of the newsmedia and among Conservative politicians and commentators (see, for example, Dennis *et al.* 2000; Green *et al.* 2000). This broader anti-Macpherson backlash found amplified expression in the overwhelmingly negative reaction to the Parekh Report (2000), which had attempted to broaden the terms of the debate about the future of multi-ethnic, multicultural Britain (see McLaughlin and Neal 2004). It also featured in newsmedia commentary on the northern riots of 2001 regarding the willingness of politically correct policing to tolerate virtual 'no-go' areas to ensure good 'community relations' and in ongoing debates about race and street crime and immigration and asylum. Direct connections were also made to the 'flags, badges and emblems' campaign being conducted by sections of the conservative press to save the RUC from post-Patten abolition (see Ellison and Smyth 2000).

Third, female and gay officers, as well as a proliferating number of staff associations, pressed to make sure that their respective interests and concerns were both included in the post-Macpherson cultural diversity agenda and recognised in their own right. This is not surprising given that there was continuing evidence of high levels of sexism and homophobia in the force (Foster *et al.* 2005). They resisted attempts by senior officers to impose an internal 'hierarchy of oppression'. Fourth, there were signs that ACPO was de-intensifying the focus on 'institutional racism'. Sir John Stevens, the Commissioner of the Metropolitan Police, applied a tough-minded realism to the problem of repairing the divisions and 'rallying the troops'. He prioritised rebuilding a sense of officer commitment by emphasising the importance of teamwork and the thicker identity of the 'police family' and concentrating on achievements rather than failures (see Stevens 2006). Officers were told to focus on the core business of delivering safer neighbourhoods; securing the capital against the post-9/11 terrorist threat; supporting the campaign for criminal justice reforms; developing effective policing strategies and implementing broader service delivery reforms; and campaigning for more resources and powers. He declared: 'Of course there will still be one or two racists in the force, and I'm determined to root them out. But we have moved on light years in the past two or three years. Even the most trenchant critics will give us that. *We are not institutionally racist*' (*Sunday Telegraph* 20 January 2002). The Commissioner received official support in January 2003 when David Blunkett, the then Home Secretary, queried the usefulness of the term 'institutional racism' (*Guardian* 15 January 2003). On the tenth anniversary of Stephen Lawrence's murder, Cressida Dick, Commander of Scotland Yard's Diversity Directorate, complicated the debate further when she contradicted both the Commissioner and the Home Secretary, saying that she could not imagine a time when the police would be able to proclaim that it was free of institutional racism (*Independent* 22 April 2003).

The intensifying 'culture wars' centred on a series of truly extraordinary disciplinary investigations involving ethnic minority officers. In August 2000, the Metropolitan Police Authority established an inquiry chaired by David Muir into how the Metropolitan Police had handled the case against Sergeant Gurpal Virdi. He had been arrested in April 1998 having been judged to have sent himself and other ethnic minority colleagues racist hate mail. Virdi stood accused of doing so because he had been turned down for promotion and planned to launch a race discrimination case. The Crown Prosecution Service subsequently decided not to proceed with criminal charges, but in February 2000 Virdi appeared before a police disciplinary tribunal. The following month he was found guilty and discharged from the Metropolitan Police.

An employment tribunal subsequently ordered the force to pay record damages of more than £150,000 for racially discriminating against the Sikh police officer. An extra £25,000 was awarded for aggravated damages in respect of the 'high-handed' manner in which he was dealt with by the Met. There was no evidence that he had sent the letters and it was found that he was the victim of racial discrimination by the Metropolitan Police, which had treated a white police officer, who was also a suspect, differently. Virdi was reinstated in November 2000 when he won an internal appeal against his dismissal. He was also offered an apology by Deputy Commissioner Sir Ian Blair and the Metropolitan Police Authority set up an inquiry into the case. The following month, Virdi and the Metropolitan Police reached a final settlement and he received an apology affirming that he had been the victim of race discrimination in the way the case was investigated. Although it had limited access to the Metropolitan Police, the Muir Inquiry established that officers were demoralised by an authoritarian managerial culture that was obsessed with procedural conformity and a 'guilty until proven innocent' disciplinary system that trapped officers. In addition, front-line supervisors and managers were not confident or competent to deal with the complex range of issues associated with diversity and difference (Muir 2001).

The case of Superintendent Ali Dizaei provided further insight into the post-Macpherson conflict raging within the Metropolitan Police. On 18 January 2001, Superintendent Ali Dizaei, one of Britain's most senior ethnic minority police officers, was suspended from duty over a variety of allegations. One of the most expensive anti-corruption investigations ever mounted concluded that Dizaei should be held to account for a barrage of well-publicised misdemeanours ranging from fiddling his expenses through to being involved in drug abuse, consorting with prostitutes and criminals, accepting gratuities and threatening national security through links to Middle Eastern diplomats. According to extensive newsmedia reports, approximately one hundred investigating officers were involved in 'Operation Helios', as were officers from MI5, Inland Revenue, Special Branch, National Criminal Intelligence Service, as well as the Drug Enforcement Agencies of California and Canada. Given the racial sensitivities associated with the case, the Metropolitan Police had involved Her Majesty's Inspectorate of Constabulary, the Crown Prosecution Service, and an independent advisory group in a consultative and monitoring role (Dizaei 2007).

The Iranian-born police officer was second in command at Kensington police station in west London, and was tipped to become the first ethnic minority chief constable or future commissioner of Scotland Yard. He was suspended just before he was due to take the Strategic Command Course, the gateway to promotion as a chief officer and take over as the head of the BPA. Dizaei had made headlines in 2000 when he accused the police service of 'ethnically cleansing' minority candidates for promotion through 'culturally biased' testing procedures. In April 2003 Dizaei was acquitted of charges alleging that he had abused his office and perverted the course of justice. Five months later the Crown Prosecution Service decided it could not proceed to a second trial relating to outstanding corruption allegations. Senior Metropolitan Police officers stood accused of orchestrating a 'racist witch-hunt' against the leadership of the Black Police Association. Dizaei, as a high-profile BPA representative who had demanded that policy be matched by action on race, was a prime target for such a witch-hunt. In addition, the covert surveillance aspects of the Dizaei investigation had allowed investigators to monitor confidential BPA business.

Following Dizaei's exoneration, he announced that he would sue the force for racial discrimination and victimisation. Negotiations for him to return to work broke down when the Metropolitan Police insisted that he would be subject to a 'service confidence procedure' which was imposed on officers about whom there were suspicions. Race relations within the Metropolitan Police reached a post-Lawrence crisis point when the BPA declared that 'the Metropolitan Police have learnt nothing from the Stephen Lawrence inquiry, not to mention its own internal cases of Singh, Michael, Locker, Virdi and Logan'. As a result of what it viewed as the deliberate attempt to criminalise Superintendent Ali Dizaei, it would not endorse efforts to recruit ethnic minority officers and would dissuade members of their communities from enrolling in the force. The BPA also demanded that the MPS drop all disciplinary allegations against Dizaei and reinstate him; a public inquiry be established to examine *Operation Helios* and other investigations by the Metropolitan Police's CIB unit; and the suspension of the officers responsible for orchestrating the witch-hunt. On the day that it was announced that Mike Fuller had been appointed Britain's first black chief constable, the BPA confirmed that it was organising a 'March of Solidarity', with ethnic minority officers marching in full uniform on Scotland Yard on 17 November 2003.

At the end of October 2003 Superintendent Dizaei was reinstated, after six weeks of negotiations. Senior police officers backed down on their original position that Dizaei could not return to operational duties because they could not vouchsafe for his integrity. In return, Dizaei dropped his race discrimination case (which it was estimated could have cost the force in the region of a £1 million settlement) and also admitted that his conduct had fallen below the standards expected of a senior police officer. The case was also subject to investigation by both the Police Complaints Authority and the Metropolitan Police Authority (MPA). Ironically, just before it was replaced by the Independent Police Complaints Commission, the Police Complaints Authority report concluded that Superintendent Dizaei should have faced disciplinary charges. The MPA inquiry, chaired by Sir Bill Morris, the former general secretary of the Transport and General Workers' Union, was tasked with investigating Metropolitan Police Service policies, procedures and practices for handling complaints and allegations against individuals, grievances and workplace disputes, as well as Employment Tribunal claims. As we shall see later in this chapter, the Morris Inquiry would publish a highly critical report in December 2004.

The hyper-racist recruits: *The Secret Policeman*

In the midst of the increasingly bitter and damaging post-Macpherson culture wars, rumours began to circulate that a BBC undercover investigation team had obtained evidence of racist attitudes and behaviour among probationary police officers that matched anything seen in the covert video footage of the five racially paranoid white men accused of murdering Stephen Lawrence.

The programme makers chose Greater Manchester Police (GMP), Britain's second largest police force, because in October 1998 David Wilmot, the then Chief Constable, had told the Macpherson Inquiry that 'society has institutionalised racism, Greater Manchester Police therefore has institutionalised racism … and it is our responsibility and duty to try and make sure that (a) that's eradicated and (b)

27

that it doesn't interfere with discharge of our responsibilities to the community' (*Newsnight*, BBC, 15 October 1998). This acceptance of 'institutional racism' came as a surprise to other chief constables and infuriated the Police Federation. Wilmot stood accused of contradicting the views of Sir Paul Condon and betraying his own officers. He also caused further controversy by insisting that GMP policies and procedures would have ensured that the murderers of Stephen Lawrence would have been brought to justice by his officers. The GMP subsequently launched *Operation Catalyst* to implement the recommendations of the Macpherson Report as well as a new recruitment campaign that emphasised that GMP was 'the best police force in the world'.

The BBC documentary wanted to find out whether the first generation of post-Macpherson officers were racially prejudiced and, if they were, whether they were prepared to ignore force policies and act upon their racial predispositions. The BBC justified its undercover investigation because of the distinct possibility that racism had been driven underground by post-Macpherson policy initiatives. In so doing, the BBC broke all the conventions that governed the relationship between the newsmedia and the police with regard to filming in training schools. It took BBC reporter Mark Daly approximately one year to infiltrate the force. During the tenth anniversary of the murder of Stephen Lawrence, Daly was approximately half-way through his basic training in Bruche Police Training Centre, Warrington, along with officers from other police forces in north-west England. In total there were 120 recruits, only one of whom was Asian. After successfully completing his training, Daly worked as a probationary constable in greater Manchester. The investigation ended in August 2003 when the reporter was arrested outside his home by GMP internal affairs officers for obtaining his police wages by deception, presenting false documents during the application process, and damaging a police uniform. The GMP officers confiscated cameras, recording equipment and notebooks from Daly's home.

In the countdown to the broadcast on 21 October 2003, there was considerable newsmedia coverage of police and Home Office anger about what was defined as the irresponsible, underhand behaviour of the BBC. Through micro-cameras hidden in his uniform, room and car, the nation was privy to covert footage Daly recorded in classrooms, the bar, canteen, various external locations and his car. However, the primary focus was his bedroom where fellow recruits hung out after the bar was closed. Here the reporter gradually turned general conversations towards the issue of race and policing.

In addition to watching covert footage of his fellow recruits, Daly also provided viewers with a video diary that filled them in on off-the-camera developments as well as his thoughts about what was unfolding around him.

Daly noted how the training centre literature made it clear that there was a zero tolerance policy with regard to racist, homophobic and sexist language and behaviour or harassment or intimidation of any form. In the first cultural diversity training class there was a discussion about racism in British society and in the police force. There was footage of recruits being warned about unacceptable behaviour, stereotyping and not to use the words 'Paki', 'nigger', 'wog' or 'coon' or they would be dismissed. A Police Federation representative reinforced the message that they should not use racist words. However, if they did they would still be represented by the Federation in any disciplinary proceedings. As was noted by Daly, this was the first time that an alert recruit would see a discrepancy between official policy and practice. The eight racist officers 'outed' by Daly in the course of his investigation were Andy Hall, Carl Jones, Tony Lewin, Adrian Harrison and Andy Turley of the GMP, Keith Cheshire and Rod Pulling of North Wales police and Steve Salkeld based in Cheshire police. In the course of a series of 'private' conversations between Daly and these officers they convey a visceral hatred of Asians, show a willingness to discriminate on racial grounds as soon as they were assigned to operational duties, and disclose strong sympathy for far right political groups.

Explaining the hyper-racist recruits

As was noted above, even before *The Secret Policeman* was broadcast, the documentary had provoked a major row between the BBC, GMP and the Home Office – fought out across the rest of the newsmedia. This programme was explosive because in spite of decades of research findings to the contrary, it indicated that racist attitudes were capable of transferring directly into discriminatory behaviour on the streets. The avalanche of newsmedia coverage of the 'racist recruits' programme in the following days contained commentary on the damage the racist-fascist views and actions shown in the programme would do to race relations; public confidence and trust in the police; internal staff relationships; recruitment campaigns; and demands that all police forces take decisive action to tackle racism. There was also a chorus of condemnation of the police and Home Office for trying to

29

censor the BBC. *The Secret Policeman* attracted international attention and respect from the broadcasting industry, with Mark Daly being voted young journalist of the year for the quality of his reporting. Detectives from two of the forces named in the *The Secret Policeman* were subsequently investigated for perverting the course of justice by the Independent Police Complaints Commission.

The programme sent shockwaves through the police and the Home Office. David Blunkett, the then Home Secretary, quickly backtracked on his criticism of the BBC, describing the programme as 'horrendous' and promising further action to eliminate racism and other forms of discrimination within the police. The chief officers in charge of the police forces implicated by the programme called press conferences to distance themselves from the rabid racist views and behaviour of their officers. Clive Wolfendale, the Assistant Chief Constable of North Wales, told reporters: 'I felt physically sick as I watched *The Secret Policeman* last night. Pulling has shamed his colleagues, his uniform and the service. He is a disgrace.' He disclosed that he would be writing to Doreen and Neville Lawrence to apologise about the attack upon them and their son. The Assistant Chief Constable of GMP, Alan Green, declared: 'The programme has greatly shocked me and made me ashamed to be part of the British police service. It saddened me greatly as there still appears to be much work to be done, despite many of the efforts we have taken to tackle racism since the Stephen Lawrence inquiry.' Because one of the officers had served with the Metropolitan Police and suggested that it was riven with racism and resentful of the Macpherson Inquiry, Sir John Stevens conceded that the words and actions of the police recruits were 'not far away' from that displayed in the covert videos of the five white suspects in the Stephen Lawrence murder case. He immediately set up an internal review of race and diversity in the Metropolitan Police Service (see Ghaffur 2004). Chris Fox, the ACPO president, subsequently accepted that the racist attitudes and actions documented in the programme evidenced that the post-Macpherson work on race and cultural diversity issues had turned out to be a 'depressing failure' (Fox 2004). ACPO committed itself to working with the BPA, CRE, advisory groups and others to re-examine recruitment, selection, training and professional development practices as well as the cultural diversity strategy. In an unprecedented move it also authored a letter to the nation expressing its determination to eradicate racism within the police service.

A variety of explanations were put forward to explain the racist views expressed in the documentary. As Rowe (2004) has noted, PC Pulling *et al.* were instantly transformed into hyper-racist 'folk devils', in a manner similar to the five white men held responsible for the murder of Stephen Lawrence. They became the 'natural born' personification of unreconstructed police racism. The dominant perspective articulated by ACPO, the Police Federation, politicians and commentators was that PC Pulling and the other foul-mouthed racist recruits were not representative of the post-Macpherson police service. To back this up, it was emphasised that Daly found no evidence of racism when he took up operational duties with Greater Manchester Police officers.

A subsidiary perspective concentrated attention on the blanket antagonism towards Asians. These officers were representative of deprived northern English localities that had fractured into racially hostile enclaves. The white population had rejected cosmopolitan multiculturalism and diversity and was increasingly intolerant of Asians as a result of 9/11. The recruits' selectively racist views were also linked with the race riots of spring and summer 2001 when simmering tensions between Asian and white communities in Bradford, Oldham and Burnley erupted into violent street confrontations. The hysterical reporting of the threat posed to the nation by asylum-seekers and refugees in the tabloid media was also blamed for fostering extremist attitudes among a generation of young whites. In a twist of this theme, the racist recruits were also paraded as evidence that far right extremist groups had managed to infiltrate the police force in order to ferment racial hatred and destroy its reputation. This was buttressed by a provocative BNP statement declaring that it did have card-carrying members who worked as police officers and that 'most police sympathise with the BNP's view that a multicultural society is not a stable society'. A final perspective was that the BBC reporter had acted as an irresponsible *agent provocateur* who had tricked immature, unthinking young men into letting their guard down.

The chair of the Commission of Racial Equality, Trevor Phillips, insisted that it was not just a matter of a few 'rotten apples' who could be screened out of the force or 'unthinking racists' who could be 'trained out' of their racist viewpoint. The documentary, for Phillips, revealed a pattern of behaviour that was pervasive, and though officially condemned was 'tacitly condoned by their peers' and not restrained by supervisors or managers. He developed his perspective in the following manner (Phillips 2003a):

It seems to me a racing certainty that these men could behave in the way they did, not because everyone else shared their views – I do not believe most police officers do – but because they knew that the *culture of their workplace* is not to grass up a colleague, no matter how repellent his behaviour. Let me return to what I said to you four years ago, which I now feel was perhaps prophetic:

In the ethos of uniformed services, a few people may do wrong, but the pressure not to 'grass' is so strong that they are protected by a vow of silence; and all too often, their success at getting 'collars' can lead others, who start with no racial bias to emulate their ways. We have to draw a line here and make it possible for the vast majority of decent officers to feel comfortable speaking out against evil, and driving those who bring dishonour to the uniform out of the service.

Six Greater Manchester Police officers, two North Wales officers and two Cheshire officers resigned and 12 officers were subsequently disciplined as a result of official investigations. ACPO committed itself to introducing a standardised 'race and diversity proof' recruitment process that would involve candidates being evaluated on seven different competencies including 'respect for race and diversity'. This competency was defined as the 'golden thread' of the new assessment procedure. In addition, there would be new tests to screen out applicants suspected of racism and the deployment of covert monitoring and integrity tests to detect racists already in post. Officers would also be encouraged to identify and marginalise colleagues displaying unacceptable attitudes and behaviour. This 'firewalling' was reinforced by banning police officers from membership of the BNP and other extremist political parties. In addition, and most alarming for the Home Office and chief officers, the police service found itself facing another round of external investigations into why post-Macpherson race and diversity policies had failed in such a disquieting manner. Given who was likely to be in charge of the inquiries it was clear that they would move well beyond the updated version of the 'rotten apple' theory to a cultural decontamination agenda.

In his speech to the BPA AGM on 30 October 2003, Trevor Phillips argued that there would have to be deep organisational transformation rather than yet more race and diversity training programmes. In the light of the disturbing evidence of racism reported in the HMIC report on GMP and the contents of *The Secret Policeman*, Phillips announced that he had written to all chief constables asking them to provide evidence that they had recruitment, vetting and training policies in place to screen out racists (Phillips 2003b). In addition, the CRE activated the recently amended race relations legislation to establish an independent inquiry to examine: the screening processes for candidates; the provision of race training for recruits; the extent of racial prejudice and discrimination; the mechanisms for the identification and management of racist behaviour among officers; the effectiveness of the race-related disciplinary process and grievance procedures; the sanctions that are used when inappropriate race-related conduct is detected; and the role of the various bodies involved in police governance in assessing how individual forces and the service in general were combating racial discrimination and complying with their race equality duty. This investigation, led by Sir David Calvert-Smith, former director of the CPS, started its deliberations in January 2004 (one month before the Morris Inquiry, discussed below) and published a final report on 8 March 2005.

'Rabbits frozen in the headlights': The Morris Report

The implementation of the post-Macpherson diversity agenda of the Metropolitan Police had a central place in the deliberations of a Metropolitan Police Authority evaluation of the MPS community and race relations training, and in the Morris Inquiry, which reported in December 2004. The Metropolitan Police Authority evaluation found that officers 'come to the training having heard negative stories and some approach the training in hostile frame of mind. In this environment, openness and honest participation can be difficult to facilitate' (2004: 3). If it was not mandatory, the majority of officers would not attend as they were not convinced of its relevance to operational policing. This report noted that the term 'institutional racism' caused such an emotional reaction among officers that it should be dropped from training programmes unless it was dealt with properly. The Morris Inquiry conducted a force-wide survey and received 1,400 documents and oral evidence from 100 individuals, during 31 days of hearings. Its members also accompanied officers on patrol, visited police stations and the training centre and operational HQ as well as Greater Manchester, Merseyside and West Midlands police forces. The high-profile disciplinary cases of Superintendent Dizaei and Sergeant Virdi were also central to the inquiry. The report provided a multifaceted analysis of the functioning of the disciplinary and complaints procedures of the Metropolitan Police. It also painted what the *Observer* (12 December 2004) described as a 'heart of darkness' picture of the force's management of race and diversity issues.

In the workplace 'diversity', while unassailable as the ethical core for policing multicultural Britain, was poorly understood, lacked coherence and was not embedded in or connected to the organisational culture. The proliferation of top-down 'buzzword' initiatives had reduced the overall message to a series of tick boxes. A sexist, homophobic, culturally insensitive rank-and-file 'canteen culture' was going unchallenged. Sitting alongside a racial obsession was a paralysing fear among front-line supervisors and managers of being branded racist or politically incorrect. 'Management by retreat' was triggering a disproportionate number of formal investigations into black and ethnic officers and fuelling a backlash as evidenced by the number of white officers lodging employment tribunal claims alleging race discrimination.

The Morris Report underlined the pressing necessity for the Metropolitan Police to develop a managerial paradigm capable of handling diversity and difference in a robust manner. It called for the elimination of discriminatory management and personnel practices, the replacement of antiquated disciplinary regulations and a review of how complaints are investigated. This fed into a separate review of police disciplinary arrangements (see Taylor 2004). Senior officers would have to take responsibility for resolving workplace disputes. Equally significantly, it also concluded that cultural diversity policies had to be devised and implemented in a way that located race in a broader equality context. This would engage 'all within the workforce of the MPS community, which would overcome the cynicism and resistance we have seen. This approach would emphasise that diversity encompasses all aspects of difference including gender, faith, disability, sexual orientation and transgender issues as well as race. It is as applicable to the majority group as to minorities' (Morris 2004: para 5.5.4).

'Ice in the heart': The Calvert-Smith Report

At the time of the release of the Morris Report there were warnings that the Calvert-Smith Report would be even more scathing in its conclusions. This CRE inquiry also focused on internal employment matters and racial discrimination rather than operational policing.

The inquiry was officially launched in March 2004 with an appeal for serving and former officers to come forward with evidence. It also threatened to cross-examine the officers who had been outed by *The Secret Policeman* in public, in much the same way as the Lawrence Five had been during the Macpherson Inquiry.

The Calvert-Smith Report (CRE 2004; 2005) concluded that the police force was 'like a perma frost – thawing on the top, but still frozen solid at the core'. Despite the commitment of chief officers 'the fact remains that every time you drill down you find that ice, and unless more is done, it won't melt any time soon' (*Guardian* 9 March 2005). Forces were either not recording the data required by the ethnic monitoring duty or were not properly monitoring this data. Nor were they carrying out race impact assessments of their policies. As a consequence, very few police forces had produced a satisfactory race equality scheme as required by the Race Relations (Amendment) Act 2000.

It was confirmed, in line with the Morris Report, that middle managers were not fully trained or properly supported on how to handle race-based grievances and complaints. There was also a fear of reporting racist incidents in case matters escalated out of control: 'such action as the service takes to deal with racist behaviour tends to concentrate on the superficial (for example, racist language) rather than the subtleties underlying racist behaviour' (CRE 2005: 16). The report declared that the screening processes were rejecting proportionately more ethnic minority than white applicants on grounds of attitudes to race, gender, homophobic attitudes and so on.

The initial race and diversity training was institutionalising racial problems. Ethnic minority recruits 'expressed concerns about the quality or commitment of the trainers, the superficial treatment of diversity issues, the "bar and alcohol" culture, the lack of proper evaluation' (CRE 2004: 43). Trainers were 'unconfident, uncommitted or even hostile to "diversity"; institutional racism remained widely misunderstood after the training and was seen as smear on the police service' (CRE 2004: 46). The training programme had alienated white officers, who believed they were 'being coerced into a "politically correct" exercise of re-programming following the Lawrence report finding, as-they-saw-it, that they were collectively racist. This gave the trainers the impossible task of dealing with resentments that arose from people who felt they were being processed rather than trained, and blamed rather then developed' (CRE 2004: 52). This was driving racial discrimination underground and allowing what was defined as a new breed of 'stealth racist' to remain undetected.

The report concluded that if the force was to move beyond a crisis management approach to race relations, it would have to create a culture 'with a clear anti-racist ethos, in which racist behaviour will be appropriately and swiftly dealt with' (CRE 2004). The 125 recommendations required changes to be made at every level of police activity, from recruitment to training, complaints and governance, in order to inculcate forces with a race consciousness. Prioritising and addressing racial prejudice and discrimination would allow the police to undertake similar work across all diversity issues and enable it to become an organisation 'less and less attractive to recruits and serving officers of the kind so graphically displayed in *The Secret Policeman*'. To reinforce this there could be a separate disciplinary offence of 'racial misconduct'. Launching the report, Trevor Phillips issued a final warning to the police: 'we don't want to be heavy-handed – we want to work with all involved in the governance of the police service to melt this ice. But if no-one's prepared to hit the defrost button, we will simply have to turn up the heat' (CRE Press Release, 8 March 2005). Failure on behalf of the police to improve their race equality and diversity schemes would lead to legal action and possibly a CRE enforcement order. If forces failed to act on such an order, it could lead to a fine or court case and even a prison sentence for the chief constable concerned.

Conclusion

There is widespread acceptance that twenty-first century policing will be required to respond to a range of perplexing community tensions, conflicts and social problems, and ever-increasing public expectations, ranging from low-level incivilities and anti-social behaviour through to violent crime, globally organised crime flows and new forms of terrorist threat. As British conurbations become ever more intensely and unpredictably diverse, drawing in more people from different cultural, religious, racial and ethnic backgrounds, the police need to be embedded within the 'multi-social' fabric and be able to understand and work with that volatile, insecure complexity. Police officers must be able to legitimately gather information and intelligence encourage the reporting of crime, identify developing crime trends as well as community tensions and potential flashpoints, and intervene using coercive force if necessary. It is now widely accepted that recruiting people from a narrow set of backgrounds and then enculturing them to think and act in a particular 'tried and tested' organisational manner is of limited value. Diversity and pluralisation of the police workforce is now defined by chief police officers and the government as an operational necessity. As Sir Ian Blair (2005) argues, the twenty-first century police force requires a highly skilled workforce capable of developing and working with new approaches, new tactics and new ways of thinking to pre-empt new criminal and anti-social threats.

The hundreds of recommendations contained in the latest set of post-Macpherson reports are intended not just to de-racialise policing but to construct a proactively anti-racist police force. There is, as we have seen, a focus on improved managerial systems for identifying problem officers; intervening to challenge unacceptable attitudes and behaviour; disciplining (and, if necessary, removing those officers who fail to conform); equalising opportunities; and modernising the complaints and grievances procedures. A crucial issue is whether it is possible to imagine a more culturally differentiated police identity that can also generate a sense of belonging, mutual obligation, interpersonal relations of trust, a sense of common purpose and a special commitment. This contingent 'inside-out/outside-in' variegated police culture might draw its strength, legitimacy and symbolism from its intersection with wider multicultural reference points. However, a series of highly sensitive matters remain to be addressed in the 'hollowing out' of traditional police culture.

First, it needs to be recognised that the defining characteristics of race-related reform programmes within the police have tended to compound rather than alleviate problems. They are drafted in a crisis management environment that invariably disconnects them from the 'lived experience' of the crisis. The 'something must be done' rush to recommendations and action plans means that little real analytical attention is paid to broader social and cultural policing conditions. The managerialist-oriented reform programmes are launched with a newsmedia fanfare alongside reassurances that the police and the public can look to the future with confidence. Internal organisational confusion and potential contestation, while acknowledged, is smothered in reams of recommendations. The next crisis generates another inquiry that invariably exposes the failure of previous reforms and uncovers workplace recrimination and disillusionment. And so it is left to another generation of reforming senior officers to preside over an ever more complicated and increasingly detailed regulatory guidance on mainstreaming race and/or diversity and/ or equality and/or human rights. As a consequence, the burden of successive reform programmes with hundreds of overly ambitious and very often contradictory 'quick time' recommendations lie like a dead weight within the organisational governance and culture of the force. And it must be recognised that the Home Office has played a highly problematic role in the reform process. At key moments its anti-mnemonic policy decisions and instrumental interventions have effectively subverted the possibility of progressive reform. What is truly remarkable is that not one of the multitude of inquiries referred to in this chapter has in any sustained manner turned its investigative gaze on the key Home Office officials and their training and community relations consultants responsible for presiding over the crisis of race and diversity.

Second, little to no analytical attention has been paid within these managerialist reports to the unspoken but obviously pivotal role that 'whiteness' has played in the nurturing and sustaining of both the formal and cultural identity of the British police. This reminds us of the need for sociological analysis of the much more complicated canvas of emotional signification and ethno-cultural identification of 'Britishness' and 'Englishness' that the public police are part of. In order to diffuse potential conflict of racial and ethnic divisions, the police will have to respond both to the cultural insecurities of white officers at the same time as meeting the needs of ethnic minority officers. And, to borrow Trevor Phillips' conceptualisation, the police will have to develop the equivalent of a 'highway code' if officers are to successfully negotiate the minefield of cultural diversity. It will also have to move beyond essentialising processes that are fragmenting workplace identities, anarchising relationships and precluding the possibility of trust-building. The establishment of a multitude of representative staff groupings foreground the very real possibility of the antagonistic balkanisation of the workplace. An allied question is how the police can manage the institutional melancholia for the hegemonic police identity that is now shredding itself to pieces on the jagged contradictions of postmodernity?

Third, the force is now grappling with 'institutional racism' and the idea of 'covert' or 'stealth' racism (and presumably 'stealth' sexism and 'stealth' homophobia) that is supposedly being 'imported' into the organisation by recruits rather than produced, sustained and in certain instances amplified by it. This has been reaffirmed by the reaction to *The Secret Policeman* documentary. This has become the justification for contracting in yet more anti-racist and diversity consultants with pre-packaged programmes, which run the risk of compounding an already paranoid work environment and reproducing a discourse in which racism is very much a 'lumpen' rank-and-file cultural problem. What is significant in the Muir, Morris and Calvert-Smith reports is that this is co-joined by a damning critique of front-line supervision and management. As a consequence, it can be seen that at the same time as probationers are being evaluated on how they intend to overcome their deep-seated, unconscious racism, supervisors and managers are being sent to private sector conferences to be familiarised with the new legislative framework governing workplace diversity issues and 'best practice' on how to mainstream diversity into service delivery and core processes. The emphasis on training and conferencing leaves little space for giving consideration to the unfolding ground-level policing strains in demanding neighbourhoods that are racialising working practices in complicated ways.

Fourth, the police seem condemned not just to have to consider the present and future but to have to live with a history of conflictual relations with ethnic minority communities and between ethnic minority and white officers within police forces. For example, in February 2005 files were released to the National Archive that revealed the true extent of prejudice Metropolitan Police officers felt towards the first generation of West Indian immigrants in the late 1940s and 1950s. The files confirmed that racist attitudes permeated all ranks of the force, with officers making links between male immigrants and criminality and benefit fraud. Officers also expressed concerns about black men mixing with white women. April 2006 represented the twenty-fifth anniversary of the Brixton riots, and one of the defining moments in the post-war history of British policing passed off with little substantial commentary or reflection. However, a BBC2 documentary *Battle for Brixton* (BBC 2006) pieced together testimony from former and serving Metropolitan Police officers and local residents. Deputy Assistant Commissioner Brian Paddick accepted that 'we were an occupying army, if you like, and thinking of the people of Brixton as the enemy, that there was not a good person among them, that they were all criminals, that blackness equated to criminality'. A former officer, Peter Bleksley, declared: 'I did not join the police as a racist, but while I was in the police I became one.' He went on to recall how the police concocted evidence on people they wanted to arrest: 'People had no chance of proving their innocence. Evidence was planted, that was a common practice, and assaulting people was almost a daily occurrence.' The content of National Archive files and the testimony given in the BBC documentary undermines comforting post-war policing as consensus histories, as Whitfield's contribution to this collection examines in more detail.

Finally, there is the question of how to realise a new overarching cultural identity in a radically unsettled and unsettling post-social context. A new generation of police officers inhabit an increasingly volatile operational context. We are witnessing multiple racialisations of 'crime' along with new ethnic tensions associated with new waves of immigration, asylum and settlement. And perhaps most significantly, this generation of officers now have to live with the long-term repercussions of the attacks on London on 7 July 2005 by homegrown suicide bombers, as well as the failed attacks of 21 July 2005 and the shooting of Jean Charles de Menezes the following day. The reignited debate on how politically correct policing is partly responsible for producing an 'enemy within' and the renewed arguments for a commonly accepted framework of citizenship and a stronger sense of British national identity have wide-ranging implications for police practice and police community relations and, of course, an ever emergent police culture.

References

BBC (2003) *The Secret Policeman*, BBC1, 21 October.

BBC (2006) *Battle for Brixton*, BBC2, 10 April.

Blair, Sir I. (2005) *What Type of Police Force?* BBC1 Dimbleby Lecture, November 17.

Bourne, J. (2001) 'The Life and Times of Institutional Racism', *Race and Class*, 43 (2): 7–22.

Bowling, B. and Phillips, C. (2002) *Racism, Crime and Justice*, Harlow: Pearson Education.

Cashmore, E. (2001) 'The Experiences of Ethnic Minority Officers in Britain: Under-Recruitment and Racial Profiling in Performance Culture', *Ethnic and Racial Studies*, 24 (4): 642–59.

Cashmore, E. (2002) 'Behind the Window Dressing: Ethnic Minority Police Perspectives on Cultural Diversity', *Journal of Ethnic and Migration Studies*, 28 (2): 327–41.

Cathcart, B. (2000) *The Case of Stephen Lawrence*, London: Viking.

Commission for Racial Equality (1996) *Race and Equal Opportunities in the Police Service: A Programme for Action*, London: Commission for Racial Equality.

Commission for Racial Equality (2005) *The Police Service in England and Wales: Final Report of a Formal Investigation by the Commission for Racial Equality*, London: Commission for Racial Equality.

Council of Europe (1992) *Police Training Concerning Migrants and Ethnic Relations*, Strasburg: Council of Europe.

CRE (2004) *The Police Service of England and Wales: An Interim Report of a Formal Investigation by the Commission for Racial Equality*, London: Commission for Racial Equality.

Dennis, N., Erdos, G. and Al-Shahi, A. (2000) *Racist Murder and Pressure Group Politics*, London: Civitas.

Dizaei, A. (2007) *Not One of us: The Trail That Changed Policing in Britain Forever*, London: Serpents Tail Books.

Ellison, G. and Smyth, J. (2000) *The Crowned Harp: Policing Northern Ireland*, London: Pluto.

Foster, J., Newburn, T. and Souhami, A. (2005) *Assessing the Impact of the Stephen Lawrence Inquiry*, Home Office Research Study 294, London: Home Office.

Fox, C. (2004) 'Diversity Matters', *Policing Today*, 9 (1): 12–13.

Ghaffur, T. (2004) *Thematic Review of Race and Diversity in the Metropolitan Police Service*, London: Metropolitan Police.

Green, D.G. (ed.) (2000) *Institutional Racism and the Police: Fact or Fiction?* London: Institute for Study of Civil Society.

Hall, S. (1999) 'From Scarman to Stephen Lawrence', *History Workshop*, 48: 187–97.

Hall, S., McLaughlin, E. and Lewis, G. (1998) *The Report on Racial Stereotyping*, Statement of Research on Racial Attitudes and Stereotyping Prepared for Stephen Lawrence Inquiry.

Her Majesty's Inspectorate of Constabulary (1997) *Winning the Race: Policing Plural Communities*, London: Home Office.

Her Majesty's Inspectorate of Constabulary (1999) *Winning the Race: Policing Plural Communities – Revisited*, London: Home Office.

Her Majesty's Inspectorate of Constabulary (2000) *Policing London: Winning Consent*, London: Home Office.

Holdaway, S. (1996) *The Racialisation of British Policing*, London: Macmillan.

Holdaway, S. (1997) 'Constructing and sustaining "Race" within the police workforce, British Journal of Sociology, 48: 19–34.

Home Office (1999) *Dismantling Barriers: The Recruitment, Retention and Progression of Ethnic Minority Offices Action Plan*, London: Home Office.

Kundnani, A. (2000) '"Stumbling on": Race, Class and England', *Race and Class*, 41 (4): 1–18.

Lea, J. (2000) 'The Macpherson Report and the Question of Institutional Racism' *Howard Journal of Criminal Justice*, 39 (3): 219–33.

McLaughlin, E. (1999) 'The Search for Truth and Justice', *Criminal Justice Matters*, 35: 14–17.

McLaughlin, E. and Murji, K. (1999) 'After the Stephen Lawrence Report', *Critical Social Policy*, 19 (3): 371–85.

McLaughlin, E. and Neal, S. (2004) 'Misrepresenting the Multi-Cultural Nation: The Policy Making Process, Newsmedia Management and the Parekh Report', *Policy Studies*, 25 (3): 155–74.

Marlow, A. and Loveday, B. (2000) *After Macpherson: Policing after the Stephen Lawrence Inquiry*, Lyme Regis, Russell House Publishing.

Macpherson, Sir W. (1999) *The Stephen Lawrence Inquiry: Report of an Inquiry by Sir Willam Macpherson of Cluny*, CM 4262-1, London: Home Office.

Metropolitan Police (1998) *Working Together Towards an Anti-Racist Police Service: Report of a Conference 18 December 1998*, London: Metropolitan Police.

Metropolitan Police (1999a) *Protect and Respect: The Met's Diversity Strategy*, London: Metropolitan Police.

Metropolitan Police (1999b) *A Police Service for All the People*, London: Metropolitan Police.

Metropolitan Police (2000) *Policing Diversity: The Metropolitan Police Service Handbook on London's Religions, Cultures and Communities*, London: Metropolitan Police.

Metropolitan Police Authority (2004) *Independent Evaluation into MPS Community and Race Relations (CRR) Training: Executive Summary*, London, Metropolitan Police Authority.

Morris, Sir W., (2004) *The Case for Change: People in the Metropolitan Police Service, The Report of the Morris Inquiry.* London: Metropolitan Police Authority.

Muir, R. D. (2001) *The Virdi Inquiry Report*, London: Metropolitan Police Authority.

Oakley, R. (1988) *Employment in Police Forces: A Survey of Equal Opportunities*, London: Commission for Racial Equality.

Oakley, R. (1989) 'Community and Race Relations Training for the Police: A Review of Developments', *New Community*, 16 (1): 61–79.

Oakley, R. (1992) 'Race Relations Training in the Police: Responses and Issues', paper presented at 21st Cropwood Roundtable Conference, Cambridge: Institute of Criminology.

Parekh, B. (2000) *The Future of Multi-Ethnic Britain*, London: Profile Books.

Phillips, T. (2003a) 'Speech to 2003 CBI Annual Conference', Birmingham, 18 November, http://193.113.211.175/media/nr_.arch/2003.

Phillips, T. (2003b) 'Address to Metropolitan Black Police Association AGM', City Hall, London, 30 October, http://www.downloads/docs/MBPA_TPspeech031030.doc.

Rowe, M. (2004) *Policing, Race and Racism*, Cullompton: Willan Publishing.

Scarman, Lord (1981) *The Scarman Report: The Brixton Disorders, 10–12 April 1981*, Cmnd 8427, London: HMSO.

Smith, D. and Gray, J. (1984) *Police and People in London*, London: Policy Studies Institute.

Southgate, P. (1984) *Racism Awareness Training for the Police*, Home Office Research and Planning Unit Paper 29, London: Home Office.

Southgate, P. (ed.) (1988) *New Directions in Police Training*, London: Home Office.

Stevens, J. (2006) *Not for the Faint Hearted: My Life Fighting Crime*, London: Phoenix Books.

Taylor, W. (2005) *Review of Disciplinary Arrangements*, London: Home Office.

Tendler, S. (1991) 'Big Mack's Tough Challenge', *Police Review*, 8 March: 484–85.

Chapter 3

Police diversity training: a silver-bullet tarnished?

Michael Rowe and Jon Garland

The Lawrence Report made many recommendations concerning community and race relations (CRR) training, or what has subsequently come to be referred to as 'diversity training'. Three of these related to the need to improve first aid training and to provide it to all 'public contact' staff. It is the further seven recommendations, relating to the provision of racism awareness training and valuing cultural diversity that form the focus of this chapter (Macpherson 1999):

48   That there should be an immediate review and revision of racism awareness training within police services to ensure:

(a) that there exists a consistent strategy to deliver appropriate training within all police services, based upon the value of our cultural diversity;

(b) that training courses are designed and delivered in order to develop the full understanding that good community relations are essential to good policing and that a racist officer is an incompetent officer.

49   That all police officers, including CID and civilian staff, should be trained in racism awareness and valuing cultural diversity.

50   That police training and practical experience in the field of racism awareness and valuing cultural diversity should regularly be conducted at local level. And that it should be recognised that local minority ethnic communities should be involved in such training and experience.

51   That consideration be given by police services to promoting joint training with members of other organisations or professions otherwise than on police premises.

52   That the Home Office together with police services should publish recognised standards of training aims and objectives in the field of racism awareness and valuing cultural diversity.

53   That there should be independent and regular monitoring of training within all police services to test both implementation and achievement of such training.

54   That consideration be given to a review of the provision of training in racism awareness and valuing cultural diversity in local government and other agencies including other sections of the criminal justice system.

The establishment of training programmes intended to meet these recommendations is explored in the context of the more general historical development of police training. Even though recommendation 53 outlined that this training ought to be monitored independently there has been little published analysis of the types of programme reviewed below. Nonetheless, key themes recur across many of the reports that review police community and race relations training. These are reviewed in the second part of the chapter, which examines the difficulties associated with providing training that explores the controversial topic of institutional racism, that provides programmes jointly aimed at police officers and other staff, and that makes use of independent local community representatives in the delivery of programmes. It also assesses strategic management issues regarding diversity training and argues that stronger leadership is needed if officers are to reap the full benefits from such training. The final part of the chapter examines suggestions that resistance among rank-and-file officers to the idea of diversity training may partly be explained by 'macho, action-oriented' aspects of police culture. The chapter concludes by arguing that while there is evidence that diversity training has brought about some discernible improvements in police behaviour (not least in the reduction in the use of racist language (Foster *et al.* 2005)), there are a number of problems with an over-reliance upon the supposed benefits of a training programme that does not tackle structural issues or those pertaining to an overarching and dominant police culture.

As other contributions to this collection note, there was certainly no lack of action in terms of the police service response to the training agenda initiated by the Lawrence Inquiry. Individual police services, the Association of Chief Police Officers (ACPO), the Home Office, police authorities, universities, management consultants, and training providers have collectively delivered a host of programmes to officers and civilian staff of all ranks. The logistical and financial implications of these provisions have been considerable. The Metropolitan Police provided a one- or two-day course for 35,000 officers and staff between October 1999 and December 2002. The direct costs of this training were £3.4 million with further opportunity costs of £10.7 million (Metropolitan Police 2005). As with most aspects of policing in England and Wales, these provisions have varied from service to service in terms of content and structure. In keeping with the more general trend in police training in the twenty-first century responsibility for the development of diversity training is devolved to local services required to operate according to central guidelines. Inevitably this means that what follows is based upon general observations about police diversity training, which might not apply to every programme developed in all services.

The historical development of police training

A characteristic feature of police training introduced in response to the Lawrence Report is that it tends to encourage officers and staff to be reflexive practitioners, able to consider how their own values, attitudes and beliefs affect their professional behaviour and how this collectively impacts upon the wider public. Although this model is becoming more deeply embedded in police training in general terms, as the Initial Police Learning and Development Programme, which replaced probationer training from 2006 onwards, emphasises the need for officers to become self-directed learners (Adult Learning Inspectorate 2005), it is significantly at odds with the approach to training that has been predominant since the creation of modern police forces in the nineteenth century. For most of the intervening period police training has been characterised as a 'military model' based upon physical training and the rote learning of police powers and practices (Knights 1988). The current training environment developed after the Second World War, to meet the demands of a police service that needed to recruit large numbers of new officers. This was a period in which chief constables still tended to be men with a military background, as were many of the trainers and new recruits, who seem to have preferred that the police service adopt a model of training established in the armed forces (Wall 1998;

HMIC 2002). In the early 1970s, perhaps mindful of the increasing multicultural and multi-ethnic nature of London, the Metropolitan Police introduced elements of 'social and humanitarian' skills into probationer training and 'race and community relations' became a specific part of the curriculum in 1973. Although this broadened the training curriculum, and by implication at least reflects that police work is about more than mechanical law enforcement, it is less clear that it departed from established approaches to training since it continued to be focused upon the imparting of knowledge and information to recruits (Southgate 1982). That training was somewhat piecemeal during the 1970s was reflected in the Scarman Report (1981), which had provided a framework for police community relations prior to the Lawrence Report. Scarman (1981: 8.32) recommended that police in-service training 'designed to develop the understanding that good community relations are not merely necessary but essential to good policing' should be made compulsory 'from time-to-time' for officers up to the rank of superintendent. It is unclear why Scarman did not feel that the compelling case for junior officers to be trained on these matters did not extend to those in senior posts, although this did reflect his view that the problem of police racism was predominantly associated with those in lower ranks.

Police training in 'community relations', as the interface between officers and minority ethnic people has often euphemistically been known, has tended to oscillate between strategies intended to impact upon behaviour and those that focus upon individual attitudes, values and beliefs. The Police Training Council (PTC), established in the aftermath of the Scarman Report to develop a more rigorous programme across the whole police service, referred to contrasting approaches to CRR training:

> It is often assumed that race relations training should aim to ensure that the attitudes of individuals towards persons of a different race are tolerant or sympathetic. Others feel it is unsound, and can be counterproductive, to seek to modify attitudes and that the focus of training should be on the overt behaviour desired. (PTC 1983: 3)

Just as the tension between focusing on attitudes or affecting behaviour continues to underpin community and race relations or, latterly, diversity training, some of the PTC recommendations remain influential. In particular the PTC suggested that such training have clearly defined aims and objectives and be provided to officers at all stages of their careers; that training ought to be directly related to the specific circumstances and demands of the police role; that minority ethnic communities be closely involved in the design and delivery of courses; and that the training be monitored and assessed in order that it can keep apace with changing circumstances (PTC 1983: 10–11). That many of these principles were subsequently endorsed by the Lawrence Report and later again in several reports from Her Majesty's Inspectorate of Constabulary (HMIC 1999, 2002, 2003) suggests not only that they are of fundamental importance but also that they have not been sufficiently operationalised in police training. In the wake of the Police Training Council recommendations, Brunel University was contracted by the Home Office to deliver a programme predicated on a 'reflective practitioner' approach intended to encourage officers to consider their relations with minority ethnic communities (Oakley 1989). The training was hampered because the police service failed to acknowledge a problem of institutional racism and due to demands for relatively short, high turnover programmes that could quickly train large numbers of staff (Oakley 1989).

While the 'Brunel model' foreshadowed the more recent emphasis on addressing the values and attitudes of police staff, the contractor that followed, Equalities Associates, adopted instead a professional standards approach focused on behaviour. Underpinning the strategy was the premise that police officer attitudes and values would develop once their patterns of behaviour had been addressed. However, it seems that the 'training the trainers' strategy, which sought to train relatively few individuals who would then act as 'champions' of anti-racism in their respective workplaces, proved problematic. While police services might have been amenable to sending a few members of their training staff on the programme, there does not seem to have been a structured approach to enable them to deliver effective CRR training based on their experience once they returned to their posts.

The most recent approach to the provision of in-service training in CRR can be seen in the work of Ionann Management Consultants, who were contracted to the Home Office to provide support to the police services of England and Wales immediately after publication of the Macpherson Report. In many respects the approach adopted by this consultancy firm was similar to that of Brunel University in that it sought to encourage officers to become reflective practitioners. However, it differed from earlier efforts in that it was operating during a period not only when institutional racism was acknowledged to be a problem for the police service but also when, partly in response to the Lawrence Inquiry, sections of the service were claiming to be developing an anti-racism policing strategy (Rowe 2004). Two other key differences that affected the Ionann Management programme was the need to co-train civilian staff and officers within the same programme and the emphasis on involving members of minority ethnic communities in the training process. What follows is an examination of these three features of recent police community and race relations, or diversity, training: the impact of training on institutional racism, the challenge of training civilian and police staff; and the ways in which community involvement in the training process has been affected. The impact of police occupational cultures upon these features is then assessed. The discussion primarily relates to 'in-service' or post-probationary training, delivered by a range of training providers to police services in England and Wales.

Institutional racism

As other contributors to this collection note, there is considerable debate about the concept of institutional racism. Giving evidence to the Lawrence Inquiry, the Commissioner of the Metropolitan Police, Sir Paul Condon, was reluctant to admit that the police service was institutionally racist since there was no consensus as to what the concept meant. In the immediate aftermath of the publication of the Lawrence Report, there was a widespread tendency to assume that the finding that the police service was institutionally racist meant that all officers were racist. When the Chief Constable of Greater Manchester Police publicly accepted that the force was institutionally racist a group of his officers threatened legal action against what they argued was 'defamation of character' (Rowe 2004: 55). As Foster *et al.* (2005) suggest, it seems likely that officers' tendency to misunderstand institutional racism stems from inaccurate media coverage of the term, which often uses it to denote a problem with racism that is particularly extensive or inscrutable within an organisation. The Lawrence Report itself explicitly rejected this interpretation as it emphasised that 'we do not accept that it [institutional racism] was universally the cause of the failure of this investigation, any more than we accept that a finding of institutional racism within the police service means that all officers are racist' (Macpherson 1999: 46.27). However, the theoretical confusion surrounding the Lawrence Report's definition of institutional racism (Solomos 1999; Foster *et al.* 2005), presented a particularly difficult challenge for the development of training sessions designed to address the problem.

Several evaluations of recent police training on community and race relations have noted that efforts to address institutional racism in such programmes have often foundered (Metropolitan Police undated b; Institute of Employment Studies 2003; Rowe and Garland 2003). Our research found that officers and civilian staff were often highly cynical about the training programmes that they were required to attend and sometimes felt that the entire process was driven by the inappropriate political agendas of chief officers (Rowe and Garland 2003). Although our findings showed that participants often reflected afterwards that the training had been more useful than they had anticipated, it was clear that introducing the issue of institutional racism into the training session often caused controversy. Since those responsible for delivering the programmes reported that the pressure of delivering a large number of courses in a restricted time period, coupled with the emotive nature of what was being addressed, meant that trainers were tempted to avoid prolonged discussion of the issue of institutional racism. The Metropolitan Police evaluation of training delivered in one borough noted that those delivering the training found the programme especially problematic to deliver (Metropolitan Police undated b: 33–4):

> The third associate trainer said that they found the training extremely difficult. 'When I started working with the police I couldn't believe the stiffness and reluctance to engage in the topic,' this trainer said. 'There was a lot of resistance, a lot of extreme views – across ranks. That was the initial shock. To actually acknowledge the concept of institutional racism – the penny still hasn't dropped.' The trainer added, 'At Croydon, in the majority of the time I was the only black person in the room. This had a tremendous impact. I would walk in and the group would be all white, mostly men, with a white police trainer'.

Although it would be understandable for individual trainers to unconsciously or consciously avoid topics that could engage them in difficult debates that might draw hostility, such a tendency clearly means that one of the central contributions of the Lawrence Report is not properly addressed in the training environment. This omission is compounded by the tendency to devise training courses that focus upon issues relating to personal values and attitudes, inter-cultural communication, and the historical context of police relations with minorities. These might be valuable topics and worth addressing in the training environment. Our research suggested that one of the features of the training that participants rated highly was that it had encouraged them to consider the language that they used in the workplace and the impact that this might have upon relations with colleagues and the public (Rowe and Garland 2003). However, these features continue to present a model whereby police community and race relations are determined by the attitudes, values and behaviour of individual staff. The balance of the curriculum used in much of the Metropolitan Police Service indicates that the focus was on the individual level, with 19 of the 20 sessions contained in the two-day programme covering historical issues, individual attitudes towards stop and search and 'inter-cultural communication', and only one session explored institutional racism (Metropolitan Police undated a: 11–12).

Not only are there concerns that training has often not addressed the issue of institutional racism, and so occasionally missed the opportunity to challenge some misconceptions surrounding the concept, it is also doubtful that training can – in and of itself – provide the means to address the broader institutional dynamics of racism, the imbalance in power relations between the police and marginalised communities, nor the structural causes that contribute towards that marginalisation. While there has been some progress in terms of responding to the Lawrence Report recommendation that training programmes ought to be rigorously evaluated, there has been less consideration given to the overall impact that training can be expected to have on police work in general or police relations with the community in particular. These concerns are elaborated further in the concluding section of this chapter.

Training features, management and occupational cultures

Both the Morris Inquiry (Morris 2004) and the Commission for Racial Equality (2005), in their separate investigations into policing and diversity, noted the requirement for positive and strong leadership from senior officers in order to reinforce and support any CRR initiatives developed since the publication of the Macpherson Report in February 1999. Both organisations' reports also warned of a 'backlash' from some white officers that could become more significant unless counteracted by police leaders. As the CRE (2005: 95) argued:

race equality training requires skilled management effectively to support its delivery. There is a real potential for 'backlash', particularly amongst some white officers, and the delivery of race equality training remains far more 'politicised' and sensitive than the delivery of other types of training. Unless the police service is prepared systematically to address these issues, then learning and development on race and diversity issues will continue to be limited.

Yet a number of authors have argued that just such a scenario has occurred due to a lack of management support for CRR training (see, for example, Loveday 2000; Whitfield 2004), with the impression gained that some senior managers are more concerned with fulfilling certain 'quota' obligations (in terms of the numbers of staff trained) while not, at the same time, devising internal monitoring systems to ensure that lessons learned from the training are carried forward into the workplace on an everyday basis. Her Majesty's Inspectorate of Constabulary (2003: 28) found a number of issues that were 'detrimental to the training's effectiveness and efficiency', including a lack of clarity and direction in the overall training strategy within the service. Also, staff appraisals did not support CRR training, inadequate supervision undermined the training's overall messages, and trainers themselves were not selected or indeed managed properly.

The same thematic inspection also found that there was a lack of consistent and robust evaluation of CRR training courses, a theme that has recurred consistently in the post-Macpherson era in the provision of training more generally (HMIC 2005). Tamkin *et al.* (2003: 48), in their examination of the delivery of CRR training in the MPS, found not only that 'very little local evaluation' was being conducted but also that 'key performance indicators [had] not been identified and data not collected on a regular basis'. Such a lack of systematic monitoring and evaluative work can have a number of detrimental effects upon the success of CRR training, including the continuation of poor training practice, a lack of analysis of learning outcomes, and a lack of understanding of how any new ideas were being transferred into workplace behaviour. Also, thorough evaluation can help to refine courses so that the skills developed by trainees can have a genuine impact upon the police's relationship with local minority ethnic groups. As Cantle noted in his assessment of the causes of the so-called Milltown disorders of 2001 diversity training can play an important role in the development of positive police relations with local minority ethnic communities. This was noted particularly in cases where 'the depth and quality of this [training] had been properly evaluated' (Independent Review Team 2001: 41).

A related issue is the inconsistent national provision of training needs analysis for officers and civilian staff (HMIC 2005). As Docking and Tuffin (2005) illustrate, this is an issue that occurs across the service; however, it is one that is of particular concern for officers who have responsibility for dealing with hate crimes or diversity issues but who have had no relevant training. This merely reinforces the point that a lack of strategic thinking on the implementation of CRR training can lead to the impression that these programmes are merely rolled out when the subject is 'flavour of the month', perhaps precipitated by a 'major event' such as the Lawrence Inquiry, but there is very little in place to sustain such training or implement it on a systematic basis over a long period. Indeed, CRR training often seems to exist on its own, as a 'stand alone' exercise that is often not followed up in staff appraisals or by refresher courses. Docking and Tuffin (2005 41) even found examples of 'officers who had been in the force for a longer period of time, i.e. before the publication of the Lawrence Inquiry, had only received a self-complete textbook with no check to make sure that it had been taken on board.'

It is worth noting that these issues are addressed in the current Home Office, ACPO, Association of Police Authorities, and Centrex sponsored 'Strategy for Improving Performance in Race and Diversity Learning', which runs until 2009. It states that all police officers, staff and special constables will be assessed for CRR competency against National Occupational Standards 1A4 and 1A5[1], and that this will be logged in their annual performance and development appraisals. However, there is still a concern that this plan, however worthy in intention, may not work in practice if it is not fully supported by line managers.

The same strategy champions the incorporation of the wider police family and civilian staff into the pool of police personnel that should receive CRR training, reinforcing recommendation 49 of the Lawrence Report (see above). However, the idea of mixing police officers and civilian support staff together is not new and indeed this type of trainee integration was commonly witnessed by us during our two-year evaluation of diversity training (Rowe and Garland 2003). Indeed, mixing staff in training was regarded as an important symbolic and strategic dimension of the programmes observed, primarily since it reinforced the message that diversity should be considered as important to all aspects of work within the police service, including administration.

Overall, our evaluative research showed that civilian reactions to the CRR training experience could be categorised in the following broad terms: some staff welcomed and rated positively the provision of joint training of this kind; some welcomed the approach in principle, but felt that it was not translated into practice effectively; and others did not value the joint provision of training to support staff and officers. However, in all of the police services observed a significant number of civilian staff tended to report that they found the content of the course difficult to apply to their roles and that most of what was imparted by trainers – many of whom were or had been police officers – was not sufficiently relevant to them. Although some stated that they found the overall content of the course interesting, a common response was that support staff felt marginalised as there was too much focus on *operational* policing issues, such as stop and search procedures (Garland *et al*. 2002). For other members of the support staff there was a perception that police officers tended to dominate proceedings by being very vocal, leaving them feeling further isolated.

Nevertheless, despite the reservations of some support staff at the constabularies observed during the research it is felt that, overall, it is a worthwhile exercise to involve officers and civilians together in the training, especially as a number of the issues raised, particularly those relating to broader diversity issues, are of relevance to all individuals, whatever their role in the organisation (Rowe 2004). Equally, the resistance that some police officers appear to have to being trained in CRR issues is unfortunately shared by some civilian staff (Tamkin *et al*. 2003), and so the benefits of emphasising the importance of such training to a class consisting of both groups together become even more apparent.

Further dilemmas: integrating community involvement and overcoming officer resistance to 'pink and fluffy' training

One of the key CRR training recommendations contained in the Stephen Lawrence Inquiry Report was that local minority ethnic communities 'should be involved in such training and experience' (Macpherson 1999: 332). By this, Macpherson intended that such communities should be integrated into the designing, delivering, monitoring and evaluation of CRR programmes, so that not only would local minority ethnic people actually feel valued as part of the training process but that their insights and experiences could inform the course curriculum.

However, HMIC, in its 2003 inspection, found that there was 'insufficient community involvement in all aspects of the training cycle' (HMIC 2003: 28), something that mirrored its findings from the previous year (HMIC 2002: 24) and also those from our own research (Rowe and Garland 2003). As Foster *et al.* (2005) noted, the process of consultation and dialogue with local communities still appears to be somewhat haphazard across the police service, with no single, uniform method of community liaison evident nor any real strategy yet to be devised of the best way to integrate local minority ethnic people into CRR courses.

Hall (1988, cited in Rowe 2004: 68) suggests that historically there have been several distinct police approaches to community involvement in CRR training, with some being more effective and nuanced than others. Two of these, the 'balancing act' and 'information focused' approaches, are similar in that they involve apportioning 'blame' for bad 'race relations': the former apportions it equally between the police and minority ethnic communities, while the latter suggests that problems have occurred because whites have failed to understand minority ethnic cultures. Another method of incorporating community input, the 'black experience' approach – in which minority ethnic individuals are invited to tell officers 'where it hurts' – was the one most commonly witnessed during our evaluation of CRR training. Such a policy, while in some ways enlightening for officers and civilian staff, could also prove problematic for several reasons, most notably because it could be stressful and upsetting for community speakers who were sometimes subjected to sceptical comments and, on occasion, hostility and ridicule from some trainees (Garland *et al.* 2002). Unless managed properly by facilitators, interface sessions could become confrontational, with a beleaguered speaker on the receiving end of officers' previously pent-up frustrations.

While this type of hostile reaction was relatively rare, a more common problem we observed were those situations in which a community representative from a minority ethnic background was expected to speak 'on behalf' of *all* minority ethnic communities – an impossible role to perform, which led inevitably to problems (Garland *et al.* 2006). Another related issue was that community guests had a narrower remit – to be the 'representative' and spokesperson for their own particular ethnic group. While this may have been an easier task to perform, it was still essentially flawed as ideas of what constitutes certain distinct communities, with all of their complexities and complications, could all too easily be boiled down into broad and easy-to-understand traits that presented a simplified and monolithic impression of communities. Speakers were often asked by officers to provide them with a definitive list of cultural practices that they should be aware of. While this has its uses, especially when there was a palpable lack of familiarity on the part of officers regarding local populations, there were occasions when it felt like officers were asking speakers to *instruct* them on how to behave in certain situations, so that they would have a blueprint that they could closely follow in the future. Thus officers could take rather basic ideas away from interface sessions that could in some ways be misleading.

In addition there was an over-reliance in some forces upon those they identified as community 'leaders', who are invited to interface sessions in order to talk on behalf of 'their' ethnic group. These sessions could prove useful to training participants, who could gain valuable insights into communities from people who could speak with a degree of authority. However, on occasion we witnessed community leaders who lacked any kind of mandate to speak on behalf of others and indeed appeared to be self-appointed spokespeople whose middle-aged or elderly male profile could mean that they were out of touch with the concerns and values of the younger community members with whom the police may have especially strained relations (Garland *et al.* 2002). This could inevitably result in a distorted understanding of the needs of these young people and create additional policing difficulties.

As Kelly (2003) describes in her study of Bosnian refugees who arrived in Britain in the 1990s, similar problems regarding representativeness may also unfold when community consultation is facilitated by way of organised community associations that may not, in fact, be representative of the views of such communities more generally. Kelly argues that some of these associations may not be genuine community-based organisations at all but instead may only be formed in order to 'conform to the expectations of the host society in order to gain the advantages of a formal community association, [although] the private face of the group remains unconstituted as a community' (Kelly 2003: 41). In cases such as these trainees may again obtain a distorted picture of the concerns of certain minority ethnic groups.

Ideally, therefore, community interface contributors to CRR training should be those people who can, in some way, claim some genuine validity to 'speak up' for their own sections of local communities, as ACPO (2005: 16) suggests:

> The input from ordinary members of communities could prove invaluable, particularly those key people that do not claim representative status but are marked by the credibility in which they are held locally, not least of all by young people.

Such an approach is in itself not without problems, however. As Tamkin *et al*. (2003) discovered during their evaluation of CRR training in the MPS, some community contributors, while having credibility in the eyes of their peers, lacked the necessary skills or knowledge of policing issues to contribute successfully to the interface sessions. This would imply that some sort of a formal selection process may need to be undertaken, in an attempt to ensure that community participants can provide the type of contribution that both they and trainees would find worthwhile. There is a danger, though, that if this selection procedure is too rigorously applied then the opportunity to learn from genuine community experiences would be lost in an effort to select only 'appropriate' speakers. Indeed, HMIC advises against such a strategy, suggesting that 'the importance of exposing learners to individual experiences and views would in all likelihood be lost if robust selection were applied' (HMIC 2003: 109), instead advocating that community contributors should only interact with learners 'under the guidance and supervision of "qualified" trainers' (2003: 105).

Interestingly, the same HMIC report noted that 'in a survey carried out for this inspection, 65 per cent of forces stated that they used external facilitators in the delivery or development of race and diversity training' (2003: 109), meaning that, by implication, around a third of forces relied upon internal contributors to deliver whole CRR programmes. While this does not necessarily imply that such internal contributors were white, resulting in diversity training being delivered by white trainers to predominantly all-white audiences, it may be safe to assume that in police forces not known for their ethnic diversity this scenario may indeed be more common than would be ideal. It may occur more frequently in rural forces and indeed was observed in an evaluative examination of CRR training in a rural constabulary in the west of England (Garland *et al*. 2002). It reflects another of Hall's (1988) historical approaches to the delivery of diversity training noted above: the discussion of the experiences of minority ethnic communities by training facilitators who do not have first-hand knowledge of the subject. This approach is, of course, inherently problematic in itself as it can easily lead to misapprehensions and misunderstandings, and is certainly not something that is being advocated here. Having said that, some forces have used a video, detailing minority ethnic experiences of policing, as a way of guaranteeing the input of people from a variety of minority ethnic backgrounds into every training session. While no real substitute for genuine face-to-face interaction between officers and minority ethnic contributors, it did provide for a range of voices from different backgrounds to be heard; something that could not be provided by individual speakers who may only be able to provide a narrow range of experiences.

In the same rural force discussed above, notwithstanding the problems of having all-white training teams, groups of three or four community contributors were employed during the interface sessions, which helped to counter the danger of trainees only hearing a range of very limited perspectives. The contributors were selected from a wide pool of around 70 or so potential contributors from minority ethnic communities local to the constabulary, exemplifying the efforts that that particular force had made to forge and cultivate genuine links between themselves and nearby 'hard-to-reach' populations. This approach also illustrated that community interface sessions within CRR training programmes should not necessarily be an end in themselves, but could be built upon to forge more positive relations between the parties concerned. As Tamkin *et al.* (2003: 36) noted in the MPS:

> Some boroughs have used this interface model to go further and develop other initiatives. This illustrates that the interface model is not only useful within the course to aid learning but outside and beyond – back in the community and back in the organisation, to spur on further projects and further communication and networking.

This more proactive way of engaging with local communities, using the training interface sessions as a starting point, could provide a model of good practice for others to follow, especially as the Home Office *et al.* have stated in their 'Race and Diversity Learning and Development Programme' for the police service (Home Office *et al.* 2004: 20) that community engagement must be 'at the forefront' of diversity policies. The Development Programme outlines several methods by which this can be done – including community placements and interaction schemes, and the 'involvement of community representatives' – and the programme is also (quite rightly) at pains to point out that police diversity agendas should cover 'race, gender, sexual orientation, disability, age and religion and belief' (2004:

8) and should acknowledge the 'full scope' of ethnic groupings, including gypsies, travellers and asylum-seekers, who are sometimes overlooked in diversity strategies. Community engagement strategies will therefore have to be innovative and above all extensive, and it will be interesting to see how successful forces will be in fulfilling the expectations of the Home Office *et al.* that they should devote significant resources to activities that have, historically, been a low priority for many police forces.

As is mentioned above, one of the key aims of CRR training in the post-Macpherson era has been to get training participants to reflect upon their own values, attitudes and beliefs, in order to understand how these can impact upon their behaviour in the workplace. Such an approach is in many ways different from the more 'nuts and bolts' training that police officers are used to receiving, during which, commonly, they are provided with instruction regarding legislation and the use of police powers (Whitfield 2004). By contrast, the post-Macpherson approach emphasises a degree of self-analysis whereby participants are often asked to consider the nature of their own core values and beliefs and how these may have formed and developed (Rowe 2004). Trainers attempt to create an 'open and honest' atmosphere in which participants are encouraged to be reflective, and are told that they will not be judged negatively if their views are not 'politically correct'. Consequently participants witness what the HMIC has referred to as 'the complete dissolution of the safe learning environment' (HMIC 2003: 107), which can leave officers and civilian staff feeling unusually exposed and vulnerable. As the authors' own research discovered, this could result in trainees reacting very warily to the course content, and, rather than participating fully within the sessions, some were seen to withdraw within themselves as the programme progressed. Such actions not only made the delivery of the training difficult but also may have resulted in attendees not getting as much out of the training as they could have done (Garland *et al.* 2002).

These feelings of vulnerability can also be reinforced by officers' heightened concerns, in the post-Lawrence era, that despite assurances to the contrary they may be punished if they were to say the 'wrong thing' in class and that trainers were there to 'tell them off for being racists' (HMIC 2003). Interviews conducted by the authors of this chapter for their research sometimes revealed that officers were worried that the training environment might be bugged and that these rumours could quickly gain currency within working environments, resulting in a heightened sense of suspicion on the part of trainees as they entered the classroom for the first session of CRR training. Despite reassurances from trainers, these suspicions often proved difficult to allay and cast a shadow over proceedings (Garland *et al.* 2002).

Another source of resistance within classrooms was the notion that CRR training was simply a 'tick-box' exercise on the behalf of senior officers that was designed to fulfil, on paper, the training obligations of the police service to the Home Office without having to deliver a product of value that would precipitate meaningful change. Indeed, there may be some evidence that this is the case in some forces, including in the Metropolitan Police Service (Morris 2004) and in some of the sites examined by the Home Office in its evaluation of the impact of the Lawrence Inquiry (Foster *et al.* 2005). The Commission for Racial Equality (2005) found that some junior officers see CRR training as being merely a politically motivated response to the Lawrence Report, and thus do not afford it the attention or credibility that it needs. It may also echo a wider suspicion of senior officers, who are sometimes viewed rather dismissively as being out of touch with, and not understanding the realities of, police work (Rowe 2004). In their eyes, the provision of 'unnecessary' CRR training was merely symptomatic of just how little senior officers know of the practicalities of day-to-day policing.

However, these views may merely reveal the fact that some officers do not take diversity issues as seriously as they should, as they do not feel that supposed 'woolly and liberal' ideas are an effective way of combating the types of criminal, anti-social or disorderly behaviour that they routinely encounter. Indeed, the preference of some officers for what they see as 'traditional', action-oriented models of police work rather than community-related methods may reflect attitudes among rank-and-file officers that CRR training is just part of yet another transient social trend that the 'beleaguered' officer has to put up with (Reiner 2000: 90). It may also exemplify the low status that community safety issues have in some forces: for example, in some of the MPS research sites Foster *et al.* (2005: 91) examined, there was the discovery that:

> [Community safety unit] staff felt their work was not valued in the wider policing environment ... It was widely disparaged as 'pink and fluffy' in contrast to the 'glamorous and sexy' work in other departments ... The importance of hate crime was still not widely understood or believed to constitute 'real police work'.

It is therefore difficult for CRR training to make significant headway, and even to be taken seriously, in environments where matters relating to diversity are generally held in little regard and where aspects of police culture 'reinforce macho and anti-diversity attitudes' (CRE 2005: 81). Foster *et al.* (2005) also found that in certain of their research locations there was a degree of residual anger among officers regarding the perceived unfairness of the Lawrence Inquiry Report (something especially noted in London), coupled with a feeling that the failings of the Lawrence murder investigations were more to do with incompetence than racism, institutional or otherwise. In some non-Metropolitan forces there was a perception that the report, being highly critical just of one force, the MPS, was not relevant to the service as a whole and therefore the recommendations that came out of it only applied to the Met. In addition, there was a fairly widespread notion in some rural forces with small minority ethnic populations that issues to do with 'race', and indeed diversity more generally, were urban concerns that did not apply in their context.[2]

Part of this reluctance to be trained in diversity issues reflects a broader resistance to being 'forced' to attend a compulsory training course, as these CRR courses are throughout the service. It also is indicative of an institutional reluctance to attend training in general, and Skills for Justice (2006: 19) found that more than half of the police and law enforcement organisations they surveyed viewed training as 'a hindrance' and that in around a fifth of such organisations employee reluctance to take up training opportunities was a 'significant barrier' to course attendance.

However, part of this reluctance is also down to a reticence among some officers and civilian staff to acknowledge the relevance or importance of 'race' and diversity issues, something that occurred in some forces to such an extent that hate mail was sent to trainers (CRE 2005). It is not the inconvenience of having to 'lose' two days' work to attend training that annoys some officers principally, but rather it is the *nature* of the subject matter that they are being trained in that is resented and this manifests itself in a kind of 'entrenched cultural resistance' to many of the post-Macpherson diversity policy initiatives (Foster *et al.* 2005: 92). Reasons for this may range from a refusal to recognise the relevance of diversity issues either to the individual or to the constabulary, to a denial that racism is a problem either locally or to the police service more generally. Individual racist attitudes and beliefs may also play a part in a small number of cases.

Conclusion: understanding the limits of diversity training

This chapter has summarised some of the key issues and dilemmas surrounding the provision of police community and race relations training. Following a discussion of the problematic historical development of such programmes, including an assessment of whether CRR training should challenge attitudes and values of officers, or merely aim to change actual behaviour, we have outlined the difficulties of incorporating the concept of institutional racism into a classroom environment that may be hostile to the notion. Flaws in Macpherson's definition, and in the way that the media reported it following the publication of the Lawrence Report in 1999, were discussed in the context of the definition being misunderstood by officers who felt that they themselves were being condemned as racists.

Other issues, such as the difficulties of incorporating community representatives into course interface sessions, were also debated, and it was suggested that it was those forces that invest time and effort into fostering strong relations with minority ethnic communities that may stand the best chance of being able to fully integrate these communities into diversity training packages. It was also argued that these initiatives need to be complemented by strong leadership from senior officers that accords diversity training programmes the priority and status that they deserve. Senior officers should also make sure that CRR training does not sit on its own, in an 'oasis of political correctness', but instead is integrated into other organisational practices such as training needs analyses, evaluation processes and individual work plans and assessments.

Despite these reservations, there is some evidence that the diversity training instigated post-Macpherson has had some impact upon the workplace behaviour. For example, Foster *et al.*'s survey of officers found that, generally, respondents thought the training worthwhile, 'primarily in terms of an increased awareness of some differences in cultural protocols' (Foster *et al.* 2005: xiii). The same research also found that consultation with local communities had improved since 1999 and that there had been a general disappearance of racist language from the service.

Worryingly, however, during their investigation into the policing of racist incidents Docking and Tuffin (2005) discovered that some officers were still unclear about the acceptability or otherwise of some terms of abuse and found it hard to understand why racist invective was any different in nature or impact from other insults that pick out certain physical attributes, such as short-sightedness or being overweight. Others admitted that they used racist terminology when talking between themselves and did not comprehend why they should not do this when they knew that young Asians, for example, employed the same terminology when talking to each other.

There may be a number of reasons for confusion, including weaknesses in the local delivery of the diversity training itself. It may also be an indicator of the structural limits on what any type of training can achieve. The frequency with which reports and reviews recommend that additional or improved training can provide the solution to identified problems suggests a lack of consideration of the broader organisational context that shapes the attitudes and behaviour of police officers. Training programmes might contribute towards affecting change but it is clear that they cannot do so in isolation. While the police service has shown that it can deliver extensive programmes of training to civilian staff and officers it is far from clear that this has been done in a strategic manner that integrates training into other mechanisms of performance management and professional development.

Often it is argued that efforts to bring about change in the police service break upon the hostile rocks of an intransigent unreconstructed police culture. While many have correctly argued that such monolithic generalisations about police culture are simplistic and unhelpful, and continue disproportionately to attribute problems to the lower ranks, there is evidence that prejudicial attitudes and discriminatory attitudes not relating to ethnicity persist. Recent work by Blackbourn (2006) and Foster *et al.* (2005) indicates that homophobic and sexist attitudes persist within police culture, which strongly suggests diversity training programmes have fallen someway short of their target of encouraging officers to become 'reflective practitioners'. This does not mean that individual training programmes have failed or that a review of content and delivery will rectify these problems. Instead a more fundamental reconsideration of the role of training within the police service is required. Additionally efforts to address police culture must recognise that this does not exist in isolation and that the values and attitudes of junior officers are likely to be influenced by senior officers, politicians and media commentators when they call for 'tough action' against criminals or suggest that targeting some minority ethnic communities might be a necessary part of the 'war on terror'.

Notes

1   National Occupational Standard 1A4 is entitled 'Foster people's equality, diversity and rights' and National Occupational Standard 1A5 'Promote people's equality, diversity and rights' (Home Office *et al.*, 2004: 38–49).
2   See Chakraborti and Garland (2004) for analyses of the policing of rural minority ethnic populations.

References

Adult Learning Inspectorate (2005) *Evaluation of the New Initial Police Learning and Development Programme (IPLDP)*, London: Adult Learning Inspectorate.

Association of Chief Police Officers (2000) *Guide to Identifying and Combating Hate Crime*, London: Home Office Police Standards Unit.

Association of Chief Police Officers (2005) *Hate Crime: Delivering A Quality Service – Good Practice and Tactical Guidance*, London: Home Office Police Standards Unit.

Blackbourn, D. (2006) 'Gay Rights in the Police Service: Is the Enemy Still Within?', *Criminal Justice Matters*, 63, pp. 30–1.

Chakraborti, N. and Garland, J. (eds) (2004) *Rural Racism*, Cullompton: Willan Publishing.

Commission for Racial Equality (2005) *A Formal Investigation of the Police Service in England and Wales*, London: Commission for Racial Equality.

Docking, M. and Tuffin, R. (2005) *Racist Incidents: Progress Since the Lawrence Inquiry*, Home Office Online Report 42/05, London: Home Office.

Foster, J., Newburn, T. and Souhami, A. (2005) *Assessing the Impact of the Stephen Lawrence Inquiry*, Home Office Research Study 294, London: Home Office.

Garland, J., Rowe, M. and Johnson, S. (2002) *Police Community and Race Relations Training: An Evaluation*, Leicester: University of Leicester, Scarman Centre.

Garland, J. Spalek, B. and Chakraborti, N. (2006) 'Hearing Lost Voices: Issues in Researching "Hidden" Minority Ethnic Communities', *British Journal of Criminology*, 46 (3): 423–37.

Hall, T. (1988) 'Race Relations Training: A Personal View', in P. Southgate (ed.) *New Directions in Police Training*, London: Home Office.

Her Majesty's Inspectorate of Constabulary (1999) *Winning the Race: Policing Plural Communities – Revisited*, London: Home Office.

Her Majesty's Inspectorate of Constabulary (2000) *Policing London: Winning Consent – A Review of Murder Investigation and Community and Race Relations Issues in the Metropolitan Police Service*, London: Home Office.

Her Majesty's Inspectorate of Constabulary (2002) *Training Matters*, London: Home Office.

Her Majesty's Inspectorate of Constabulary (2003) *Diversity Matters*, London: Home Office.

Her Majesty's Inspectorate of Constabulary (2005) *Managing Learning: A Study of Police Training*, London: Home Office.

Home Office, Association of Police Authorities, Association of Chief Police Officers and Centrex (2004) *A Strategy for Improving Performance in Race and Diversity 2004–2009: The Police Race and Diversity Learning and Development Programme*, London: Home Office.

Independent Review Team (2001) *Community Cohesion: A Report of the Independent Review Team chaired by Ted Cantle*, London: Home Office, pp. 10–11.

Institute for Employment Studies (2003) *A Review of Community and Race Relations Training in the Metropolitan Police Service*, Brighton: Institute for Employment Studies.

Kelly, L. (2003) 'Bosnian Refugees in Britain: Questioning Community', *Sociology*, 37 (1): 35–49.

Knights, E. (1988) 'Foreword', in P. Southgate (ed.) *New Directions in Police Training*, London: Home Office.

Lawrence Steering Group (2005) *Update on Progress Against Recommendations of the Stephen Lawrence Inquiry Report*, Sixth Annual Report, London: Home Office.

Loveday, B. (2000) 'Must Do Better: The State of Race Relations', in A. Marlow and B. Loveday (eds) *After Macpherson: Policing After the Stephen Lawrence Inquiry*, Lyme Regis: Russell House Publishing.

Macpherson, Sir W. (1999) *The Stephen Lawrence Inquiry: Report of an Inquiry by Sir William Macpherson of Cluny*, CM 4262-1, London: Home Office.

Metropolitan Police (2005) Freedom of Information Request No.2005120000532, personal communication.

Metropolitan Police (undated a) *Interim Report: Evaluation of the Diversity Training Programme, Merton Borough*, London: Metropolitan Police.

Metropolitan Police (undated b) *Interim Report: Evaluation of the Diversity Training Programme, Croydon Borough*, London: Metropolitan Police.

Morris, Sir W. (2004) *The Case for Change: People in the Metropolitan Police Service*, London: Metropolitan Police Authority.

Oakley, R. (1989) 'Community and Race Relations Training for the Police: A Review of Developments', *New Community*, 16 (11): 61–79.

Police Training Council (1983) *Community and Race Relations Training for the Police: Report of the PTC Working Party*, London: Home Office.

Reiner, R. (2000) *The Politics of the Police*, 3rd edn, Oxford: Oxford University Press.

Rowe, M. (2004) *Policing, Race and Racism*, Cullompton: Willan Publishing.

Rowe, M. and Garland, J. (2003) 'Have You Been Diversified Yet? Developments in Police Community and Race Relations Training in England and Wales', *Policing and Society*, 13 (4): 399–411.

Runnymede Trust (2000) *Commission on the Future of Multi-Ethnic Britain*, http://runnymedetrust.org/projects/meb.html.

Scarman, Lord (1981) *The Brixton Disorders: 10–12 April 1981 – Report of an Inquiry by the Rt Hon Lord Scarman OBE*, London: HMSO.

Skills for Justice (2006) *Sector Skills Agreement: Stage 1 Skills Needs Assessment – Policing and Law Enforcement*, Sheffield: JSSC Ltd (Skills for Justice).

Solomos, J. (1999) 'Social Research and the Stephen Lawrence Inquiry', *Sociological Research Online*, 4 (1).

Southgate, P. (1982) *Police Probationer Training in Race Relations*, Research and Planning Unit Paper 8, London: Home Office.

Tamkin, P., Pollard, E., Djan Tackey, N., Strebler, M. and Hooker, H. (2003) *A Review of Community and Race Relations (CRR) Training in the Metropolitan Police Force*, Brighton: Institute for Employment Studies.

Wall, D. S. (1998) *The Chief Constables of England and Wales: The Socio-Legal History of a Criminal Justice Elite*, Dartmouth: Ashgate.

Whitfield, J. (2004) *Unhappy Dialogue: The Metropolitan Police and Black Londoners in Post-war Britain*, Cullompton: Willan Publishing.

Chapter 4

Understanding Institutional Racism: the Stephen Lawrence inquiry and the police service reaction

Anna Souhami

Introduction

Policing in England and Wales has been regularly beset in recent decades by accusations of discriminatory treatment and practice in relation to local minority ethnic communities. Among the most significant of these in recent times were events surrounding the investigation of the murder of Stephen Lawrence in south-east London in 1993 in what an inquest jury later described as a 'completely unprovoked racist attack'. Following a flawed initial investigation and a deluge of 'extraordinary' and 'unsatisfactory' police activity (Macpherson 1999: 2.1:3), the case attained increasing political momentum (Rock 2004), becoming both symbolic of the problem of racist violence in Britain and the inadequacy of policies to address it, and the focus of concerns about problematic police–community relations more broadly (Bowling 1999; Downes and Morgan 2002).

Reflecting the wider resonance of the case, the focus of the subsequent public inquiry, chaired by Lord Justice Macpherson, was simultaneously particular and general. It was concerned to examine the circumstances of Stephen Lawrence's murder and the details of the police service's response to the incident and their handling of the investigation thereafter. More generally, however, the inquiry turned its attention to the broader issues of police–community relations and to the question of police discrimination both within the service itself and in its policies and practices more broadly. The inquiry was hugely critical of the Metropolitan Police Service (MPS) and made a number of damning statements about policing in England and Wales more generally. It concluded that there had been a series of fundamental flaws in the investigation and that these resulted from 'professional incompetence, institutional racism and a failure of leadership by senior officers' (Macpherson 1999: 46.1:317). Its assessment of all three was excoriating. However, it has been the third element of the Lawrence Inquiry's diagnosis – the application of the term 'institutional racism' to the Metropolitan Police particularly, and the police service more generally – which has generated the greatest debate since the publication of the inquiry report.

Since its development in the American black Civil Rights Movement in the 1960s, the term 'institutional racism' has come to be adopted in numerous contexts on both sides of the Atlantic, absorbing multiple meanings and levels of analysis (Singh 2000). Recognising the contested nature of the concept (Macpherson 1999: 6.6:20), the Lawrence Inquiry attempted carefully to specify the meaning it was attributing to the term and the reasons for its application to the specific case of the investigation. In particular, as I will show, the inquiry took great care to distinguish between the processes of discrimination generated by the structural workings of the police organisation (institutional racism) and the actions, deliberate or otherwise, of individual officers (individual racism). In doing so, it made plain that it was the former that was its primary concern and that it was of crucial importance that the application of the term 'institutional racism' should not be mistaken for an allegation that it was police officers as individuals, rather than the police organisation, that were being labelled racist. However, in the event, this was precisely what occurred.

Drawing on a major study of the impact of the Lawrence Inquiry on policing throughout England and Wales (Foster *et al.* 2005), this chapter explores how the inquiry's application of the term 'institutional racism' was received within the police service and explores why the term continues to be so comprehensively misunderstood. In particular, it looks at the way that the application and definition of the term within the inquiry report itself may have exacerbated its central ambiguities.

Racism and institutional racism

The issue of racism was described by the inquiry as having 'permeated' its investigations (Macpherson 1999: 6.1:20). From the allegation by Mr and Mrs Lawrence that racism was integral to the failure of the investigation, Stephen Lawrence's murder, the role of the police in the investigation and the subsequent campaign itself became increasingly firmly framed in the terms of race and racism as the case gathered political momentum (Rock 2004). As Rock (2004) argues, this potent context inevitably had a powerful influence on the shape and focus of the subsequent Inquiry (2004: 440).

Noting the sensitivities of the concept 'of racism' and the dangers inherent in its misuse, the Lawrence Inquiry carefully set out its understanding of the term and its particular application in the case of the police investigation into Stephen Lawrence's murder. Racism, it said, consisted of 'conduct or words or practices which disadvantage or advantage people because of their colour, culture or ethnic origin' (Macpherson 1999: 6.4:20). It could take different forms. First, it could be overt, namely language, actions or processes that were deliberately intended to discriminate against Black and Minority Ethnic (BME) people because of their ethnicity (Tonry 2004). Although little evidence of overt racism was found, the inquiry noted a number of instances of the use of inappropriate language (Macpherson 1999: 44.11:310) and was concerned to ensure that the allegation that 'racism infected the MPS' (Macpherson 1999: 46.26:321) was fully investigated. However, the inquiry noted that racism could also take a 'more subtle form' which was just as damaging. In particular, it was concerned to investigate the ways in which processes at the level of institutional policies and practices could systematically discriminate against minority ethnic communities.

The Lawrence Inquiry took evidence from several experts as to the importance of distinguishing the discriminatory practices of organisations from the actions of individuals. It gave specific consideration to the deliberations of Lord Scarman's Inquiry into the 1981 'disorders' in Brixton, south London. While there were many differences between the Scarman and Stephen Lawrence Inquiries, in terms of the incidents that gave rise to them, the speed with which they were called, and their recommendations (Bowling 1999), both became a focus for problematic police–community relations more broadly and had a lasting impact on the policing landscape. The urban unrest of the early 1980s had highlighted the deterioration that had taken place in relations between the police and many communities, particularly minority ethnic communities, and this was therefore a central concern for the Scarman Inquiry.

Scarman was critical of the policing of Brixton and especially the heavy-handed 'Swamp 81' 'street saturation' operation. He concluded that the behaviour of some officers, front-line staff in particular, could be deliberately 'racially prejudiced' and 'ill considered' (Scarman

1981: 4.62:64). Yet, he argued, discriminatory behaviour could also result from 'unthinking' racist stereotyping (Scarman 1981: 4.63:64). Further, he found that the routine 'attitudes and methods' of the MPS had not been adjusted to meet the needs of an ethnically diverse community (1981: 4.70:66). In particular, the MPS had not understood the centrality of community relations to policing in a 'multi-racial society' (1981: 4.80:68). Consequently, despite their efforts to the contrary, policing had been insensitive and inappropriate, resulting in a breakdown of relations between the police and minority ethnic communities (1981: 4.70:66).

The Scarman Inquiry therefore detailed a number of facets of discrimination that, as described below, were similar to those later identified by the Lawrence Inquiry. However, Scarman explicitly rejected 'institutional racism' for the problems that had precipitated the inquiry. For Scarman, the term referred to a process that 'knowingly, as a matter of policy, discriminates against black people' (1981: 2.22:11). By this understanding, he argued, neither the MPS nor British society more broadly could be described as institutionally racist. However, he added:

> If, however, the suggestion being made is that practices may be adopted by public bodies as well as private individuals which are unwittingly discriminatory against black people, then this is an allegation which serves serious consideration, and, where proved, swift remedy. (Scarman 1981: 2.22:11)

The Lawrence Inquiry was critical of Lord Scarman for acknowledging the existence of 'unwitting' or 'unconscious' racism yet confining the idea of 'institutional racism' to overtly racist policies and practices that are deliberately designed to discriminate. This narrow conception of the term had left the more complex and insidious forms of discrimination beyond the scope of police attention.

> Whilst we must never lose sight of the importance of explicit racism and direct discrimination, in policing terms if the phrase 'institutional racism' had been used to describe not only explicit manifestations of racism at direction and policy level, but also unwitting discrimination at the organisational level, then the reality of indirect racism in its more subtle, hidden and potentially more pervasive nature would have been addressed. (Macpherson 1999: 6.15:22)

Having recognised the importance of bringing these wider processes within its scope, the Lawrence Inquiry offered a new definition. Acknowledging the complexity of the phenomena at hand, it was careful to note that the definition was not intended as a 'final answer to the question' but rather to set out their standpoint so that the application of the term in the context of the investigation could be understood. Institutional racism, it said, consists of:

> The collective failure of an organisation to provide an appropriate and professional service to people because of their colour, culture, or ethnic origin. It can be seen or detected in processes, attitudes and behaviour which amount to discrimination through unwitting prejudice, ignorance, thoughtlessness and racist stereotyping which disadvantage minority ethnic people. (Macpherson 1999: 6.34:28)

Through this definition, the inquiry broadened its scope of interest in at least two important ways. First, it brought within its gaze not just those behaviours that were intended to disadvantage minority ethnic people, but those that did so unconsciously or unwittingly. So, for example, 'unwitting racism' could arise from actions that were thoughtless, patronising or ignorant, even if they were well intentioned (Macpherson 1999: 6.17:22). In this way, the inquiry accepted that actions could be defined as racist regardless of their intention. It thus drew attention to the potential for divergence in the way that policing is perceived by officers, and the way it is experienced by local communities. Indeed, a core theme throughout the inquiry and its recommendations is that an appreciation of the viewpoint and perception of those subject to racism is paramount to understanding it and thus responding appropriately. So, for example, the inquiry stated that a racist incident should be considered to be 'any incident which is perceived to be racist by the victim or any other person'.

Second, the definition attempted to shift attention away from a preoccupation with the behaviour of individual officers, towards problems generated at the level of institutional policies and practices. In so doing, it brought within its scope a number of areas of policing activity. It focused attention on the operation of institutions and structures as well as the actions of individual officers; processes, routines and customs as well as specific acts and instances of racism; and, as the existence of 'institutional racism' can be assessed by discriminatory outcomes (Bowling 1999), it directed attention not just to policing actions but their effects.

Having set out its standpoint, the inquiry concluded that institutional racism had been an important component of the failure of the investigation into Stephen Lawrence's murder. It detailed instances of 'unwitting racism' that had marred the investigation, including Inspector Groves' behaviour at the scene, the condescending and inconsiderate approach of officers at the hospital, the sidelining of Duwayne Brooks and Stephen Lawrence's parents, and the refusal by some officers to believe that the murder was racist. Centrally, it considered that the routine practices and processes adopted in the MPS had been characterised by a 'colour blind' approach, which failed to take account of the different needs and expectations of the diverse communities they policed. As a consequence, race relations had been underplayed at all levels of the way the case was handled. Furthermore, the inquiry broadened its assessment beyond the murder of Stephen Lawrence and its aftermath and beyond the policies and practices of the Metropolitan Police to the police service generally. It stated that 'institutional racism ... exists both in the Metropolitan Police Service and in other Police Services and other institutions countrywide' (Macpherson 1999: 6.39).

In drawing this conclusion, the inquiry made plain that it was vitally important that its accusation of institutional racism should not be mistaken for allegations of individual racism. It stated emphatically:

> We hope and believe that the average police officer and average member of the public will accept that we do not suggest that all police officers are racist and will both understand and accept the distinction we draw between overt individual racism and the pernicious and persistent institutional racism which we have described. (Macpherson 1999: 6.46:30)

The official response to the inquiry

The initial response to the inquiry suggested that Macpherson's attempts to distinguish between discrimination at the level of organisational policies and practices and individual racism had been successful. After first standing firm against the charge of institutional racism, the Commissioner of the Metropolitan Police, Sir Paul Condon, eventually accepted the definition used by the Lawrence Inquiry. His initial reaction, reported widely in the press, was to deny that his force was 'institutionally racist' or that institutional racism had contributed to the failure of the investigation of Stephen Lawrence's murder, arguing that 'by any ordinary use of those words' (Part 2, day 3: 307–8) the term suggested the majority of his staff were racist and that the MPS pursued policies that were deliberately discriminatory. In a public statement, the Commissioner revealed that he had been unhappy with the range of earlier definitions used during the inquiry and had written to Sir William Macpherson about these concerns. The response, he said, was the production of a 'new and demanding definition'. In doing this, the Lawrence Inquiry had:

> addressed my specific concern and fear that the old definitions could be used to label most police officers as deliberately racist. They are not and the new definition, which will apply to all public bodies and the wider community, makes this clear. That is why I accept its application to the Metropolitan Police Service.[1]

Condon's statement was welcomed and endorsed by the Home Secretary. In his first speech to Parliament after the publication of the inquiry report, Jack Straw said:

> That is a new definition of institutional racism, which I accept – and so does the Commissioner. The inquiry's assessment is clear and sensible. In my view, any long-established, white-dominated organisation is liable to have procedures, practices and a culture that tend to exclude or to disadvantage non-white people. The police service, in that respect, is little different from other parts of the criminal justice system – or from Government Departments, including the Home Office – and many other institutions. (Hansard 1999)

Indeed, the publication of the Lawrence Inquiry appeared to unleash a process of catharsis by which heads of police services, criminal justice agencies and local government organisations more broadly 'queued up to declare their organizations institutionally racist' (Tonry 2004: 76; see also Singh 2000: 33). In large part, it appeared that Macpherson's efforts to shift the focus away from individual staff towards collective organisational processes had made the term easier to accept. The problem was cast as something universal and impersonal: organisational members could feel assured that the source of discrimination was, as Tonry puts it, 'in the system, but not in them' (2004: 77). Indeed, the inquiry's use of the term has been criticised on the basis that it allowed practitioners to deny responsibility for their actions. Macpherson's definition implied a problem so endemic and pervasive that police services or other organisations could neither be held responsible nor expected to bring about any change. In other words, it let the police service, and other organisations, off the hook. For example, in 2003 the then Home Secretary David Blunkett argued that the term risked allowing managers to 'duck their responsibilities, to be able to offload their feelings by believing it's the system or a process' (*Guardian* 2003a). Echoing this, Trevor Phillips, the Chair of the Commission for Racial Equality, later that year described the term as a 'cop-out' for large public bodies, arguing 'what they will say is: "well, we hold our hands up to institutional racism". What they mean by that is, "somehow it is the system. But it is nothing to do with us, is it? We don't actually have to do anything"' (*Guardian*, 2003b).

Understanding the Lawrence Inquiry

However, it appears that the reaction to the term 'institutional racism' within the police service was very different. Far from feeling that the term exonerated them by relocating the problems of discrimination to the level of institutional policies and practices, many staff thought that the inquiry had accused them, as individuals, of racism. As a result, the inquiry was met with profound resentment and hostility by many within the police service.

Drawing on a major study of the impact of the Stephen Lawrence Inquiry on policing in England and Wales (Foster *et al.* 2005), the following pages explore the way the term was received and understood among police staff and attempts to examine why it should have been so comprehensively misunderstood.

The research reported here was conducted between 2002 and 2004. Centrally, it involved in-depth ethnographic research in eight police force areas selected on the basis of policing context (city, town, urban, rural); composition of their populations (with a variety of high and low minority ethnic settlement and different types of minority ethnic communities); force size; and geographical spread. The study also involved three national surveys to establish a picture of the inquiry's impact at a national level: a survey of approximately 1,300 interviews with officers in 17 forces, a postal survey of 98 ACPO staff, and a postal survey of over 130 police authority members.

Reactions to the inquiry

It was clear from the research that the Lawrence Inquiry had generated intense feelings of anger within the police service and these remained even five years after its publication. During the qualitative fieldwork, a considerable amount of resentment about the Lawrence Inquiry was expressed by police officers in all research areas. The strength of reaction appeared to be particularly powerful in London sites, where the inquiry and its immediate aftermath were described in strongly emotional terms. One officer described how after the publication of the inquiry 'everyone felt really low, we lost a lot of people, people didn't want to come to work, sickness was spiralling'. Front-line officers felt personally criticised by the inquiry and said that it was 'awful', 'terrible' and staff felt 'shocked and kicked'. One officer said, 'We've been slagged off, week after week, month after month. That, more than anything, broke my morale.'

The intensity of feeling in London was perhaps predictable given that the inquiry had focused primarily on the Metropolitan Police. In contrast, the inquiry appeared to have less resonance in other police force areas. For example, a detective sergeant in a large urban force said, 'It was remote. It was something that was in the press and belonged to London.' Yet while the inquiry may have seemed more distant in forces outside London, it still appeared to have generated considerable anger. For example, a detective constable (DC) in a rural area said the inquiry 'discredited the police generally. We all got tarred by it.' An inspector in another force area said, 'it had a terrible impact'.

Understanding institutional racism

Much of the anger officers felt about the Lawrence Inquiry stemmed from the term 'institutional racism'. This appears to have been the single most powerful message that police officers received from the inquiry. In all research sites it was immediately associated with the term, even in those areas where knowledge of the inquiry was otherwise poor. Yet despite the resonance of the term among officers in all case study sites, it was almost always misunderstood. The vast majority of officers conflated ideas of institutional and individual racism, thinking that the term referred to a widespread problem of racist attitudes and behaviour among police staff.

In light of this pervasive misunderstanding, it is perhaps not surprising that the term institutional racism created such widespread resentment and anger. For example, one PC said, 'The term institutional racism was being bandied about, that really annoyed me. I never have been, I never will be [racist]. When you join the police, you don't get sent on a course to be a racist.' In this context, the eventual acceptance of the term by Sir Paul Condon and other senior officers was viewed as a betrayal by some staff:

I thought about resigning. It was like, 'you should be hung and burnt at the stake, you're all racists'. (Detective constable, county force)

I thought 'how dare they'. I felt really aggrieved. I still do. I'm still angry about it. (Detective inspector, county force)

This widespread misunderstanding was acknowledged by respondents to the survey of Association of Chief Police Officer-rank (ACPO) staff, who were asked how well they thought officers in their own force understood the term 'institutional racism'. Only two thirds (67 per cent) thought middle managers in their force understood the term 'very well' or 'well' and this figure fell to 24 per cent for front-line officers. Indeed, only three out of 98 ACPO respondents believed their front-line officers understood the term 'very well'. However, the vast majority (94 per cent) said their ACPO colleagues understood the term either 'well' or 'very well'. In this assessment, ACPO staff appeared to reflect the observation of the Scarman Inquiry that there was a gulf between senior officers and front-line staff in relation to the degree of understanding and sensitivity towards questions of racism and police–minority community relations (Scarman 1981: 4.63:64). Yet the difference between ACPO and other staff was perhaps less apparent in the qualitative fieldwork, where there seemed to be considerable misunderstanding of the meaning of 'institutional racism' among officers at all ranks. For example, one ACPO officer described his reaction to the term in the aftermath of the report's publication in the following way:

'I didn't feel that I was racist. You know, you may on hard analysis have done something which you are not fully aware of, but in terms of accepting the mantle of being a racist ... with all that it entails, I think ... [there were] lots of concerns regarding that.

Officers' association of the term with individual racism appeared to have been reinforced by the way that the term was understood by the wider public. Officers in all research sites reported being called racist by the people they encountered. For instance, one Met officer said that after the inquiry, 'I had a group of black kids shouting "murderer" at me.' Such encounters were not just with local BME communities, but reported to be with 'middle class' or 'local English white residents' as well. In other words, some officers appeared to feel that the effect of the term was so powerful that they had become labelled as racist by parts of the population with whom antagonistic relations were not expected.

In particular, the association of the inquiry with individual racism seemed to have been reinforced by media coverage, which appeared to have had a powerful role in shaping officers' understanding of, and opinions towards, the inquiry. Indeed some officers thought it helped to distort the meaning of 'institutional racism', contributing to the widespread misunderstanding among both police staff and the public more widely. In the ACPO survey three-fifths of respondents felt the way the inquiry had been presented in the media was negative. In the officer survey many respondents reported being affected by media coverage and three-fifths (60 per cent) felt it had a negative impact on their jobs. Staff reported feeling under intense and negative scrutiny:

> I can remember clearly there was a period following Stephen [Lawrence]'s death and the publication of the Macpherson Report where it just hammered on about the police, you couldn't pick up a paper without there being negativity around police action, inaction, police response, it was a real time of beating the police up. (Senior officer, MPS)

> When all of this was going on ... you'd go to the pub and they'd say, 'I read the paper today, and you are institutional racists.' And if they think that, then what are the public thinking? (PC, MPS)

Misunderstanding institutional racism

In this way, the deployment of the term institutional racism was by no means unproblematic. Despite the inquiry's efforts to distinguish between systematic, collective discrimination and the actions of individual officers, and despite Macpherson's belief that the inquiry 'made it crystal clear that, because we call the Metropolitan Police institutionally racist, not every policeman is a racist' (*The Times*, 1 April 1999, cited in Rock 2004) the term was nevertheless interpreted by the majority of police staff as accusing them, as individuals, of racism. Moreover, the term appeared to be misunderstood consistently among all ranks and in all forces throughout England and Wales in which research was conducted.

In part, the reporting of the Lawrence Inquiry on television and in the press, together with the reaction of some key stakeholders, appeared to be important factors in this misreading of the inquiry's intent. However, arguably there are also aspects of the term and its particular application to the Lawrence case that were less than helpful in the face of such potential misunderstanding. In particular, it appears that the inquiry's own approach and use of the term may have contributed to the confusion over the crucial distinction between individual and institutional racism.

The following pages briefly outline three potential sources of difficulty: the application of the term to the specific case of the murder investigation; the complexities inherent in the dynamics of institutional racism; and, finally, the ways in which its use and definition in the inquiry report may have not only failed to clarify the meaning of the term but exacerbated its central ambiguities.

Institutional racism and murder investigation

The first area of difficulty concerns the application of the term 'institutional racism' in the context of an analysis of the actions and role of the police in the investigation of Stephen Lawrence's murder.

As an inquiry into a specific murder investigation, the Lawrence Inquiry was concerned both to investigate and understand the actions of particular police officers at the scene of the murder and during the subsequent investigation. Both the report itself and an analysis of the failures of the investigation therefore necessarily focused on the behaviour of individual officers in a specific series of encounters. Thus, the inquiry's conclusion that the investigation was marred by professional incompetence and poor leadership located its failings in the actions of individual officers as well as broader processes of systemic discrimination.

The difficulty, as Lea (2000, 2003) argues, is that it is not always easy to infer the workings of institutional processes from the actions of a single group of officers. This is particularly problematic when it is shown that the investigating officers acted in ways that may not have been typical of their colleagues. For example, as he points out (Lea 2000), the inquiry shows that while the murder was not characterised by the attending officers as racist, others, including the senior investigating officers, 'plainly' recognised it as such (Macpherson 1999: 19.38:146). In other words, one group of officers behaved in ways in which their colleagues did not.

The extent to which wider institutional processes can be distinguished from the failures of a single group of officers, and failures deriving from racism can be distinguished from incompetence, therefore needs careful explanation. However, the report's discussion of institutional racism 'suffers from crucial ambiguity' in this regard (Lea 2003: 50). It does not precisely specify which behaviour is generated by individuals and which by institutions; or which institutional dynamics encourage racism. It is thus unclear how, for example, the inquiry reached the conclusion that officers' failure to categorise Stephen Lawrence's murder as racist stemmed from 'unwitting collective racism' (Macpherson 1999 19.37:146) rather than the inappropriate or inadequate responses of the specific officers concerned.

In the context of such ambiguity, it appears that the failings at the level of individual officers took on particular prominence to those interpreting the report. As Lea argues, when the analysis of the investigation focuses on the level of individual actions, the institutional element is necessarily backgrounded (2000: 221). In addition, while it is relatively difficult to specify the precise contribution of racism in the failure of the investigation, the instances where officers were incompetent and made mistakes are both more immediately apparent and more easily understood.

Reflecting this, police officers' assessments of the inquiry's findings prioritised the failings of the individual investigating officers. Officers in all research sites thought that the failure of the inquiry was unrelated to institutional racism, or even individual racism, but was indicative of the incompetence of the Metropolitan Police at that time. For example, a detective sergeant (DS) said:

> I'd be surprised if [the investigation was poor] because Stephen [Lawrence] was black, I just think it was incompetent ... The police will investigate murders with the utmost ferocity. I can't imagine a whole team of detectives going 'OK bugger it', 'cause he's black. I can imagine the SIO being incompetent, and going down the wrong track,

but not 'cause he was black'.

Similarly, a senior officer in London said:

The suggestions of racism and the fact that we'd ignored him because he was a black boy were ridiculous ... What they showed was that the police were dreadful ... [and] the murder investigation was poor ... all the way through... he got poor first aid, the family were dealt with dreadfully, but had they been a Puerto Rican family or a white family, they would have got a dreadful service.

Some officers, in all sites, also questioned why the focus had fallen on the murder of Stephen Lawrence in particular. For example, a PC in a London site said:

It angered me because it was one murder where the police made mistakes, but what about all those other murders where the police made mistakes, what about all those other families, all those victims.

Further, many officers could not understand how the failings of this one investigation reflected practices in the police service more broadly. For these officers, an investigation led by the Metropolitan Police was the main focus of criticism of the Inquiry. How then could the problems of this one case be extrapolated to forces elsewhere, particularly given the perceived incompetence of the MPS at this time? As a sergeant in a small county force explained:

Who was Stephen Lawrence? He was a black lad killed in London who the Met made many cock-ups about. It was bad publicity for the police that was generated by the Met. They made cock-ups, and we're all paying for them as we always do.

Or as a DS put it in another site, 'the bloody Met always bollocks things up'.

In other words, the suggestion was that the main problem experienced in the Lawrence case was not institutional racism but incompetence – the implication, often made very explicitly, is that incompetence is 'colour blind'. Of course, this was a means by which officers individually, and forces collectively, were able to distance themselves from the inquiry. It is possible that the stigma attached to its perceived charge of racism was such that a conclusion of incompetence was easier to accept. However, officers' understanding of the failings it identified may also have been an inevitable consequence of the way that the scope of the inquiry shifts between the investigation of a single case and problems at the level of the police service more broadly. At the least, the failure of the report to specify precisely the contributions of each to the problems in the conduct of the investigation did little to clarify the crucial distinction between individual and institutional processes, incompetence and racism.

Institutional racism, institutions and individuals

A further source of confusion in police officers' understanding of institutional racism appears to have derived from the complexity of the concept itself. Officers appeared to find it difficult to locate what, exactly, was 'institutional' about institutional racism.

First, it appeared that many staff found it difficult understand how attributes of an 'institution' – and indeed the notion of an institution itself – could be separated from the individuals who comprise it. Even those officers with a more sophisticated understanding of the term 'institutional racism' said they were confused. As a DS in a London site asked, how can an organisation be racist and individuals not when 'the organisation is the people in it'.

In part, officers' confusion reflects the ambiguity inherent to the concept. Institutions and the individuals that constitute them are not wholly distinct. First, as Lea puts it (2000: 221), the workings of institutions are, of course, 'encountered as the actions of individuals'. In other words, it is through police officers that organisational policies and practices are carried out and become embedded. Second, organisations are created and shaped by their members. They are thus dynamic processes as well as structures with policies and rules. As Holdaway puts it:

> institutions emerge, they are not static, do not wholly transcend and are not finally determinant of action. They emerge from taken for granted ways of working together; from related, taken for granted ways of thinking; and from taken for granted categorisations and self-definitions of identity. (1999: 3.2)

It appears to be this relationship between the policies of an institution and their generation by the staff within them that led to a criticism of the concept of 'institutional racism' by the Home Secretary David Blunkett in 2003:

> I think the slogan created a year or two ago about institutional racism missed the point. It's not the structures created in the past, it's the processes to change structures in the future and it's individuals at all levels who do that. ... it isn't institutions, it's patterns of work and processes that have grown up. (*Guardian* 2003a)

The difficulty of distinguishing the police organisation from the staff who comprise it appears likely to have contributed to officers' misunderstanding of the concept of institutional racism. By implication, labelling the police service institutionally racist in effect was understood as labelling its staff.

But the crucial difference between the discrimination generated by individuals and by institutions appeared to have been blurred by the way in which the aspects of institutional racism prioritised in the report are both experienced by officers and manifested in practice.

As Singh (2000) shows, the concept of institutional racism has been conceptually 'stretched' over different levels of analysis, variously referring to structural processes, groups of social actors, and individual attitudes and prejudices. In its account of institutional racism, the inquiry appears to have given primacy to a particular interpretation of the concept that focuses on 'quasi-psychological' (Singh 2000: 32) factors, such as 'attitudes and behaviour', 'unwitting prejudice', 'ignorance', 'thoughtlessness' and 'racist stereotyping' (Macpherson 1999: 6.34:28).[2] The inquiry gave careful consideration to the way that these facets of institutional racism were mediated in the occupational culture of the police service. Thus, it stated that such attitudes derived from an 'inflexible police ethos' and were able to 'thrive' in a 'tightly knit community'. In particular, it stated that the 'police canteen can too easily be its breeding ground' (Macpherson 1999: 6.17:22).

The way that police culture can mediate service delivery is one that has been the focus of much research (Banton 1964; Bittner 1975; Skolnick 1966; Shearing and Ericson 1981; Reiner 2000; Chan 1996, 1997, 2003, to name but a few). In particular, research has explored the ways in which particular organisational tasks or working environments shape the ways members experience and understand their social world and their role within it: in other words, the way institutions shape the way their members 'think' (Douglas 1986: 112). These informal values, beliefs and assumptions become manifested in the way in which officers employ informal 'recipe knowledge' (Chan 1996) in decision-making, and it is these that may lead to inequitable outcomes; as the inquiry described in the conduct of the police inquiry into Stephen Lawrence's murder.

The difficulty appears to have been that, because of the pervasive and subtle effects of these processes – shaping the way police officers understand social reality – and their manifestations as discretionary decision-making in particular contexts, they were not easily recognised or identified as 'institutional' processes. So, for example, those staff who were familiar with the case denied that the investigating officers' dealings with Duwayne Brooks at the scene of the murder were shaped by 'institutional racism'. Instead, their actions were thought to be understandable responses to a particular instance of suspicious and difficult behaviour. Officers had heard that Brooks was, for example, a 'mouthy, anti-police so and so, which didn't help at all'; 'he wasn't a particularly nice character'. His behaviour therefore led him to be perceived, as one officer put it, as 'trouble'. In other words, he was thought to be pathologised by the officers not because he was black but because he was a 'bad boy'. This was not understood as an institutional process but, as one officer put it, as an 'instinct thing'. For example, one officer explained that the behaviour of the investigating officers reflected his own practice. He said that often when he stopped a car and 'asked a few questions', black men would become extremely abusive 'so you'd think, right then, and you'd try to get them for what you can. That's not racist.' In his view, police officers' dealings with Duwayne Brooks was understandable: 'he was very abusive, very aggressive at the scene, that wasn't brought out'.

Of course, this articulation of the processes by which Duwayne Brooks was not treated as a primary victim but a suspect demonstrated the very processes Macpherson and others have identified in the 'racialisation' of the investigation into Stephen Lawrence's murder: for example, the categorisation of minority ethnic groups as 'unrespectable' (Waddington 1999) and thus 'police property'; the dismissal of 'race' as irrelevant to the case (Holdaway 1999); and the lack of recognition of how an expectation of discrimination and mistrust can affect the ways in which police actions are understood by minority ethnic communities, thereby resulting in a cycle of escalating mutual hostility (Foster *et al.* 2005). The difficulty is that the subtlety and pervasive nature of the ways these processes occur were not *experienced* by officers as being generated institutionally.

Instead, the coding of the protagonists in the Lawrence case and the responses of the officers concerned were understood solely in terms of the professional decision-making of individual staff: a result of the understandable responses of the officers involved to provocative and suspicious behaviour. The labelling of this process as 'institutionally racist' was therefore understood in terms of individual racism.

Again, this understanding of the actions surrounding the Stephen Lawrence case led some officers to think that their interpretation by the inquiry was unfair. Some staff thought that the perception that racism played a part in officers' decisions at the scene demonstrated that the inquiry didn't understand policing. As one officer put it, 'everything they didn't have an answer for, they blamed on racism'.

Institutional racism and the Lawrence Inquiry Report

In this way, while the inquiry took care to differentiate between institutional and individual racism, this distinction was not recognised or understood by many within the police service. Although the inquiry stated explicitly in more than one passage that its application of the term 'institutional racism' did not imply that there was a widespread problem of racism among individual staff, the term was understood in precisely this manner. It appears that in part this widespread misunderstanding may have resulted from the manner in which the focus of the inquiry shifted between questions of individual conduct in a murder investigation and organisational processes more broadly; further, some confusion is likely to have arisen from the complexities inherent in the concept itself, particularly those aspects of institutional discrimination prioritised in the inquiry, which are manifested through the actions and attitudes of individual officers. The imprecision of the processes described in the inquiry report could provide little resolution to such confusion.

However, there were aspects of the use of the term within the report itself that may not only have failed to clarify the meaning of the term but also contributed to the confusion over the crucial distinction between individual and institutional racism.

In particular, a difficulty arises in the way the report shifts between different levels of analysis. As I have outlined, the remit of the inquiry was both particular and general: it was concerned both to investigate and to understand the actions of particular police officers at the scene of the murder and during the subsequent investigation as well as to examine the broader practices and policies of the Metropolitan Police

Service. In doing so, it identifies not one process – 'institutional racism' – but three. First, it describes overt or deliberate racism: behaviour, language or processes that are deliberately intended to discriminate against BME people because of their ethnicity; second, 'unwitting' or 'unconscious' racism, that is, behaviour of individual officers that unconsciously and unintentionally discriminates against minority groups; and third, systemic, collective racism generated by the way that institutions function.

As discussed above, these three processes are not always discrete and distinct. However, they are analytically separate and, as Tonry puts it, are 'ethically quite different' (2004: 77). The difficulty is that they are not clearly identified in the report as such. Instead, there is considerable confusion in the way they are employed throughout the inquiry report.

First, the differentiation between these three processes is not always clear. Indeed, they are, on occasion, used interchangeably. For example, the use of 'inappropriate and offensive language' is described as an instance of 'unwitting racism' (Macpherson 1999: 46.28:322). Yet, as the inquiry itself suggests in an earlier paragraph (1999: 6.3:20), the use of 'inappropriate expressions' that are 'well known to be offensive' is perhaps more commonly understood as overtly racist. This rather implies a lack of clarity as to the meaning of what is or is not 'unwitting' racism. Similarly, Inspector Groves' assumptions at the scene of the murder that Stephen Lawrence and Duwayne Brooks had been involved in a fight, and his consequent failure to assess or respond to Duwayne Brooks as a primary victim, are described variously as an instance of all three processes. In one paragraph it is cited both as an example of 'unwitting racism' in which it was not believed that 'discrimination or disadvantage was overt' (1999: 46.28:322), and 'insensitive and racist stereotypical behaviour' which implies conscious and overt racism; and elsewhere in the report it is described as an example of 'institutional racism' (1999: 6.45:29–30).

Second, the definition of 'institutional racism' offered in the Lawrence Inquiry Report may have contributed to the widespread misunderstanding of the term. A number of critics have highlighted what they perceive to be its shortcomings and one, Michael Tonry (2004: 76), has described the definition as 'extraordinarily artless, and almost incoherent'. He is critical of the terms it uses to describe the facets of institutional racism. For example, he argues that 'unwitting prejudice' is oxymoronic – actions that are based on prejudice cannot be 'unwitting'. Similarly, 'racist stereotyping' is not an instance of institutional racism but is, *per se*, racist. Further, the construction of the statement that institutional racism consists of a collective failure 'to provide appropriate and professional service to people *because of* their colour, culture or ethnic origin' (emphasis added) is again more suggestive of overt racism: it describes failures based on, or motivated by, perceived ethnicity. In this way, the three processes of conscious, unwitting and systemic racism that the inquiry was attempting to capture are elided within the definition itself. As a result, the definition did little to clarify the crucial distinction between institutional and individual discrimination, but instead reflected the central ambiguities of its use in the report.

The problem of institutional racism

A final area of difficulty concerns the term 'institutional racism' itself. As we have argued elsewhere (Foster *et al.* 2005), it seems that the widespread confusion between institutional and individual discrimination appears in part to have stemmed from the simple fact of the inclusion of the word *racism* within the term. The word 'racism' is so highly powerful and emotive, and carries with it such a deeply embedded social stigma, that when it is deployed, even within a term such as institutional racism that carries different meanings, it is very difficult to dissociate it from the actions of individuals. In other words, it seems likely that even if the inquiry report had more precisely located the dynamics of the institutional processes it was attempting to describe, the resonance of the word 'racism' within the term would almost inevitably have generated a sense among officers that issues of individual racism were at least in part the focus of attention.

In part, the resonance of the term appears to have given the inquiry particular potency. Indeed, Tonry argues that the appeal of the term for the inquiry was precisely in its emotional charge: as he says, 'accusations of racism are galvanizing and attract attention' (2004: 77). The application of such a powerful term certainly appears to have been an important catalyst for change in some important areas of the police service (see Foster *et al.* 2005). Yet at the same time, the power of the term appears to have been problematic. By inadvertently drawing attention to the more potent and better understood problems of racist attitudes and behaviour, and by the insufficient clarity in its use, the inquiry's application of the term 'institutional racism' seems to have deflected police attention from the very problem of embedded organisational practices and policies that it was actually intending to capture.

Notes

1 Available at:
   http://www.guardian.co.uk/Lawrence/Story/0,,208692,00.html
2 Indeed, as Reiner (2000) argues, despite Scarman's 'misplaced' emphasis on overt and deliberate acts of individual racism, it was he who had the better grasp of how discrimination by the police was intrinsically connected to wider structures of racial and social inequality.

References

Banton, M. (1964) *The Policeman in the Community*, London: Tavistock Press.

Bittner, E. (1975) *The Functions of the Police in Modern Society: A Review of Background Factors, Current Practices, and Possible Role Models*, Seattle: University of Washington Press.

Bowling, B. (1999) *Violent Racism: Victimisation, Policing and Social Context*, Oxford: Oxford University Press.

Chan, J. (1996) 'Changing Police Culture', *British Journal of Criminology*, 36 (1): 109–34.

Chan, J. (1997) *Changing Police Culture: Policing in a Multi-Cultural Society*, Cambridge: Cambridge University Press.

Chan, J. with Devery, C. and Doran, S. (2003) *Fair Cop: Learning the Art of Policing*, Toronto: University of Toronto Press.

Douglas, M. (1986) *How Institutions Think*, Syracuse: Syracuse University Press.

Downes, D. and Morgan, R. (2002) 'The Skeletons in the Cupboard: The Politics of Law and Order at the Turn of the Millennium', in M. Maguire, R. Morgan and R. Reiner (eds) *The Oxford Handbook of Criminology*, 3rd edn, Oxford: Clarendon Press.

Foster, J., Newburn, T. and Souhami, A. (2005) *Assessing the Impact of the Stephen Lawrence Inquiry*, Home Office Research Study 294, London: Home Office.

Guardian (2003a) 'Blunkett dumps "institutional racism" ' 14 January.

Guardian (2003b) 'Institutional racism used as an excuse for doing nothing, says CRE Chief'. 1 September.

Hansard (1999) *Parliamentary Debates*, 24 February, col. 391.

Holdaway, S. (1999) 'Understanding the Police Investigation of the Murder of Stephen Lawrence: A 'Mundane' Sociological Analysis', *Sociological Research Online* 4(1), http://www.socresonline.org.uk/socresonline/4/lawrence/holdaway.html

Lea, J. (2000) 'The Macpherson Report and the Question of Institutional Racism', *The Howard Journal*, 39 (3): 219–33.

Lea, J. (2003) 'Institutional Racism in Policing: The Macpherson Report and its Consequences', in R. Matthews and J. Young (eds) *The New Politics of Crime and Punishment*, Cullompton: Willan Publishing.

Macpherson, Sir W. (1999) *The Stephen Lawrence Inquiry: Report of an Inquiry by Sir William Macpherson of Cluny*, CM 4262-1, London: HMSO.

Reiner, R. (2000) *The Politics of the Police*, 3rd edn, Oxford: Oxford University Press.

Rock, P. (2004) *Constructing Victims' Rights: The Home Office, New Labour and Victims*, Oxford: Clarendon Press.

Scarman, Lord (1981) *The Scarman Report: The Brixton Disorders, 10–21 April 1981*, Cmnd 8427, London: HMSO.

Shearing, C. and Ericson, R. (1981) 'Culture as Figurative Action', *British Journal of Sociology*, 42 (4): 481–506.

Singh, G. (2000) 'The Concept and Context of Institutional Racism', in A. Marlow and B. Loveday (eds) *After Macpherson: Policing after the Stephen Lawrence Inquiry*, Lyme Regis: Russell House Publishing.

Skolnick, J. (1966) *Justice Without Trial: Law Enforcement in Democratic Society*, New York: Wiley.

Tonry, M. (2004) *Punishment and Politics: Evidence and Emulation in English Crime Control Policy*, Cullompton: Willan Publishing.

Waddington, P. A. J. (1999) 'Discretion, "Respectability" and Institutional Police Racism', *Sociological Research Online*, 4 (1): http://www.socresonline.org.uk/socresonline/4/lawrence/waddington.html

Chapter 5

Black Police Associations and the Lawrence Report

Simon Holdaway and Megan O'Neill

The Macpherson Inquiry and subsequent Lawrence Report are usually associated with relationships between the police and the service they offer to ethnic minorities (Macpherson 1999). One important outcome from the inquiry findings was that all police policies and practices needed to be scrutinised for negative, racial bias. An (inevitably) all-encompassing notion of 'institutional racism' was at the heart of the analysis of the Metropolitan Police Service, suggesting that the other 42 constabularies of England and Wales might be described similarly. All constabularies and policies were thus brought within the scope of reform.

One area of policy where institutional racism had a particular grip was the police response to allegations of racial attacks; the relationship between the police and the families of murder victims was another. A less familiar and, publicly, almost imperceptible subject included in the report's recommendations addressed rather different victims of racialised discrimination and prejudice. These were police officers and support staff from minority ethnic groups.

The Lawrence Report thus gave an impetus to change racialised relations *within* constabularies.[1] Of particular significance was Macpherson's recommendation that Black Police Associations (BPAs) be established in all constabularies which Jack Straw, then Home Secretary, endorsed without qualification during his introduction of the report to the House of Commons. The consequences of that endorsement will be considered in this chapter. First, we will chart briefly the history of BPAs before Lawrence. A consideration of new articulations of race within constabularies and their consequences follows. In particular, the creation and sustaining of boundaries to frame an essential notion of black officers' experience of police employment is discussed. Finally, a change from the dominance of overt racism to its covert articulation, which BPA officials have identified, will be analysed.[2]

1997 – New Labour

The Lawrence Report placed race relations firmly on New Labour's agenda. It could not be ignored, joining a wide range of areas subject to Labour's approach to the management of the public sector. In brief, race relations, including relations within constabularies, were defined as a matter for management by chief constables and their staff.

The Home Secretary's endorsement of BPAs encouraged their wider establishment in constabularies. Minority ethnic staff no longer had to present a special case to form an association. The government had given them a warrant, recognising the marginalisation of minority ethnic officers and support staff, who could be the subjects of prejudice and discrimination. Indeed, research studies funded over a number of years by the Home Office had demonstrated the vulnerability of black and Asian officers, and senior officers' very patchy responses to allegations of prejudice and discrimination (Holdaway 1991, 1997; Holdaway and Barron 1997). Some resisted, but many more had developed a personal strategy of accommodation to what was a routine aspect of a black or Asian police officer's working life (Holdaway 1997).

The Home Secretary had now recognised this state of affairs and, through his endorsement of BPAs, made a clear statement that racial prejudice and discrimination of any type within constabularies was not acceptable. The statement was strengthened further by the Home Office funding of the National Black Police Association, which canvassed support from minority ethnic staff in many constabularies. Associations formed in constabularies before 1997, the Metropolitan Police Association for example, also gave encouragement to their peers, who had perhaps met informally for a time, to now become members of a recognised group. The subject of 'race' was therefore given a sharper focus and greater legitimacy after the publication of the Lawrence Report, and BPAs were to influence the form in which it would be articulated within constabularies.

The ways in which BPAs moulded race relations will be considered later. First, recognition should be given to a further factor that structured their action. This is New Labour's managerial approach to the public sector in general and race in particular, which provided BPAs with the new resources chief officers might have needed if they were to fulfil the objectives the government set for them. In his speech introducing the Lawrence Report to the House of Commons, Jack Straw endorsed BPAs and recommended that all chief constables encourage their development in every constabulary. This brought formal recognition to existing BPAs, providing them with an added status and, more generally, sending a signal that chief officers would have to give a new emphasis to recognised and unacknowledged problems of race relations.

New Labour's now well known and continuing approach to the management of the public sector has been for central government to set targets related to various activities, and to monitor outcomes from the action local agencies take to meet them (Rhodes 2000). The direction and required outcomes of policy are set by central government. Local institutions, constabularies in this case, decide how they use their resources to achieve the targets set. As far as race relations within constabularies were concerned, targets for the recruitment, retention, and promotion of minority ethnic staff were put in place and to be realised.

Chief constables now found themselves having to meet challenging targets in a difficult area of work that could benefit from minority ethnic officers' advice. BPAs were an obvious source of help. This position gave BPA officials further valuable resources. They could claim to be an important source of advice for chief officers formulating not only recruitment and retention policies but also policies related to race generally – and just about every policy could have such a feature. To ignore the advice of BPAs could be evidence of a chief's failure to accept Macpherson's findings and, maybe, of 'institutional racism'. Indeed, after Macpherson it was calamitous for a chief constable to do anything that risked any such thing. A number of them lined-up to agree that their constabulary was institutionally racist (Holdaway and O'Neill forthcoming).

One upshot of the government's targets was therefore to give BPAs resources needed by chief officers, including a seat at policy tables and other influential fora. With their BPA at the table, chiefs could provide evidence that they were consulting with and responding to the needs of their minority ethnic staff. Indeed, in our study of BPAs, which included interviews with assistant chief constables with responsibility for race policy, we found that the inclusion of BPAs in formal and informal discussion of policy and practice was welcomed.

In the vast majority of constabularies, BPAs are now represented on many committees, but mostly those concerned with personnel and related matters. Further, they are often involved in training and advice about the provision and quality of police services to minority ethnic groups. This work has been of such substance that many constabularies have provided offices and equipment for their BPA, and dedicated staff time for the chair or secretary to work specifically on BPA matters.

Changing articulations of 'race' and ethnicity

Several consequences have flowed from these circumstances. The first is that the articulation of 'race' within constabularies and, consequentially, the position of minority ethnic officers changed after Lawrence. The managerial categorisation of race, and subsequent development of BPAs, has influenced its meaning within constabularies. Once solely the characteristic of an individual, it was now also to acquire a more collective significance within the police workforce.

There is a sense that whenever anyone is categorised as the member of an ethnic or racialised group they are attributed with a collective status.[3] The particular point made here is a rather different one, however. Research studies carried out in English constabularies during the decade before Lawrence indicated that minority ethnic officers felt isolated within their workplace. They had little power and, therefore, few resources other than personal determination to challenge routinely expressed racist jokes and banter, to be regarded as a full member of their team of colleagues, and for their difficult situation to be recognised by senior officers as a first step to its resolution. To be a police officer from a minority ethnic group was to be marked out as an individual who was different from the ethnic majority. Minority ethnic officers were not associated with or part of a representative group within constabularies. 'Race' and 'ethnicity' were individualised.

The growth of BPAs after Lawrence has begun to change that situation. Although we do not know the number of minority ethnic officers who are members of BPAs, and cannot assume the majority are, the government's recognition drew them together symbolically and instrumentally: symbolically in that BPAs were to represent the voice and recognised status of minority ethnic officers as a distinct group within the workforce, and to declare it clearly to colleagues;

and instrumentally in that minority ethnic officers became integral to aspects of police policy-making and the monitoring of practice, often with direct access to a chief officer, if needs be. 'Race' appeared as a categorisation extending beyond individuals to a formally recognised and identifiable group within the workforce.

Second, 'race' became increasingly a subject for management by chief and senior officers. This meant that resources and the authority of senior officers could and should be brought to bear upon and change it. Manifestations of racialised inequality could be managed to equality through the deliberations of working groups and committees with a remit to develop policy, and to allocate resources to, for example, BPAs advising about recruitment campaigns designed and targeted precisely on work with ethnic minorities. Policy documents related to centrally set targets, action plans, good practice guides, and evaluation reports have thus increased, all dealing with aspects of the management of race.

The basis of these various regulatory and managerial phenomena has generally been an implicit notion of equal outcomes from police interventions for all ethnic groups. It has nevertheless been the case that many rank-and-file officers have interpreted such developments as examples of positive discrimination (Foster *et al.* 2005). Many officers have viewed BPAs as an alternative to the Police Federation, the official police union, viewed, incidentally, as the 'White Police Association' by many minority ethnic officers. Policies to create unequal outcomes have been interpreted as tipping the balance in favour of 'ethnics'. A mood of caution has developed, deterring supervisors from tackling problems associated with race positively during their daily work. If they get it wrong, they risk allegations of 'racism', and disciplinary action. This has proved to be a difficult context of work for many lower-ranked supervisors, leading to a lack of confidence and hesitancy when dealing with race policy (Foster *et al.* 2005).

Policies have therefore been managed within this environment, chief officers taking the lead in policy development but reliant on lower ranked supervisors, mostly inspectors and sergeants, to relate them to practice on the streets and in the station. Race has become a managerial category often dealt with hesitantly by police supervisors, watchful of the consequences of error, whether unwitting or deliberate.

Representing black staff

BPA officials understand a key aspect of their role to be the representation of minority ethnic staff views to their senior command. For most associations, 'black' is regarded as an adequate descriptor of all minority ethnic staff that, to a more distanced eye, is potentially contentious, failing to capture different ethnic identifications.

During our recent research project about the role of BPAs in English and Welsh constabularies, we asked BPA chairs and deputy chairs if their criteria for membership of their BPA excluded some minority ethnic staff. We also asked why some visible minority officers were not members of their association, expecting insight into any problems the single designation 'black' might have raised.

The majority of associations used the title 'Black Police Association' because it signified that visible minorities had a single experience of racism (Phillips 2005). To admit publicly divisions between different minority ethnic groups working within constabularies would weaken an association's bargaining power and authority when representing members. BPA interviewees, however, also appreciated that this designation might exclude members of a visible minority who did not identify themselves as black. One adopted solution was to create associate membership, allowing members' white partners, white officers, and members of the public who sympathised with an association's objectives to join. Their proxy ethnicity allowed attendance at BPA meetings and social events but not constabulary committees and working groups.

This was a partial solution, however, because it could not accommodate, for example, potential members of South Asian or Middle Eastern origin who placed their distinct, shared culture ahead of any experience of discrimination or prejudice. A denial of the importance of their culture by BPA officials could appear a refutation of their ethnic identity and a trivialisation of assertions of membership of an ethnic group.

The widely shared claim to an essential experience of racism nevertheless remained in the ascendancy within most BPAs. During interviews, some chairs and deputy chairs of BPAs were resolute about it, justifying their perspective in a number of ways. This chair, for example, described the essence of 'blackness', ironically using the example of a member of mixed heritage, and therefore cultural origins, to justify a common experience of racism.

Because the issue of blackness is so key to what we are about, because it should go to those people that fall within that category of the term black. We have full members that, if you look at them they are white. Or, as the term white is understood. And they are of mixed heritage but because they meet the criteria or, because of their experiences, they have suffered racism based on the fact that emphasis has been placed on their, say the fact that half of their heritage is Pakistani or Bangladeshi or Chinese or whatever. They fit into the criteria. Those that don't fit within that criteria actually still have the ability to become an associate member, which offers all the same rights and privileges except they can't vote, whereas a full member can. And that's how we dealt with that we decided very early on that we don't want to water down the issue, we want people to know what we are about and there is no other word that encapsulates that than black. And it's about the visual aspect of it.

Another chair explained further that the context of working within the police was particularly important when understanding this common experience of racism. There may be differences between minority ethnic staff outside of the context of employment. However, a common experience dominates within it.

… under the term of 'Black', which is primarily a, it's not an assessment of colour, but the sharing common experience of people from African Caribbean and Asian origins. So, they have to be a member of the police service. But it's around minority ethnic people sharing common experience and being part of the police service.

Other officials justified a single experience of racism by looking beyond the police service to encompass the history of black people living on many continents. There was an imperative to embrace it; failure to do so could indicate a less than full appreciation of the history of ethnic relations in the UK generally and the police in particular, which should not be forgotten. Another chair emphasised that history's racialised, global dimensions:

… the term black has a history. And it's a term that was adopted by most people from that experience. So, you know, it's a social political term that's been adopted, not only in the UK but in America, Africa. It's got a history that speaks around that shared and common experience.

Black colleagues who were not members of a BPA thus failed to realise that their association was part of a history of conflict. This BPA secretary put it that they do not

fully recognise the history of the Black Police Association or the history of black people. And they sort of say, so you know we're not really black you know, we are almost white so this isn't for us. It's something that we will work on; it's something that we will work on in the future in terms of education about our members. I mean lots of people out there don't realise the hard work, because they are not involved in the organisation they think that everything is smooth running. They don't recognise the difficulties that we have had in the past as an organisation.

Other chairs could not muster such confidence. They realised that any notion of ethnicity within a BPA's membership criteria was potentially precarious and open to deconstruction. For this next chair, the relational and contrasting character of ethnicity was central, marking a boundary between black officers and the culture of the ethnic majority workforce, which is a 'white culture, a white institution'.

I mean, I'm ethnic, you're ethnic, we all have an ethnicity, but it's the colour of our skin and the experiences, our shared experiences. Em, but yeah, we've had people who have said, 'These people should be members and these people shouldn't be because they're all ethnic minority' and we say, 'Well no, they're not an ethnic minority as such because it's a white culture, a white institution we work for and we are really the minority.' Em, but yeah, it has been sort of raised as a sort of, 'Why can't these people be full members?'

A number of associations had changed their name to 'Black and Asian Police Association', widening membership, which some chairs viewed as a weakening of their strategic position within a constabulary. However, this chair thought it was important to add Asian to his association's title.

I asked somebody, 'Why can't we just be called BPA?' They said, 'No because I am proud to be Asian.' Black denotes something completely different to some. I don't like being, I am not a black man. I am an

Asian, yet I'm an African. Africans always assume that Africans are black; I have experienced racism from blacks and from whites. I am a second generation African, I am more African that the black people that live in ... yet I cannot be African because I am brown skinned. So therefore I will celebrate the fact that I am brown and I will call myself Asian if that is what you want me to be, even though I am very proud to be an African. In fact, Africa courses through my veins, but I am not allowed to be that. And there are a lot of Asian officers want to be called Asian and not black.

BPAs therefore face something of a dilemma if they are to be a fully representative group. 'Black' can summarise the single experience of racialised discrimination faced by members of minority ethnic groups, a perspective with its origins in the American Black Power movement during the 1960s (Carmichael and Hamilton 1968). On the other hand, some minority ethnic officers identify themselves with reference to their cultural or religious origins. Some of those who focus upon cultural origins have dark skins and some, Jewish officers for example, do not. This has presented an ongoing difficulty that will not be resolved easily.

Recent government and constabulary policies have compounded this tension between 'race' and culture, because they focus upon 'diversity' and 'multiculturalism'. The celebration of culture has become a keynote of New Labour policy, in tension with Macpherson's central, analytical concept of institutional racism. The former admits to a workforce including a wide variety of minority ethnic groups, each with a claim to representation based on cultural or faith-based criteria. The inclusion of all minority ethnic groups is at its heart. The latter places a strong emphasis on a unified identity and racialised grouping, based on a distinct history, visibility within the workforce, and other unifying criteria. Cultural diversity is subordinate to membership of a racialised group.

This tension between racialised and cultural representations has developed within the London Metropolitan Police Service, where a considerable number of police associations have been formed. The policy encouraging this development has been precisely one of recognising diversity, allowing claims of representation to Italian, Jewish, Turkish, Greek, Sikh, Hindu, Muslim, Christian and Irish officers.[4] All these groups have their own association, meeting with chief officers in one committee, vying and yielding to claims for representation, reform and, therefore, the same resources.

The officials of non-black associations were interviewed during our research. It was noticeable that they stressed distinct cultural and religious traits of direct relevance to their employment. Jewish officers talked about the demands of religious observance, dietary requirements, not working on the Sabbath, as well as their majority colleagues' prejudice and discrimination. Muslim officials referred similarly to diet and the need for a prayer room in stations. Others, the Greek association for example, focused upon close family and kin relationships that could be fostered to assist police investigations of crime within their community. These and related features took precedence over what was viewed as the 'political' stance of the Black Police Association, that was often perceived as self-serving, confrontational and unhelpful. Officials of the Black Police Association viewed their colleagues in these other associations as misunderstanding the essential unity between them. They recognised the importance of cultures but saw them as secondary to the overriding problem of racism.

All the officials described their claim to membership with reference to an essential feature of their minority group. There was something essentially different about the employment experience of 'black' officers, an experience reaching back to a long history of racialised discrimination and prejudice. Similarly, there was something essentially different about, for example, the experience of officers of Greek origin. Their shared, unified culture bound them together. The basis of the claims differed from group to group but each offered an argument based on essentialism.

Social science research has challenged notions of essentialism, arguing that they are deterministic, unsophisticated and stereotypical, giving licence to racist thinking, and the presentation of a certainty about human characteristics shielding how racialised identities are constructed and sustained as essential. Identities are much more varied, more precarious.

A notion of essentialism is at the heart of racism. BPA officials knew this but their particular blend of essentialism was based on political objectives. To be divided into many minority groups was to lose influence and power during negotiations, allowing chief officers to dispute their claim to represent all black officers within the workforce. This was a strategic position, using 'race' as a political resource to gain authority and power (Fuss 1989). The tensions between a focus upon racism and upon culture and faith will not disappear. Essentialisms are constructed socially, and therefore fragile. BPAs will have to visit their criteria of membership time and again as chiefs respond to the claims of culturally based groups within and outwith their constabulary.

Covert racism

The notion of essentialism is pertinent to a further change that has followed the publication of the Lawrence Report. Our BPA interviewees told us that overt racism has given way to covert racism. In their recent evaluation of the impact of the Lawrence Report on policing, Janet Foster and her colleagues also documented a falling away of overtly racist language but did not probe what minority ethnic officers meant when they referred to continuing, different forms of racism, which are presumably covert (Foster *et al.* 2005).

By definition, criteria to identify covert racism in the workplace are elusive, presenting a very difficult problem for supervisory officers who have to assess them. As one BPA chair explained:

> You can't see it, you can't smell it, you can't taste it, but you know if you go for a job you ain't going to get it because it is always internal. And you can't put your finger on what, but you know in your heart of hearts why and those sorts of things.

Claims to be the subject of covert racism need an adequate measure of supporting evidence, which might not be readily available if, as the chair pointed out, 'you can't put your finger on it'. And this problem is compounded if, as an assistant chief constable who was interviewed explained, the perpetrators of covert racism are 'becoming a lot more clever. We don't have overt racists in the Police Service. We have a lot of covert ones. Very mobile, very articulate, and very clever in the way they operate.'

Two points are of initial relevance to the view that covert racism is prevalent and that there are a lot more covert racists within the police service.[5] The first is a lasting, institutional memory of overt racism. Macpherson's challenge to overt racism within the ranks, and the Home Secretary's and many chief constables' endorsement of his view, has not eradicated its vivid presence within memories shared by many officers. In this sense, covert racism lives on, raising officers' awareness of the present, not least as they reflect upon their relationships with white colleagues.

Second, Macpherson defined institutional racism in very wide terms indeed. He included 'unwitting', 'ignorance', actions and attitudes, and more within it. Further, the idea of an institution acting in a discriminatory way is sufficient to allow widely differing interpretations of racism. We understand immediately the notion of an individual acting but the idea of an institution as similar is elusive and much more difficult to comprehend. It was nevertheless an idea that the police were required to grasp post-Macpherson, allowing ambiguous evidence of racism to be considered:

> Institutionalised and covert are very much related. Certain things, institutionalised racism, you can put down to, you know, you can put your finger on it. It's black and white. Other things, you know, there's a whole lot of grey area. And when you start getting that grey area that's where I feel that covert racism can operate and it operates very well in that. (BPA chair)

When the uncertainty of Macpherson's definition and the strength of an institutional memory of racism are associated, a schema of interpretation to identify covert racism is created. Schemas, similar to Goffman's notion of 'frame', include knowledge and related ways of identifying and understanding covert racism (Goffman 1974). They are taken for granted, helping us to make sense of experience because they round-out ambiguity, are culturally specific (in our case related to work within constabularies) and constrain officers. They are not only associated with the interpretation of immediate situations but also raise expectations of what will be identified and interpreted in particular contexts; they relate interpretations of past experience to the present, embody shorthand, stereotypical views of groups, and enhance a view of the social world in which ethnic and racialised categories are in the ascendancy.

What, then, were the clues that BPA officials cited when they identified covert racism? First, the spatial context within which covert racism might have been expressed was mentioned. There are secluded places where white officers can articulate racist views. For example, a recent undercover documentary television programme, *The Secret Policeman*, revealed how recruits expressed one view about race within the setting of the police training school classroom but another, very different one, when in the private space of a bedroom. Similarly, BPA officials sometimes suspected that some of their colleagues articulated acceptable views in their presence but, when at home, in a bar with colleagues or a wholly private space they would say very different things.

> *You might get three or four white officers when they are out together and have a few drinks and might make a comment, you know a racist comment about black people. That is more covert, rather than in the workplace, in the canteen sort of having a general conversation when I could be sitting on the next table. (BPA chair)*

There was a consequential lack of trust in colleagues, who might present a view of acceptance to their minority ethnic colleagues but harbour very different, private opinions. In this context, minority ethnic officers had developed a clear framework to assess whom they could trust, as this chair explained:

> *I have been on this planet a number of years, I know people I am safe with, I know people I can say anything to. I know people who I'm not safe with and I don't big grey box everything. And when I walk in a room I for one think, and I think many others are processing, which box do they fit in? Constantly reassessing and moving them up and down the step. And on different issues they fit in different boxes, and by non-verbal and verbal, comfortable factors, all sorts of things make you assess this and you think 'Yes, I think that person might have a problem.' But you never know whether that is a race problem or it's because you are a young inspector or they remember something when you told them off once. You never know exactly what it is, so what you end up doing is processing a lot of rubbish and getting nowhere. That's really tiring if you want to bother doing it, and you can't stop yourself doing it. I know a lot of people who do it, it's a mental process, and you can't stop it.*

The constant reflection on personal experience this officer described draws on a memory of open racism and a close assessment of clues evident in an immediate encounter with a colleague. Although we all reflect upon and check such clues in everyday life, the breach of trust created by racism within the police service had heightened a constant concern about being its victim.

Black officers therefore drew on a range of selected indicators to identify and make sense of their experience of police employment, including covert racism. This assumed a privileged, essential standpoint from which to assess another's demeanour, use of language, action and other signs of racism. There might be a conversation between officers from ethnic minority and majority groups. A bystander overhearing or observing it would be unlikely to sense that this was an encounter with undertones of racism. It would appear to be mundane, just two people talking to each other. Any knowledge of the subjects discussed or observation of the participants' gestures, tone of voice or chosen words would not be interpreted as signs or symbols of racism. From the standpoint of the ethnic minority officer, however, something very different was occurring. That officer's interpretation brings covert racism to the surface, facilitated by a particular schema of interpretation related directly to employment as a minority ethnic police officer. The participants' experience of police employment is *essentially* different. This chair illuminated in brief compass the way in which he interpreted mundane encounters:

Well, it might be words or gestures that people might use to describe somebody or something, and you know full well by the meaning that, what they're saying ... What they wouldn't do is come out with it. And if you pull them up on it, they'd you know, they'll deny it. But it's there, it's there and I think it's going to take a long while before that changes.

Another way in which black officers sensed racism was through the type of questions white people asked occasionally. These were based on an assumption of fundamental, often stereotypical differences between ethnic minority and majority people:

I mean the best one I have ever heard, covert racism, is a question people are always itching to ask. It's a stupid question really: 'Could you speak English when you came here?' I mean, you know that they are always thinking of that question because English is a white man's language. How can a brown-skinned person speak it so well? You know, and these are stupid nonsensical sort of comments you hear, and it always makes me laugh because those people are basically ignorant. (BPA chair)

Other evidence signalling covert racism included judgements about senior officers' reluctance to provide resources to a BPA; a failure to advertise vacant posts beyond a constabulary enabling outside ethnic minority officers to gain access to it; posting black probationer constables with a black mentor, which meant that any difficulties would be blamed on him rather than on a white officer; and a general, negative pressure felt by black officers when they 'raise their head above the parapet' to make a complaint about an aspect of policy or practice.

Finally, a lack of action by white supervisory officers when a black officer made a complaint could be a further indicator of covert racism. This chair described such a situation and pointed to a wider evidential base that could bring a number of similar cases together, to identify and bring covert racism to the surface:

But I know it's racism because when I complain they don't want to know. My work colleague, who I should have spoken to to sort it out, didn't want to know. And then suddenly he found a very trivial and stupid allegation and suddenly you have a problem with me. And there's another of my BPA colleagues going through the same thing at the moment.

Evidence based on the assumption of an essential, privileged position to make sense of mundane acts, interpreted as covert racism, is insufficient to secure formal proof of an allegation of racism. More is required – recurring, comparable incidents, for example. Assistant chief constables were therefore guarded about such privileged evidence, but aware that they had to be watchful.

My view is there isn't a lack of willingness to tackle it, but sometimes the evidence does not always support the particular case and you can't nail people to the wall if there isn't the evidence that supports it. And one of the real difficulties with bullying and harassment, people generally don't do it in front of other people, you know. So when you are looking for evidence and you look for corroboration quite often nothing is there. You might have an individual who has been very damaged, very, you know, has suffered inappropriate treatment, and you know, you don't doubt what they are telling you. But you have to have the evidence to actually pursue it and there is none there. (ACC)

In a small number of constabularies, mostly where there was a personal relationship of considerable trust between an ACC and a BPA chair, what might seem to be discrete incidents were documented as part of a vigilant approach.

And we are trying to work out who they are, and that is where the BPA and the links that I have with them, the informal links, you know we can't prove this. That this has happened in such and such a section. At least it is something that is logged in my database so I can start to do a little bit of further probing on it. (ACC)

ACCs did not therefore rule covert racism as beyond their control. Measures to deal with it, however, would be tested by the evidence of BPA officials' essential experience of being black and employed in a constabulary.

Assessment – the future of BPAs

Ethnicity and race as ways of seeing

One of the reasons we wanted to undertake research about Black Police Associations was because they pose challenges to criminological analyses of 'race'. Most studies of aspects of race and racism within the criminal justice system, including the police, have not been about how the phenomenon of race is constructed. They have been concerned with inequalities of outcome from the use of legal powers and services. Mirroring so much of what goes under the banner of contemporary criminology, key theoretical questions have been ignored completely. That, of course, is folly because theory is implicit within all analyses of the social world, including evaluations of policy that dominate so much of what passes for intellectual criminological work.

The changing articulation of race and relationships between officers and other police staff that have been analysed in this chapter suggest that attention should be given to 'race' and 'ethnicity' as ways of seeing the world. We need to describe and analyse further the schemas of interpretation drawn upon by minority ethnic staff working in criminal justice agencies; to compare and contrast them; to relate them to the contexts of employment within which they have arisen and to other, related settings; and to determine how they inform and might be embedded within new relationships between members of different ethnic groups.

One further point to make about the focus upon schemas is that, as Roger Brubaker has argued, it helpfully dissolves away analytical distinctions between race and ethnicity (Brubaker *et al.* 2004). A realist status is not afforded to either race or ethnicity. Race and ethnicity are not dissolved away as if they are merely rhetoric, style or some other feature of what those who write about 'new ethnicities' might, with lashings of jargon, call a 'bricolage of racialised presentations' (Cohen 1993; Cohen and Bains 1993; Back 1995; Brah and Coombes 2000). Rather, the notion of race and ethnicity as ways of seeing the world begins to reveal their similarities, including, for example, the normative use of stereotypical thinking, and a belief in essentialism. Similarity, rather than difference, may therefore be revealed when the cognitive structure of perceptions and related articulations of race and ethnicity are analysed. The contexts within which they are articulated and related to action, however, will differ, as will relationships based upon them. This linking of ideas to context is crucial because, without an understanding of the albeit often fragile connection between cognition, relationships and action, race and ethnicity seem to float in the ether rather than be based on terra firma.

Essentialism

We have seen how the early BPAs developed and persisted with a notion of essentialism, marking them off from their white colleagues under the unifying banner of being black. Crucially, this was a strategic, political stance related to their claim to be a distinct group within the police workforce, with a right to be included in discussions about policy and to be provided with resources. In a nutshell, any signs of division based on different ethnic groups having different views of the world weakened BPAs' claims.

The presentation of essentialsm has caused, and in the future will continue to cause, BPAs difficulties. Despite their apparent sturdiness, all essentialisms are fragile and open to dispute. Officers from an Asian background may not view themselves as black, and troublesome arguments about who can be members of a BPA are provoked. Some Asian officers might place their ascription as Muslims (or Hindus) in the ascendancy. Neither accepts wholly that prejudice and discrimination within the workplace is based on their being 'black' or having a skin of any hue. Rather, religious belief and practice are their causes. BPAs have therefore patrolled ethnic boundaries that define 'black', aware that this is a political activity with the potential to threaten their status and authority within a constabulary.

Within this context other groups, also claiming an essential experience of police employment, have made their own pitch for recognition and resources to remedy their dissatisfaction as a disadvantaged group within the workforce. The London Metropolitan Police Service, for example, has Black, Muslim, Christian, Jewish, Sikh, Hindu, Italian, Greek, Turkish, Irish and more associations. Each one makes a claim to special representation based on essentialism. The Black Police Association claims essentialism related to racism, the Muslim, Sikh, Jewish and Hindu associations to religious belief and related cultures, and the Turkish and Italian associations to culture.

BPAs would rather all these associations were linked under one banner signifying the experience of and challenge to racism within constabularies. Their colleagues in other associations, however, view this perspective as partial, excluding their distinct understanding and experience of police employment and wider societal relationships framing their membership of an ethnic group. Recognition of and respect for diversity and difference, not the one experience of racism, are at the core of their claims.

Chief officers find themselves pulled by this tension between racism and cultural difference, between a unified and a diverse presentation of minorities within the workforce. Indeed, Home Office policy has done little or nothing to clarify or deal with it. The roots of much BPA policy lie in anti-racism. The other associations draw on multiculturalism. Both are based on essentialist foundations; both lead to different policies. Indeed, it can be argued that a focus upon multiculturalism enhances a view that humankind can be defined into groups that are essentially different. The recognition and accommodation of their culture declares as much. The future of BPAs is very likely to be one that requires them to establish their essential claims in comparison to the ethnic majority and cultural/religiously based groups within constabularies.

Notes

1 There is not space in this chapter to discuss the notion of 'racialisation', which is central to the analysis presented. Discussion of it in relation to 'race' generally and Black Police Associations in particular can be found in Holdaway 1996.

2 The chapter is based on research untaken under the auspices of ESRC Grant R000239360. Interviews were conducted with the Chairs and Deputy Chairs of BPAs, Assistant Chief Constables with responsibility for BPAs, and Human Resource Directors in this two-year project.

3 We do not make an analytical distinction between 'race' and 'ethnicity' in this chapter. There is not room here to explain the reasoning for this position. See Brubaker 2002; Brubaker et al. 2004.

4 More groups might have developed.

5 This officer's view was of individuals who are racists, which is obviously incompatible with the notion of institutional racism. I do not probe different 'lay theories' of racism in this paper.

References

Back, L. (1995) *New Ethnicities, Multiple Racisms: Young People and Transcultural Dialogue*, London: UCL Press.

Brah, A. and Coombes A. (2000) *Hybridity and its Discontents*, London: Routledge.

Brubaker, R. (2002) 'Ethnicity without Groups', *Archives of European Sociology*, XLIII(2): 163–89.

Brubaker, R., Loveman, M. and Stamatov, P. (2004) 'Ethnicity as Cognition', *Theory and Society*, 33: 31–64.

Carmichael, S. and Hamilton, C. V. (1968) *Black Power: The Politics of Liberation in America*, London, Jonathan Cape.

Cohen, P. (1993) *Home Rules*, London, New Ethnicities Unit, University of East London.

Cohen, P. and Bains, H. S. (eds) (1993) *Multi-Cultural Britain*, Basingstoke: Macmillan.

Foster, J., Newburn, T. and Souhami, A. (2005) *Assessing the Impact of the Stephen Lawrence Inquiry*, Home Office Research Study 294, London, Home Office.

Fuss, D. (1989), *Essentially Speaking*, New York and London: Routledge.

Goffman, E. (1974) *Frame Analysis*, Harmondsworth: Penguin.

Holdaway, S. (1991) *Recruiting a Multi-Racial Police Force*, London: HMSO.

Holdaway, S. (1996) *The Racialisation of British Policing*, Basingstoke: Macmillan.

Holdaway, S. (1997) 'Responding to Racialised Divisions within the Workforce – the Experience of Black and Asian Police Officers in England', *Ethnic and Racial Studies*, 20 (1): 69–90.

Holdaway, S. and Barron, A.-M. (1997) *Resigners? The Experience of Black and Asian Police Officers*, Basingstoke: Macmillan.

Holdaway, S. and O'Neill, M. (2006) Institutional Racism after Macpherson: an analysis of police views, *Policing and Society*, 16 (4): 349–69.

Macpherson, Sir W. (1999) *The Stephen Lawrence Inquiry: Report of an Inquiry by Sir William Macpherson of Cluny*, CM 4262-1, London: HMSO.

Phillips, C. (2005) 'Facing Inwards and Outwards?', *Criminal Justice*, 5 (4): 357–77.

Rhodes, R. A. W. (2000). 'The Governance Narrative: Key Findings and Lessons from the ESRC's Whithall Programme,' *Public Administration*, 78(2): 345–64.

Chapter 6

Policing Muslim communities

Neil Chakraborti

The lives of Muslim communities have been subjected to extended political and media intrusion during recent times as events worldwide have conspired to focus the spotlight upon their religious and cultural identities, and more often than not the extent to which these identities supposedly differ from 'mainstream' Western ideology. A recent illustration of their newsworthiness was provided by an extraordinary series of contemporaneous but coincidental news stories during February 2006, a month described by Bunting (2006) as a 'mensis horribilis' for British Muslims, which provoked considerable anger and resentment among, and against, the Muslim communities. This month first saw government plans to afford Muslims and other faith groups the same protection as that available to Sikh and Jewish communities, under existing racial hatred legislation, defeated by just one vote in the House of Commons.[1] The decision to reject the government's proposals to create a new offence of incitement to religious hatred through 'abusive' or 'insulting' behaviour, and instead to approve House of Lords amendments restricting the applicability of these provisions to only 'threatening' behaviour, was welcomed by jubilant opposition MPs and freedom of speech campaigners who had mounted a concerted high-profile lobbying effort against the proposals. However, it was lamented by groups such as the Muslim Council of Britain who felt that the law as passed would continue to perpetuate the inequalities of existing legislation and would fail to meet the needs of Muslim communities (Gledhill 2006).

Barely a few days later, the debate between freedom of expression and protection of religious sensibilities was further fuelled by the publication in a Danish newspaper of satirical cartoons depicting the prophet Mohammed in a variety of 'terrorist' guises. Widely condemned as offensive to the Islamic faith, the cartoons' publication nonetheless raised serious questions over the legitimacy or otherwise of repressing opinions, however insulting and repellent. The nature of ensuing Muslim protests against the cartoons, which in some instances took the form of violent demonstrations and visible support for future suicide bombings in the West, was seen to have potentially worrying implications in reinforcing stereotypes about the oversensitivity of Muslim communities and the suspected incompatibility of Muslim and non-Muslim values (Joseph 2006; Ramadan 2006; Stubbs 2006).

The position of Muslims again came under scrutiny in that same month following the conviction of Abu Hamza al Masri on charges of soliciting murder and inciting racial hatred. The radical Islamist cleric, seen by many as the epitome of Islamist extremism in Britain (Campbell *et al.* 2006), was convicted on 11 out of 15 charges after a month-long trial, sentenced to seven years' imprisonment and was set to face extradition to the United States on kidnapping and terrorism-related charges. While this verdict itself was widely welcomed by both non-Muslims and Muslims alike, accusations of double standards did emanate from some elements of the Muslim communities when drawing comparisons between the result of the Hamza trial and the very different outcome of another racial hatred trial which had come to its conclusion only a few days previously. Nick Griffin, leader of the British National Party (BNP), walked free from court having been partially acquitted along with his co-defendant Mark Collett on incitement to racial hatred charges,[2] despite having been filmed by an undercover BBC documentary team making openly inflammatory remarks about Muslims and the Islamic faith in speeches during the build-up to local and European elections in West Yorkshire.[3] However one views the rights and wrongs of this decision, the overlapping timing of two high-profile trials centring on principles of free speech and incitement of racial hatred thrust the contentious nature of the incitement debate into ever sharper focus, and reignited British Muslims' concerns over the ambiguous, and for some contradictory, legal provisions governing the 'preaching of hate' (Bunting 2006).

The implications in policing terms of this increased focus upon Muslims are not always clear-cut and easily discernible; indeed, to some extent it could be argued that recent debates have centred more on perceptions of Muslims' identity and sense of belonging rather than any actual or tangible change in their policing requirements both as victims and as perpetrators. However, this chapter argues that the headline grabbing news stories of February 2006, allied to the prolonged deliberations over the position of Muslim communities following the 2001 and 2005 terrorist attacks in the US and UK respectively, are symptomatic of the growing levels of concern over the threat posed *to* Muslims as targets of racially and religiously motivated prejudice and *by* Muslims as potential sources of 'terror' and scourges of national identity. As such it is this twofold concern that has implications for the police as they seek to discharge the functions of protecting British Muslims from hate crime and defending the state against the extremist Islamic threat often associated with terrorist activity.

Nevertheless, the title of this chapter is in some respects misleading. On the one hand it may suggest that Muslim communities have a different set of policing requirements from non-Muslim communities, thereby setting them apart from white people and from their minority ethnic counterparts in the UK. Moreover, the title to some extent homogenises Muslim communities in inferring that as a collective group they have a distinct set of shared policing requirements. As a number of authors have rightly asserted (see for example Spalek 2002; Macey 2002; Garland *et al.* 2006) greater attention should be paid to acknowledging the heterogeneity and diverse characteristics of the British Muslim population, as it is both difficult and dangerous to generalise about the policing of Muslim communities without affording suitable recognition to the very real differences in background, belief, experience and need among British Muslims.

That said, it is clear that Muslims have been the subject of extensive conjecture, scrutiny and misapprehension within academic and political discourse, and as such their policing does require careful and specific consideration, particularly in the light of increased media demonisation, growing fears over the spread of Islamic extremism and concerns about 'Islamophobic' prejudice. Moreover, these policing requirements have changed somewhat in the post-Macpherson era: while debates surrounding police relations with minority ethnic communities have tended to focus more on relations with the African Caribbean and black British communities, factors such as those cited above have seen greater prominence afforded to police relations with British Muslims. This chapter, therefore, seeks to analyse the distinctive position of Muslim communities within British society by examining why, and how, we should police both the needs of, and the threat posed by, British Muslims. Focusing upon some of the more problematic features of the ongoing debate that has seen Islam's importance shift from personal faith to a politicised and constructed identity, the chapter examines the manner in which the state has sought to balance the competing claims of policing this perceived need and threat, and seeks to identify more progressive ways in which the policing of Muslim communities can address the very real fears of Muslims and non-Muslims alike.

Shifting perceptions of the Muslim identity: from personal faith to politicised construct

As has already been asserted, Islam is by no means a monolithic concept and the British Muslim population, which currently stands at approximately 1.6 million, is far from a 'straightforward' homogenous community with a singular set of beliefs, values and needs. The diversity of this population derives in no small part from the long-established tradition of Muslim migration to Britain from a number of different areas, mainly South Asian, which stretches back over 300 years (Runnymede Trust 1997; King 1993). Although Muslim communities emerged over the course of the eighteenth and nineteenth centuries through the formation of small settlements in port towns and cities across Britain, large-scale migration began in earnest in the 1950s as a result of post-war labour shortages, with Muslim workers coming principally from the districts of Azad Kashmir in Pakistan and the Sylhet area of north-eastern Bangladesh, as well as from Gujarati districts of India (Runnymede Trust 1997). Later decades saw further widespread Muslim migration from Turkey, the Middle East and North Africa, and more recently Somalian, Kosovan, Kurdish, Iranian and Bosnian communities have established themselves across the UK, highlighting the culturally and ethnically diverse make-up of the present-day British Muslim population, whose population is supplemented still further by the relatively large number of white converts to Islam identified in the 2001 Census[4] (Smith 2004).

The spiritual diversity of this population is also often unappreciated, as followers of Islam can broadly be split into two main camps – Shi'a and Sunni. The vast majority of Britain's Muslims are Sunni Muslims, widely regarded as adaptable and politically moderate groups willing to adhere to the notion of secular government and a multicultural society if left free to practise their religion, although even within that tradition alone lie a number of different and evolving movements, with this diversity in belief and interpretation referred to by King (1993: 34) as 'the fragmentation of Islam within Islam' (see Spalek 2002 and Rex 2002 for a more complete overview of the spiritual diversity of Islam).

However, while the Islamic faith may in itself be interpreted in varying ways by its followers in the UK, their religious (as opposed to strictly ethnic) identity has assumed increasing significance for Muslims as a way of distinguishing themselves from other South Asian migrants, establishing themselves in an alien and at times hostile environment, and reinforcing their sense of self-belief in light of their ongoing social and economic disadvantage (McLouglin 2005; Runnymede Trust 1997). As Modood *et al.* (1997) found in their fourth national survey of ethnic minorities, approximately three-quarters of Muslim respondents felt that their religion was very important to the way they live their lives, and the intensity of Muslims' religious beliefs and practices has prompted suggestions that their social and cultural impact is far greater than their numbers in isolation may initially indicate (Rex 2002: 53). At the same time, though, rather than being viewed exclusively as a positive means of spiritual empowerment, the embracing of their religious identity has increasingly become a source of concern within some sections of non-Muslim British society. Suspicion abounds with regards to the 'alien' characteristics of the Islamic faith, its perceived threat to monoculturalist images of the 'British' way of life, and the appeal of radical Islamic anti-Western discourses to younger generations of estranged, 'non-integrated' Muslims, to the point where it seems that identifiably racist expressions of resentment towards Muslim groups are becoming ever more normalised. As Kundnani (2005) puts it:

> The result is a mindset which makes Muslims into potent symbols for an apparent loss of national belonging. Instead of asking how society excludes Muslims and how this exclusion contributes to a process of ghetto-isation, the questions asked are about Muslims refusing to integrate; Muslims as a political problem; Muslims having to become more British. It is their 'alien' values that are the problem rather than our racist values.

It would appear that public (mis)understanding of Islam has shifted its meaning beyond personal faith to a fiercely politicised identity readily associated with the menace of global terrorism (Younge 2005; Kundnani 2005). For commentators such as Kundnani, alarmist media narratives have combined with punitive political rhetoric to amplify the threat posed by Muslims and to create a new folk-devil, an object of hostility that bears the brunt of social anger and that concretises moral anxieties (Cohen 1973). This process has created a culture of suspicion against Muslims throughout Europe, whose presence is widely perceived to be a threat as the 'enemy within' in the war on terror and whose adherence to Islam is seen as a direct challenge to the very notion of 'Europeanness' and symptomatic of Huntington's (1993) predicted 'clash of civilisations' between Western and non-Western societies (Fekete 2004: 4; Huntington 1993). Such constructions of Muslim identity have furthered their alienation from not only the white non-Muslim world but, increasingly, from their minority ethnic counterparts. Indeed just as British Muslims have tended to identify themselves through their faith and not through their ethnic identity, a similar trend has recently begun to emerge among other South Asian groups, with the secular term 'Asian' often now replaced as a means of self-identification by reference to religious identity as a way of setting groups such as Sikhs and Hindus apart from Muslims, and thereby enabling people from these groups to escape the increased scrutiny and stigmatisation directed towards Muslim communities.[5]

Anti-Muslim prejudice, or Islamophobia to use the phrase commonly employed to describe this prejudice, had been a significant concern even before the onset of this latest moral panic. The nature of Islamophobic prejudice has been explained by the Runnymede Trust (1997: 4) in the following terms:

> The term Islamophobia refers to unfounded hostility towards Islam. It refers also to the practical consequences of such hostility in unfair discrimination against Muslim individuals and communities, and to the exclusion of Muslims from mainstream political and social affairs ... The word 'Islamophobia' has been coined because there is a new reality which needs naming: anti-Muslim prejudice has grown so considerably and so rapidly in recent years that a new item in the vocabulary is needed so that it can be identified and acted against. In a similar way there was a time in European history when a new word, anti-Semitism, was needed and coined to highlight the growing dangers of anti-Jewish hostility.

As the Trust's report highlights, Muslims have faced forms of Islamophobic prejudice over the course of many centuries, and their fear of attack has been well documented even before the culmination of recent events had placed the spotlight on the Muslim communities. Clancy *et al.* (2001), for instance, highlighted the vulnerability of Pakistani and Bangladeshi households to crime, finding that these groups are highly fearful of crime, face the highest risk of being a victim of a racially motivated offence and are generally the least satisfied of all minority ethnic groups with various aspects of the police response to sought contact. Unquestionably, though, it is the terrorist attacks of 11 September 2001 in the US and 7 July 2005 in the UK that have accentuated problems of British anti-Muslim prejudice, and that have accelerated the process of what Werbner (2004: 464) describes as the 'spiralling progressive alienation' of Muslims in the West. Certainly, these events have had a pronounced impact upon their perceived vulnerability, sense of well-being and experiences of victimisation (Garland *et al.* 2006; Ansari 2005; ECRI 2004). For instance, in the months following the events of September 11, McGhee (2005: 102) reports that Muslim communities, along with Sikh and other Arab and Asian groups in the UK, endured a four-fold increase in the number of racist attacks, with Asians in the Tower Hamlets district of London experiencing as much as a 75 per cent increase in attacks. He also notes the simultaneous growth in far-right activity and propaganda directed against Muslims at this time, citing concerns voiced by the Forum Against Islamophobia and Racism over the preponderance of publications distributed by the BNP in the aftermath of September 11, which they felt were designed specifically to incite hatred against British Muslims (2005: 104). This Islamophobic 'call to arms' has by no means been reserved for an exclusively white audience: anti-Muslim sentiment is so strong among some Asian fringe movements that the BNP can be conceived in some ways as a potential ally, and at least one small Sikh faction, the Shere-e-Punjab grouping, are known to have co-operated with the BNP on their campaigns against Islam (Kundnani 2002: 72–3).

Moreover, these problems have merely intensified following the July 2005 bombings in London. In the three weeks immediately after the bombings, police figures showed a six-fold increase in the number of religiously motivated hate crimes reported in London, with the vast majority being directed at Muslim households and places of worship, while in excess of 1,200 suspected Islamophobic incidents were recorded by police across the country in this same three-week period (BBC 2005; Dodd 2005a) Similarly, a UK-wide poll of Muslim households conducted in the aftermath of the London attacks indicated that as many as 63 per cent were considering leaving Britain amid fears of retaliatory violence and an anti-Muslim backlash (Dodd 2005a). The continued polarisation of Muslim and non-Muslim identities, coupled with the long-term nature of the so-called 'war on terrorism' intimates that these experiences of violence, harassment and abuse are likely to continue for the foreseeable future.

Policing the needs/threat conundrum

In the wake of high-profile episodes of Islamic terrorism, Muslim communities' need for added protection against a heightened risk of Islamophobic attack has been more pronounced than ever. However, their plight has not gone unnoticed by the state, and some headway has been made with regard to reducing levels of racism and policing the needs of British Muslims. Docking and Tuffin's (2005) evaluation of the post-Lawrence Inquiry response to racist incidents, for example, suggests that positive progress has been made in the reporting, recording and handling of incidents following the introduction of the Home Office *Code of Practice* (2000), which sought to establish effective and consistent reporting and recording procedures; to build levels of trust in the police; to increase victim satisfaction, and to aid in the prevention of racist incidents (Docking and Tuffin 2005: iv). This progress has implications for all minority ethnic groups, including Muslims, and is illustrative of the post-Macpherson drive to develop sustainable responses to problems of institutional racism and racist victimisation (for a more detailed overview, see Rowe 2004; Bowling and Phillips 2002).

The government has also sought to extend legislative protection to cover religiously motivated, as well as racially motivated, crime. Racially aggravated provisions in the Crime and Disorder Act 1998 were supplemented by the introduction of nine new religiously aggravated offences in the Anti-Terrorism, Crime and Security Act 2001, which went some way towards affording greater recognition to faith groups and 'faith-hate' with these sentence enhancement provisions. At the same time, however, the eleventh-hour rejection of Clause 39 – the incitement of religious hatred proposals – by the House of Lords during the Bill stage of this piece of legislation exacerbated many Muslims' concerns over the lack of available protection against Islamophobic attack (McGhee 2005: 102). These concerns appeared to reaffirm the government's determination to push through additional safeguards extending the coverage of existing racial hatred provisions[6] to include the incitement of religious hatred. Ultimately, the government's proposals on this issue have been watered down to some extent as a result of prolonged objections and House of Lords amendments (as discussed above), but even in their more restricted guise, the new incitement provisions do give Muslims added protection against attacks on their religious identity.

It is conceivable that the government's efforts to strengthen the law might have had a positive impact on the relationship between

Muslims and the British state. However, much of this goodwill may arguably have been nullified by the government's equally determined efforts to address the perceived threat of Muslims to notions of shared citizenship and national security. Governmental concerns over the 'Muslim threat' first came to prominence following the outbreaks of unrest and disorder in the northern towns of Oldham, Burnley and Bradford (among others) during the summer of 2001, which witnessed violent confrontations between white and predominantly Muslim communities, widespread destruction of property and attacks against the police. The government's response to these disturbances, set out within the report of the review team chaired by Ted Cantle, saw renewed emphasis placed upon the concept of community cohesion as a way of engendering a set of common principles that would enable all communities to work together towards a unified purpose (Home Office 2002: 10–11). Establishing a greater sense of citizenship, it was felt, would help to resolve the residual breakdown in contact between different cultural, religious and ethnic groups, and would act as a catalyst to improve levels of mutual trust and understanding among divided and segregated communities.

Taken on its merits, the *idea* of community cohesion, with its calls for further inter-community dialogue, is appealing. However, there are several problematic features with the term that have served to antagonise Muslim communities. While presented as a solution to the build-up of tensions between communities that spilled over during the 2001 disturbances, the explanatory potential of community cohesion has been criticised for dismissing the influence of equally significant contributory factors such as the rising levels of unemployment among Asian communities in the affected areas; residential segregation; discriminatory deployment of police powers; and the destabilising effect of far-right ideology (Burnett 2004). Moreover, in overlooking such factors, this 'solution' was seen as overly simplistic by seemingly condoning the violence of white communities as representative of frustration and instability, but condemning the violence of Muslims as representative of their unwillingness to accept the norms of national identity (Burnett 2004: 9; CARF 2002: 5). Consequently, governmental attempts to induce a sense of common citizenship based upon acceptance of shared notions of 'Britishness' could in some ways be seen as counter-productive if perceived to be a way of manipulating Muslim communities' feelings of identity. If expected, as in a revised version of Norman Tebbit's infamous 'cricket test'[7] to realign allegiances in accordance with imaginary and ill-defined constructions of national identity, Muslim feelings of cultural 'otherness' are likely to intensify, as are problems of marginalisation and self-segregation.

The push to police the threat to national security has in many ways already exacerbated those problems. The graphic nature of the September 11 terrorist attacks, and indeed those that have followed throughout the world since, predictably led to the development of more sophisticated and wide-ranging anti-terrorism measures to counter the perceived threat of Islamic extremism. Moves to step up the policing of this specific 'terror threat' in the UK are understandable. Following the July 2005 bombings in London, public fears over home-grown terrorist activity rose sharply, while commentators have highlighted the growing attraction of the more puritan strands of Islam among some sections of Muslim youth disenchanted with what they see as the subordination of Muslims across the world and with their own experiences of social and political marginalisation (Kundnani 2002: 75–6). However, the excessive mobilisation of the rhetoric of security, or 'the securitisation agenda', to coin Fekete's (2004) description of recent government policy, has invited counter-allegations of 'state terrorism' from some critics (see, for example, Sivanandan 2006; Fekete 2004; Ansari 2005), which while arguably an exaggerated claim, at least highlights the alarm that has arisen from this agenda's impact upon British Muslim communities.

Since the turn of the millennium, the United Kingdom has adopted two key pieces of legislation to combat the threat of terrorism: the Terrorism Act 2000 and the Anti-Terrorism, Crime and Security Act 2001.[8] The 2000 Act was introduced in response to what the government saw as the changing face of international terrorism, and had already introduced a raft of measures designed to create new terrorism-related offences and to give the police new counter-terrorism powers before the advent of '9/11' heralded the passing of a new stream of provisions under the 2001 Act. That a second piece of legislation was deemed necessary so soon after the introduction of what had been envisaged at the time to be comprehensive form of anti-terror protection (McGhee 2005: 98) is not altogether surprising: as Walker (2002: ix) observes, 'legislation aimed against terrorism has been established in Great Britain for well over two decades ... often, the laws have been prompted by a crisis and represent both a symbolic and practical response to a phenomenon which is seen as a grave menace to liberal democracies and their citizenry'. More unexpected was the contentious nature of many of the provisions introduced under the 2001 Act, which caused consternation among critics for their potentially unjust implications for Muslim communities, and the equally controversial nature of proposals that fall under the government's subsequent terrorism bill, which represents yet another attempt to police the supposedly increased threat of extremist activity following the London bombings of 2005. As Walker (2002: 15) goes on to note, while it can be justifiable for a liberal democracy to employ special powers against groups engaged in political or paramilitary violence, this does not entail permitting the government *carte blanche* to respond in any way it chooses; there must be an adherence to principles that reflect the values of individual rights, constitutionalism and democratic accountability.

The furore surrounding the legitimacy of some of the government's more recent anti-terror proposals suggest that those principles have not been adhered to. These proposals have faced a torrid passage through Parliament, none more so than the 'glorifying of terrorism' clause, which finally received approval in the House of Lords, at the third attempt, following extensive criticisms from backbench government rebels, opposition parties and peers. Legislating against the 'glorification' of terrorism – which sees individuals imprisoned for up to seven years for directly or indirectly encouraging or inducing acts of terrorism – was referred to explicitly by the Prime Minister in the immediate aftermath of the London bombings as a key component of the government's strategy to 'pull up this evil ideology [of Islamic extremism] by its roots' (Jeffery 2006). However, the term may arguably have more potency as a rhetorical device used to illustrate the government's 'toughness' on the perceived threat of extremism. As the conviction of Muslim cleric Abu Hamza has shown, existing powers are already in place under the Public Order Act 1986 to police the threat of incitement, and if further powers are justifiable then it seems highly inconsistent for the House of Lords to override the principles of freedom of speech in cases involving the incitement of terrorism, but not for the incitement of religious hatred. On this basis it would seem that guarding against the potential threat posed by Muslims has greater political significance than the protection of their needs.

Some of the other more controversial proposals contained within the government's anti-terror legislative package that have provoked dismay among critics on account of their unjust implications for Muslim communities relate to detention without trial, and stop and search powers. Provisions under the terrorism legislation of 2001 allowing for the indefinite detention of foreign nationals suspected of involvement in international terrorism had already been condemned as discriminatory in a House of Lords ruling in 2004 and contrary to the UK's obligations under the European Convention of Human Rights (ECRI 2004: 31), but rather than abandoning this policy the government instead issued control order legislation, involving house arrest and electronic tagging, to replace detention without trial. As Sivanandan (2006: 5) observes, government pledges to extend these orders to British nationals as well as foreign nationals under its new counter-terrorism measures signify an intent to police the threat of both the 'enemy within' and 'the enemy at the gate'. Such a move, particularly when considered in the context of renewed efforts to detain terrorism suspects for up to three months without charge, has been criticised for encouraging an aggressive police stance based more on 'fishing expeditions' than on substantive intelligence, which would further alienate and criminalise Muslim communities (Ansari 2005).

Similarly, the wider stop and search powers available to the police under section 44 of the Terrorism Act 2000 have raised fears over the unfair targeting of Muslim communities (Woolf 2005; Cowan and Travis 2004; Freedland 2005; McGhee 2005). It should be noted that some degree of caution must be exercised when analysing the impact of stop and search figures upon Muslims specifically: Garland *et al.* (2006: 3), for instance, argue that claims of institutional anti-Muslim bias from the Muslim Council of Britain, arising from the release of the 2002–03 Home Office statistics reporting a 302 per cent increase in the number of stops and searches conducted upon Asians, cannot be justified on the basis of those statistics alone as the police employ a crude 'Asian' category to record stops and searches of all those from the South Asian communities. For Garland *et al.*, therefore, allegations of police scapegoating of Muslims cannot be substantiated until recording mechanisms become more sophisticated in their differentiation of specific religious and ethnic identities. Nonetheless, irrespective of how legitimate claims of institutionalised Islamophobia may be, perceptions of discriminatory targeting among the Muslim communities have serious implications for the strength of their relationship with the police. With this in mind, the government has consistently sought to emphasise that their 'war' is against extremism and terrorism, not Islam. For instance, during a series of meetings over the summer of 2005 with Muslim community leaders, the then Home Office minister Hazel Blears repeatedly denied that she had ever endorsed racial profiling, claiming instead that stop and search operations were 'intelligence-led', despite having gone on the record earlier in the year to suggest that Muslims had to accept as a 'reality' that they would be stopped and searched more frequently (Oliver

2005). Perhaps unsurprisingly, these denials have done little to dilute fears of excessive targeting, and the manner in which broad-ranging powers have been hastily introduced, allied with the deployment of divisive soundbites and an ensuing moral panic over Islam, has left many British Muslims feeling over-policed and under-protected.

Identifying a way forward in the policing of Muslim communities: cohesion through consultation

The current climate of fear and recrimination has done little to dilute public suspicion over the Muslim 'other'. The polarisation of Muslim and non-Muslim identities, so apparent during media reporting of the urban disturbances of 2001 (Burnett 2004), has continued with the publication of the Cantle Report and with the subsequent wave of legislation brought in to protect the British public from the dangers of Islamic extremism. This continued 'them and us' situation, however, has created an unhelpful context in which to police the real, and not constructed, threats and needs of Muslim communities, where progressive policies can become submerged by regressive rhetoric.

For some, the celebration of difference that lies at the heart of multiculturist standpoints is to blame for the current state of affairs. The concept of multiculturalism, which takes its values from a post-Enlightenment respect for the plurality of cultural, religious and ethnic identities that define contemporary societies, has been widely used as a descriptive term to identify the characteristics of modern-day Britain and as a prescriptive tool to categorise the policies necessary to manage diverse communities (Malik 2005a). However, the post-Cantle drive towards community cohesion policies, together with increased fears over the threat of 'home-grown' terrorist activity, have raised questions over the merits of multiculturalism. The Cantle Report's calls for greater inter-community and interfaith interaction cast an element of doubt over what Smith (2004: 198) refers to as 'the wisdom of a *laissez-faire* approach to celebrating religious and ethnic diversity', which could result in a potentially hazardous polarisation. Instead, as discussed above, this report and subsequent government policies have pushed for more integrationist strategies that encourage Muslim communities to adopt shared notions of common citizenship. For some commentators, aspirations to a common set of values have been injudiciously abandoned in the name of multiculturalism, resulting not only in divided communities but, more worryingly, in a passive tolerance of extremist anti-British sentiment (Phillips 2004; Malik 2005a, 2005b; Burchill 2005).

In some respects such a stance is understandable: much of the tension that surrounds the position of the Muslim 'other' stems from a general misunderstanding (and misrepresentation) of Islam, and attempts to lessen this tension through the promotion of social cohesion may be of value in making people aware of the similarities, and not just the differences, between Muslim and non-Muslim communities. At the same time, though, the balance must be delicately struck if calls for the greater integration of Muslim communities are to be free of the monoculturalist overtones emanating from the citizenship lessons, language classes, allegiance pledges and other related mechanisms for inducing shared values put forward by the government in recent years. Certainly, the seemingly 'everyday' profiles of the perpetrators of the July 2005 London bombings, which included for some of them university education, being a follower of cricket, teaching children with learning difficulties and, in the case of one, being married to a white English woman, suggest that the clamour for the further integration of Muslim youth may in itself be insufficient when it comes to policing the threat of an extremism rooted not in multiculturalism but in alienation (Sivanandan 2006). Seemingly moderate 'Cantle-esque' requests for greater acceptance of shared values are arguably devoid of any real clarity, and can be used to give legitimacy to the 'assimilate or else' demands made by some sections of the media (see, for instance, Burchill 2005) that reinforce the polarisation of Muslims and non-Muslims, as Smith (2004: 198) acknowledges:

> What is evident in this [community cohesion] discourse is that there are tensions, if not direct contradictions, between a liberal benevolence towards religious diversity and a growing fear that religious identity could present a serious threat to community cohesion. There is some lack of clarity in the government discourse and policy and a suspicion of 'spin', as politicians try to be all things to all people. There is also a level of confusion and some justifiable resentment among urban believers regarding the use of 'faith community' as a code word for 'ethnic minorities' or perhaps more specifically for 'those Muslims and other minorities who are making things difficult for us in the inner cities'.

In order for Muslim communities to feel less alienated and to engage more with the wider public sphere, it would seem that they must first be able to identify more readily with key public institutions, which could provide them with a greater sense of empowerment (Fulat 2005; Kundnani 2002). In this sense their relationship with the police is of paramount importance. As discussed above, measures have been introduced in the years following the Stephen Lawrence Inquiry to help build stronger relationships between the police and minority ethnic communities, but there remains scope for improvement. For instance, Muslims' fears over their treatment at the hands of the police could, to some extent, have been mollified through the establishment of the Independent Police Complaints Commission (IPCC), which provides the added safeguard of an avenue of independent appeal should a complainant feel dissatisfied with the level of information given by the police or with the outcome of a police investigation. However, a continued lack of confidence within some quarters can be seen in the findings of an IPCC survey highlighting that almost a third of all Asian respondents fear being subjected to police harassment if they issue a complaint against their force (Cowan 2006), while the legitimacy of the complaints process has itself been questioned by the Islamic Human Rights Commission who have criticised the IPCC for 'failing minority victims' (Waseem 2005: 4) on the basis of what the commission perceived to be an unsatisfactory investigation into a police raid on the home of a British Muslim.[9] Similarly, misgivings about the police may have been confounded by recent calls by the Association of Chief Police Officers (ACPO) to reconsider targets to recruit more minority ethnic officers, one of the key reforms introduced by the Macpherson Report. While researchers had originally welcomed the progress identified by Her Majesty's Inspectorate of Constabulary (HMIC) in recruiting a more ethnically diverse workforce, particularly as an increased and sustained Muslim presence in the police service could have a pronounced impact in fostering a more enlightened appreciation of Islam within the service (Sharp 2002; HMIC 2000), this progress appears to have stalled because of a failure, to use the words of ACPO's spokesman on race and diversity issues, 'to get across the business and operational case for diversity' (Dodd 2006).[10]

A further source of discontent among many British Muslims relates to the manner in which the police engage with them. Research has drawn attention to the importance of developing a process of consultation with minority ethnic communities that encourages two-way dialogue with all sections of these communities (Garland et al. 2006; Chakraborti and Garland 2003) and such an approach is likely to be pivotal if Muslims are expected to acquiesce with some of the policing measures introduced as part of the government's anti-terrorism proposals discussed above. Unfortunately, community consultation often tends to be dominated by police-led agendas rather than being oriented towards community interests and concerns (Foster *et al.* 2005; Jones and Newburn 2001), and this has been particularly evident during the consultation process undertaken with British Muslims in the aftermath of recent terrorist activity. Innes (2006: 13), for example, has noted the inherent weaknesses of the police's strategic engagement approach, arguing that the identification of particular individuals as leaders and/or opinion formers raises questions over the representativeness of their views and the extent to which so-called leaders are in touch with people most at risk of alienation and radicalisation. Likewise, visits conducted by government ministers across the UK supposedly in search of grassroots Muslim opinion following the July 2005 bombings have attracted criticism from Muslims and non-Muslims alike for being stage-managed in their conception and delivery (Ward 2005), while similar charges of tokenism have been levelled at the establishment of Muslim working groups set up as a way of involving Muslim communities in the process of tackling extremism but given only six weeks to recommend initiatives to tackle the problem (Oborne 2006).

Gaining the trust of Muslim communities forms an indispensable part of strategies designed to police both the threat posed to Muslims as targets of Islamophobic prejudice and by Muslims as instigators of criminal activity. The sensitivity of the present political climate dictates that the police develop imaginative and sophisticated consultative strategies that allow them to earn this trust, and recent criticisms of heavy-handed anti-terrorism policing measures among senior figures within the police service suggest that the development of strong relationships with Muslim communities is starting to establish itself as a policing priority.[11] In many respects there is considerable overlap between the types of measures outlined above that may help to engender levels of trust and some of the recommendations made in the Macpherson Report. The recruitment of a more diverse police workforce, improved communications between the police and minority ethnic communities and a more effective police complaints system are all features of the reform agenda set out in the Macpherson Report, and in that sense there are strong similarities between mechanisms for improving police relations with minority ethnic groups both then and now. However, it is also true to say that debates have moved on quite significantly in the 13 or so years that have passed since the murder of Stephen Lawrence, most notably with regard to the politicisation of Muslim identity and the policing implications that result therein. With this in mind, post-Macpherson policing initiatives need to be considered in the context of their potential impact upon Muslims as a specific group in their own right, and not just as part of a broader network of minority ethnic communities.

As this chapter has sought to highlight, the policing of the needs/threat conundrum presents a formidable challenge that cannot realistically be taken on without the engagement of British Muslims as willing actors in the process. Despite the problematic history of police/minority relations and the punitive overtones of government policy, there is evidence to suggest that British Muslims still hold considerable trust in the role of the police as a source of protection and that they would welcome the expansion of consultation schemes that enable their communities to engage directly and openly with the police (Bolognani 2005; Dodd 2005). Therefore, in line with Innes's (2006) suggestions, if implemented less narrowly than is often the case to include a wider spectrum of Muslim voices, strategic consultation schemes could trigger a real improvement in relationships between the police and Muslim communities that gives Muslims a greater opportunity to present their concerns and vulnerabilities to the police, while simultaneously generating enhanced intelligence opportunities for the police. When conceived in such a manner, improving the channels of communication between the police and Muslim communities through more progressive strategies of consultation seems to be a crucial, and arguably the only, sustainable way of policing the conundrum and eroding the mistrust that has developed on both sides.

Notes

1 Under existing racial hatred legislation, Sikhs and Jews are defined as ethnic groups (as opposed to faith groups) and are therefore afforded the same legislative protection as any other ethnic group. In both cases their membership has historically been drawn from just one cultural group, whereas the world's Muslim population is made up from numerous ethnically and culturally diverse groups (McGhee 2005: 97).

2 Nick Griffin was acquitted on two charges relating to speeches filmed by the BBC undercover documentary team, and the jury failed to reach verdicts on two other charges. Mark Collett was cleared of four similar charges of stirring up racial hatred, and the jury failed to reach verdicts on a further four counts in his case. Both men have since been cleared of all charges in a second trial held during November 2006.

3 This included claims that crimes such as rape and paedophilia against non-believers in Islam were countenanced by the Qur'an, allegations that white girls in West Yorkshire were being groomed for sex by Muslim men, and references to Islam as a 'wicked vicious faith' (Herbert, 2006).

4 According to the 2001 Census, out of a total Muslim population of 1,546,626 more than one in ten described themselves as white (179,773), of whom 63,042 were British, 890 Irish and 115,841 'other' whites.

5 Kundnani (2002: 72) for instance describes how in January 2002 a leading Asian radio station *Sunrise Radio* went as far as to ban the word 'Asian' as a result of long-running campaigns led by Hindu and Sikh groups keen to disassociate themselves from Muslims.

6 As specified in section 17 of the Public Order Act 1986.

7 The 'Tebbit test' refers to comments made by the former Conservative MP Norman Tebbitt in April 1990 questioning the loyalty and allegiance of Britain's ethnic minorities who chose to support their countries of origin in cricket matches in preference to the English national team.

8 At the time of writing the government's most recent anti-terrorism bill is in the process of being passed into law as the Terrorism Act 2006.

9 The Islamic Human Rights Commission based its conclusions upon a report into the IPCC's investigation into the raid on the home of Babar Ahmed, a British Muslim arrested under the Terrorism Act 2000, and his subsequent complaint of serious police misconduct. Particular concerns were raised by the Commission over the transparency and accountability of the investigation process, and over the IPCC's perceived failure to take account of vital evidence (Waseem 2005).

10 Peter Fahy, Chief Constable of Cheshire Police and ACPO spokesman on race and diversity issues, claimed in his comments to the *Guardian* newspaper that the police service had 'lost the diversity argument with [its] own staff, the popular press and public overall. They see it purely in terms of political correctness' (Dodd 2006).

11 ACPO, for example, are known to have opposed a number of the government's anti-terrorism proposals announced after the 2005 London bombings because of the damaging effects they would have upon Muslims' confidence in the police (Dodd, Norton-Taylor and White 2005), whilst Peter Clarke, deputy assistant commissioner of the Metropolitan Police and head of Scotland Yard's anti-terrorist branch, has publicly acknowledged the need for stop and search powers under the Terrorism Act 2000 to be more tightly focused if they are to avoid alienating Muslim communities (Travis 2006).

References

Ansari, F. (2005) *British Anti-Terrorism: A Modern Day Witch-Hunt*, Wembley: Islamic Human Rights Commission.

BBC News Online (2005) 'Hate Crimes Soar After Bombings', 3 August http://news.bbc.co.uk/1/hi/england/london/4740015.stm

Bolognani, M. (2005) *Research Findings: Attitudes Towards Crime and Crime Prevention in the Bradford Pakistani Community*, Leeds: Centre for Ethnicity and Racism Studies, University of Leeds.

Bowling, B. and Phillips, C. (2002) *Racism, Crime and Justice*, Harlow: Longman.

Bunting, M. (2006) 'It Takes More Than Tea and Biscuits to Overcome Indifference and Fear' *Guardian*, 27 February.

Burchill, J. (2005) 'Why Should We Tolerate These Islamofascists Who Hate Us All?' *The Times*, 16 July.

Burnett, J. (2004) 'Community, Cohesion and the State', *Race and Class*, 45 (3): 1–18.

Campaign Against Racism and Fascism (CARF) (2002) 'Community Cohesion: Blunkett's New Race Doctrine', *CARF Newsletter No. 66*, February/March: 5–6.

Campbell, D., Dodd, V. and Branigan, T. (2006) 'Guilty: The Cleric Who Preached Murder as a Religious Duty', *Guardian*, 8 February.

Chakraborti, N. and Garland, J. (2003) 'Under-researched and Overlooked: An Exploration of the Attitudes of Rural Minority Ethnic Communities Towards Crime, Community Safety and the Criminal Justice System', *Journal of Ethnic and Migration Studies*, 29 (3): 563–72.

Clancy, A., Hough, M., Aust, R. and Kershaw, C. (2001) *Crime, Policing and Justice: the Experience of Ethnic Minorities. Findings from the 2000 British Crime Survey*, Home Office Research Study 223, London: Home Office.

Cohen, S. (1973) *Folk Devils and Moral Panics*, St Albans: Paladin.

Cowan, R. (2006) 'Fear Deters Complaints from Ethnic Minorities', 20 February, *Guardian*, 20 February.

Cowan, R. and Travis, A. (2004) 'Muslims: We Are the New Victims of Stop and Search', *Guardian*, 29 March.

Docking, M. and Tuffin, R. (2005) *Racist Incidents: Progress Since the Lawrence Inquiry*, Home Office Online Report 42/05, London: Home Office.

Dodd, V. (2005a) 'Two-thirds of Muslims Consider Leaving UK', *Guardian*, 26 July.

Dodd, V. (2005b) 'Special Branch to Track Muslims Across UK', *Guardian*, 20 July.

Dodd, V. (2006) 'Diversity Target is Unrealistic Say Police Chiefs', *Guardian*, 31 March.

Dodd, V., Norton-Taylor, R. and White, M. (2005) 'Lords Threaten Rough Ride for Anti-Terror Bill', *Guardian*, 21 November.

European Commission against Racism and Intolerance (ECRI) (2004) *Third Report on the United Kingdom*, Strasbourg: Council of Europe.

Fekete, L. (2004) 'Anti-Muslim Racism and the European Security State', *Race and Class*, 46 (1): 3–29.

Foster, J., Newburn, T. and Souhami, A. (2005) *Assessing the Impact of the Stephen Lawrence Inquiry*, Home Office Research Study 294, London: Home Office.

Freedland, J. (2005) 'In the Grip of Panic', *Guardian*, 22 January.

Fulat, S. (2005) 'Recognise Our Role in Society', *Guardian*, 21 January.

Garland, J., Spalek, B. and Chakraborti, N. (2006) 'Hearing Lost Voices: Issues in Researching "Hidden" Minority Ethnic Communities', *British Journal of Criminology*, 45 (3): 423–37.

Gledhill, R. (2006) 'Rowan Atkinson Celebrates Government Defeat', *The Times*, 1 February.

Herbert, I. (2006) 'BNP Leader Walks Free as Race-Hate Prosecution Fails', *Independent*, 3 February.

Her Majesty's Inspectorate of Constabulary (2000) *Winning the Race: Embracing Diversity*, London: HMIC.

Home Office (2000) *Code of Practice on Reporting and Recording Racist Incidents. In Response to Recommendation 15 of the Stephen Lawrence Inquiry Report*, London: Home Office.

Home Office (2002) *Community Cohesion: A Report of the Independent Review Team Chaired by Ted Cantle*, London: Home Office.

Huntington, S. (1993) 'The Clash of Civilisations?', *Foreign Affairs*, 72 (3): 22–49.

Innes, M. (2006) 'Policing Uncertainty: Countering Terror through Community Intelligence and Democratic Policing', *Annals of the American Academy of Political and Social Science*, 605: 1–20.

Jeffery, S. (2006) 'Q&A: The Glorification of Terrorism', *Guardian*, 15 February.

Jones, T. and Newburn, T. (2001) *Widening Access: Improving Police Relations with Hard to Reach Groups*, Police Research Series Paper 138, London: Home Office.

Joseph, S. (2006) 'The Freedom That Hurts Us', *Guardian*, 3 February.

King, M. (1993) *Muslims in Europe: A New Identity for Islam*, European University Institute Working Paper No. 93/1, Florence: European University Institute.

Kundnani, A. (2002) 'An Unholy Alliance? Racism, Religion and Communalism', *Race and Class*, 44 (2): 71–80.

Kundnani, A. (2005) 'The Politics of a Phoney Britishness', *Guardian*, 21 January.

Macey, M. (2002) 'Interpreting Islam: Young Muslim Men's Involvement in Criminal Activity in Bradford', in B. Spalek (ed.) *Islam, Crime and Criminal Justice*, Cullompton: Willan Publishing, pp. 19–49.

Malik, K. (2005a) 'Making a Difference: Culture, Race and Social Policy', *Patterns of Prejudice*, 39 (4): 361–78.

Malik, K. (2005b) 'Multiculturalism has Fanned the Flames of Islamic Extremism', *The Times*, 16 July.

McGhee, D. (2005) *Intolerant Britain? Hate, Citizenship and Difference*, Maidenhead: Open University Press.

McLoughlin, S. (2005) 'Mosques and the Public Space: Conflict and Cooperation in Bradford', *Journal of Ethnic and Migration Studies*, 31 (6): 1045–67.

Modood, T. and Berthoud, R., with the assistance of Lakey, J., Nazroo, J., Smith, P., Virdee, S. and Beishon, S. (1997) *Ethnic Minorities in Britain: Diversity and Disadvantage. The Fourth National Survey of Ethnic Minorities*, London: Policy Studies Institute.

Oborne, P. (2006) 'The Politics of Fear', *Independent*, 15 February.

Oliver, M. and agencies (2005) 'Blears Backs Away From Racial Profiling', *Guardian*, 2 August.

Phillips, T. (2004) 'Multiculturalism's Legacy is "Have a Nice Day" Racism', *Guardian*, 28 May.

Ramadan, T. (2006) 'Cartoon Conflicts', *Guardian*, 6 February.

Rex, J. (2002) 'Islam in the United Kingdom', in S. T. Hunter (ed.) *Islam, Europe's Second Religion: The New Social, Cultural, and Political Landscape*, London: Praeger, pp. 51–76.

Rowe, M. (2004) *Policing, Race and Racism*, Cullompton: Willan Publishing.

Runnymede Trust (1997) *Islamophobia: A Challenge For Us All*, London: The Runnymede Trust.

Sharp, D. (2002) 'Policing After Macpherson: Some Experiences of Muslim Police Officers', in B. Spalek (ed.) *Islam, Crime and Criminal Justice*, Cullompton: Willan Publishing, pp. 76–95.

Sivanandan, A. (2006) 'Race, Terror and Civil Society', *Race and Class*, 47 (3): 1–8.

Smith, G. (2004) 'Faith in Community and Communities of Faith? Government Rhetoric and Religious Identity in Urban Britain', *Journal of Contemporary Religion*, 19 (2): 185–204.

Spalek, B. (2002) 'Religious Diversity, British Muslims, Crime and Victimisation', in B. Spalek (ed.) *Islam, Crime and Criminal Justice*, Cullompton: Willan Publishing, pp. 1–18.

Stubbs, S. (2006) 'It's About Discretion and Good Taste', *Guardian*, 3 February.

Travis, A. (2006) 'Use of "Stop and Search" Terror Law Alienating Muslims, Warns Yard', *Guardian*, 17 February.

Walker, C. (2002) *Blackstone's Guide to the Anti-Terrorism Legislation*, Oxford: Oxford University Press.

Ward, D. (2005) 'Muslims Tell Blears of Price They're Paying, Their Anger and Fears', *Guardian*, 3 August.

Waseem, S. (2005) *The Independent Police Complaints Commission: Who Will Guard the Guardians?*, Wembley: Islamic Human Rights Commission.

Werbner, P. (2004) 'The Predicament of Diaspora and Millennial Islam: Reflections on September 11 2001, *Ethnicities*, 4 (4): 451–76.

Woolf, M. (2005) 'Anti-Terror Police Told to Target Asians', *Independent*, 13 September.

Younge, G. (2005) 'We Can Choose Our Identity, But Sometimes It Also Chooses Us', *Guardian*, 21 January.

Chapter 7

Macpherson, police stops and institutionalised racism

Kevin Stenson and P.A.J. Waddington

Facts and narratives of truth

Facts do not appear unbidden before us, neatly dressed in the garments of officially accredited 'truth'. Both in the worlds of academic disciplines and in everyday culture, what count as 'facts' and 'truth' are the product of artful rhetoric (that is persuasive devices) and logical argument. Truths do not simply inhere in a body of argument and data, they involve an interaction between those making truth claims and the audiences they target (Smith 1978). Academics favour conceptually precise, emotionally low key, rational language. By contrast, the language of law, order and race employed by politicians and the mainstream mass media is more likely to be emotionally charged, figurative, metaphorical and involve personal stories held to signify wider truths (Shearing and Ericson 1991).

In volatile political climates, politicians tend to abandon the rhetoric about the need for 'evidence based' crime control policies and create new policies on the hoof. These initiatives often reflect the ways in which politicians and journalists in the mass media discuss issues of crime control in terms of individual, sensationalised cases and/or lobbying by interest groups. It is an old legal adage that 'hard cases make bad law'. Yet we should recognise that cases, such as murders of children, attracting much public debate and media attention play a major influence on the construction and implementation of law and policy (Jewkes 2004). Hence, official initiatives may respond to emotive media reaction and wider moral panics to notorious crimes, perceivably lenient sentences, inefficiency or malpractice by the police or other criminal justice agencies.

Metaphors do not just embroider language or rational conceptual arguments. They have powerful emotional force as calls to action, and operate in clusters to structure our thoughts and understanding of social relationships (Lakoff and Johnson 1980: 5). Moreover, these rhetorical constructions must find ways to play down alternative ways of framing information. Their success depends on the extent that they become the default position. This is the taken-for-granted received wisdom about how things are and should be – what other ideas have to combat. In the sphere of law and order, this struggle over truth is manifest in a politics of crime and crime control that links the ways we define and manage them. As we shall see, this is particularly so in public discussions about policy and policy-making in relation to race, crime and policing. However, there are variations in the extent to which the contest over ideas is visible to a particular cultural community or wider public (Stenson 1991). A key problem for criminologists, much agonised over within the academic community, is their lack of public visibility and lack of overall clout in the circuits of power in which ideas about crime and control are shaped.

Hence, criminologists struggle to be heard in the cacophony about crime and try to be careful about the evidential basis of their explanations. This is their key selling point in marketing their knowledge about crime and order to policy-makers and the public. There is conflict within the discipline about what should be considered to be the proper standards of evidence and methodology. The Home Office generally favours studies using quantitative methods (Gelsthorpe and Sharpe 2005; Stenson and Edwards 2004). However, there is another side to the picture. The Home Office has also commissioned in recent years qualitative research leading to policies that signify what could be termed a 'cultural' or anthropological turn in official criminology. These attempt to address issues of local culture and context. This chapter first explores this cultural turn. With a focus on the contentious issue of police stop and search, it then examines the tensions and ambiguities in the notion of institutionalised racism, and the race relations and racism narrative in which it is embedded. This narrative reveals and highlights examples of racism that had hitherto been under-acknowledged by officialdom. However, it confuses race, based on visible physical characteristics, with ethnicity, based on shared cultural characteristics. It obscures much of the complexity of inter-ethnic and other intergroup relations. It also detaches the study of policing and other forms of social control from the study of the behaviour of offenders and the circumstances that impact on them. This chapter emphasises the need to bring these issues back together and provides an alternative narrative that recognises the increasing demographic complexity of modern urban life. The narrative of race relations and racism, on its own, is ill-equipped to make sense of this complexity.

Cultural turn: signal crimes, statistics and policing

This new direction recognises that the emotive reaction to crime and justice is not simply foisted on the public by the media. The media help shape, and also reflect, popular ways of perceiving and reacting to crime that focus on particular, dramatically and voyeuristically presented events (Wilkins 1991). The tendency to focus on particular cases is perhaps most visible at local level. At this level, much of the information that people receive about crime, including presentation of local and national official crime statistics, is screened out as 'noise'; perception is necessarily selective (Innes 2004). People tend to focus not on crime statistics, nor weighty arguments about how to interpret them. Rather, they focus on particular 'signal' crimes, such as a brutal murder, a spate of callous street robberies, rapes, spectacular acts of criminal damage, anti-social behaviour by youths, assaults on small shops, and acts of terrorist violence. This is because these attain iconic status, crystallising widespread local anxieties, tensions and misgivings about patterns of demographic, environmental, economic and cultural change in localities. What is true locally may also be so nationally. This notion of signal crime can help us understand why the media and public debate prioritise particular types of crime, offender and victim, according them iconic status within the broader culture.

Hence, we can extend the notion of 'signal' crime further to embrace 'signal statistics'. These are often repeated figures, usually drawn out of context from complex data, that become key rhetorical tools in argument. Central government has recognised that published figures showing an overall decline in total crime since 1995, as measured both by police statistics and also the annual British Crime (victim) Surveys, have not reassured the public, because they do not resonate with personal perception, experience and anxieties, and media images (ODPM 2004). The personal and media focus remains on indications of rises in violent and sexual crimes, a small, and perhaps temporary, proportion of the total. This official recognition underpins the

development of the national 'reassurance policing' agen
the roll-out of neighbourhood police teams committed t
and responding to local concerns and maintaining a
patrolling presence.

In addition, there are both positive (good) and negative (ᵘᵃᶜ,
'signal' modes of policing, negatively crystallised in notorious cases.
These instances of policing are depicted as metaphors for types of
policing, for example in relation to minority communities. In the UK,
the most notorious example is the poorly conducted investigation
of the murder in 1993 of the black teenager Stephen Lawrence. The
subsequent Macpherson Report into his death echoed the claims
of the anti-racist lobbies active during the inquiry in labelling this
case an instance of institutionalised racism within the police service
and British society more generally. This was followed by legislation
requiring the police and other public agencies to monitor their
practices for signs of racism and to develop policies to prevent and
reduce it. In the case of the police, this involves, among other things,
monitoring the degree to which police stops and searches of citizens
are proportionate to the numbers of residents living locally, in
particular racial categories as defined and measured by census data.
There has been much debate within the police service and academia
about the extent to which the 'bungled' investigation was an instance
of racism or chronic inefficiency in police practice that may have
similarly affected the families of other lower-class homicide victims
(see Souhami, and Roycroft *et al.* this volume).

Institutional racism

The Macpherson Report famously highlighted and popularised
the notion of 'institutional racism', focusing particular attention on
the alleged disproportionality of police stops of black people. The
report emphasises police stops, given that they are often the most
sensitive encounters between the representatives of state power and
the public. This is especially so with racial and ethnic minorities,
often located at the lower reaches of society, where people may be
suspicious and resentful of the use of these powers by police officers.
This may be particularly marked among those minorities originating
from countries without community policing traditions and in which
citizens see the police as a brutal oppressive force. Macpherson
claimed that disproportionate stops, like other discriminatory practices
by police and criminal justice personnel, are the result not simply

of intentionally prejudicial behaviour by individual officers. Rather, the most significant forms of racism stem from routine institutional practices, often 'unwittingly' undertaken by those who would not necessarily describe themselves as racist. However, as we have argued elsewhere, Macpherson's approach to racism is contradictory and ambiguous. Notwithstanding this notion of unwitting, institutional racism, he does in fact claim that disproportionate police stops and searches arise from selective, intentionally prejudiced behaviour by officers (Waddington *et al.* 2004). Therefore, Macpherson's definition of racism oscillates between the notions of the unwitting, institutional impact of policy and practice, and intentionally prejudicial behaviour by individuals and groups.

Predictably, therefore, a recently published Home Office report on the impact of Macpherson found deep hostility and resentment, especially in London, among police officers to what they saw as Macpherson's unwarranted claims about their pervasive racism (Foster *et al.* 2005). The Home Office report claimed that officers did not understand the subtleties of the notion of institutional racism. Yet, given the way it defined racism the Macpherson Report *did indeed* claim that officers were intentionally racist in how they stopped people. This helps to explain their resentment and misgivings about the impact of Macpherson in painting an officially endorsed, negative public picture of officers' attitudes and behaviour. The report was seen by officers as amplifying and providing justification for negative feelings and prejudice against the police by black minorities and reinforcing a hostile, unco-operative stance by sections of the black population when officers tried to patrol and maintain order.

The readiness in minority and liberal circles to view the Stephen Lawrence case within the frame of racism rather than, for example, incompetence or individual instances of corruption, resonates with interpretive frameworks or dominant narratives, developed between the late 1960s and early 1980s by anti-racist lobbies (Pitts 1993). These intellectual elements were drawn upon by the networks of advocacy groups that were involved in the campaigns for justice for the family of Stephen Lawrence (Rock 2004). Interestingly, in an officially funded and endorsed report, one of Macpherson's key concepts is rooted in these radical structural critiques of state power, developed originally by self-organised and funded radical campaign and advocacy groups and their academic allies. These groups can be described as constituting 'circuits of power', with agendas of 'governance from below'. In resisting state power, they generated, in their shifting alliances, ways of describing and explaining the world and images of how to improve it. These forms of knowledge, constructed as truth, are developed and communicated through talk and texts. They are key elements deployed to build and mobilise support in a range of campaigns by advocacy groups, or sites of governance from below (Stenson 1991, 2005). In this case, these lobbies claimed that in areas of black settlement, the police undertook indiscriminate stops and searches of black people and commonly engaged in criminally unprofessional practices such as assaults in police custody and planting evidence on black suspects in order to secure convictions (Cohen and Bains 1988; Solomos 1993).

While criminologists, for research purposes, may wish to focus narrowly on the analysis of police stops, this is more difficult to do in the framework of this dominant narrative. Within this story-line, the discriminatory overuse of stop and search is but one element in a continuum of discriminatory practices by police officers, criminal justice, prison and other penal agency personnel. These went beyond the intentionally prejudiced behaviour of racist individuals, rotten apples in an otherwise healthy barrel. Rather, these practices are seen as manifesting a systemic bias against black people, associating them disproportionately and unfairly with emotive crimes like street robbery, sexual and other violent assault, drug trading and pimping (Clancy *et al.* 2001). At the same time, the police and justice system are seen as failing to protect black people from criminal or racist attack by white offenders from a dominant society, hostile to those perceived as unwelcome, strangers, or 'other', in their midst. The disturbances in Brixton and other areas of UK black settlement in 1981 and later in 1985 were, hence, depicted by anti-racist radicals as a boiling over of rage and resistance to this treatment by representatives of the state.

Race relations and racism narrative

Within the academy, the publication of *Policing the Crisis* (Hall *et al.* 1978) marked a watershed in assembling the intellectual building blocks of the anti-racist movement. This work in the academy was a counterpart to vigorous political activity within communities. Though their claims to be voices of the community were always contestable, the purveyors of the earlier versions of anti-racist narratives in the 1960s and 1970s had some effective representation in urban, left-wing Labour local authorities, and many lived in areas of minority settlement. They were involved in trade unions and in a variety of self-funded campaign groups rooted in the neighbourhoods and lifestyles of poor minority groups (Sivanandan 1990). The new political narrative acknowledged some links between poverty and oppression and everyday, street-level criminal conduct. It emerged and crystallised in the aforementioned landmark text, and was reinforced in *Race and Class* and other radical publications.

However, the weight of explanation assembled neo-Marxist structural explanations of the economic crises of late capitalism, labelling and other radical social theories. In essence, the explanatory emphasis shifted from policing as a response to heightened levels of crime, disorder, deviant lifestyles and illegal economies in deprived areas and minority populations. That explanatory narrative had been rooted in liberal, welfare state explanations highlighting, in Robert Merton's terms, 'anomie'. This explained crime and disproportionate involvement in the criminal justice system among the poor resulting from poverty, inequality, inadequate schooling and other diminished life chances, and discrimination. These explanations also emphasised, as in Chicago between the world wars, intense competitive struggles between ethnic groups trying to survive in the city. More generally, the explanatory focus was on a gap between societal success goals and the means available to achieve them.

The new paradigm, by contrast, focused more on discriminatory social control, unwarranted by the conduct of those being controlled. This marked a significant break in the tradition of explanation and narrative stream in terms of what elements could be comfortably brought together by academics who wished to guard their liberal credentials and avoid damaging *ad hominem* charges of racism. The moral panics over black street criminality in the late 1970s, and the goad to aggressive police patrolling that was said to come in its wake, were, in these terms, seen as useful distractions. Against the backcloth of British colonialism, they unfairly scapegoated the UK black minority for the tensions and anxieties of a society downwardly spiralling into economic and cultural decline. This form of analysis helped to provide warrant for the distancing – or even complete separation – of the study of racist social control of minorities by the police and criminal justice, from the study of disorder, illegal economies, criminal behaviour and lifestyle within minority groups. Within the world of progressive UK liberal criminology, and their counterparts in other countries, this narrative has helped to create a new explanatory position dominant more generally within the field. This is especially so in relation to the provision of teaching materials for the burgeoning numbers of students of criminology (Bowling and Phillips 2002).

This evolved into what can be described as a Race Relations and Anti-Racism model, or narrative, that was increasingly accepted as a default position by the Home Office from the mid 1980s. This highlights the struggle for power along racial fault lines and plays down spatial variations, as if the same dynamics operated everywhere from Lands End to John O'Groats (Stenson *et al.* 1999). This model pictures the population as consisting of a dominant white population which controls the resources and key positions of cultural and material power. Within this model, there is a predisposition to depict conflict between people of different races or ethnicities as involving powerful white offenders attacking vulnerable non-white victims. Underneath this dominant mass lies the black population. As Gurchand Singh (2000: 35) argued, institutional racism is couched in a particular theory of social stratification:

> Although there are variations, the description usually put forward identifies two main 'classes' in the social formation: 'blacks' and 'whites'. These two classes are placed within a hierarchical relationship: 'black' people are identified as a subordinate class, or even underclass, while 'white' people are seen to be a dominant and exploitative class ... However, there are several problems with this theory of stratification. Firstly it ignores the fact, and cannot explain why 'black' and 'white' people occupy different class positions ...

> Secondly, this particular theory of social stratification assumes that 'black' people are the sole objects of racism. However, this ignores certain historical instances where 'white' people have become the objects of racism. For example, the Irish ... Jews, gypsies, and travellers have also been the objects of racist discourses and violence.

In the 1970s and early 1980s, in urban Labour local authorities and other left liberal circles, race was defined in political rather than cultural terms. It was conceptualised as made up of groups that, whatever their cultural differences, shared the common experience of racist oppression and a history of colonial domination. The assumption was that the specific ethnic and other cultural identities that may have divided the various non-white minority populations would erode and be replaced by a common identity based on the shared experience of racist oppression. This was reinforced by census and other state systems of population classification. These tended to bury white cultural, ethnic minority groups, such as the Irish, Cypriots, Poles and Jews, within the catch-all, 'white' category (Waddington *et al.* 2004).

This way of picturing society also displaced lower-class, urban, indigenous white populations from the foreground. Let us briefly consider these populations. By contrast with the 1970s, when the skinhead cult was ascendant, demographic and other changes have eroded their local economic, political, cultural and physical powers. They are, hence, increasingly removed, culturally and economically, from the upwardly mobile classes of all ethnicities. This is largely a consequence of the well-documented flight from the cities of many affluent middle-class and skilled working-class families, in the child-rearing age ranges, to rural and outer suburban areas. The poorer white populations left behind have their specific experiences of crime, policing, inequality, inter-ethnic relations, unemployment and access to public services and labour markets. They are also rendered less visible to officialdom and the favoured ideological concerns of the liberal middle classes. This marginalisation is reinforced by the rise of New Labour, which has tended to neglect these constituencies and their concerns. It has created a vacuum of representation increasingly filled by the British National Party and other groupings on the far right. Their far right narratives on websites and campaign literature highlight, through emotive stories of individual cases of violence and perceived oppression, the claimed risks to these populations of competition from migrants, and in particular from criminal victimisation by young males from ethnic minorities (Webster 1996; Home Office 2001; Dench *et al.* 2006).

However, to return to the story of the development of the race relations and anti-racism narrative, the brunt of economic decline in the 1970s and New Right economic reforms and unemployment in the 1980s impacted heavily on inner-city minority populations. The riots of 1981 and 1985 and festering discontent led to attempts by the central state to re-connect with these populations. During the 1980s and 1990s, the race relations and anti-racism model evolved and moved from being the rallying cry of fiery radicals, acting outside the state, to an ideology shared by activists who evolved into salaried professionals, funded by the public purse, and who became increasingly involved with the liberal reaches of the state. This race relations and racism narrative, like its purveyors, became embedded within the liberal governmental elites. New policy networks emerged linking, for example, liberal media, civil servants in the Home Office, with the Commission for Racial Equality, local race equality councils and lobbies of minority lawyers, police officers, and others involved in the criminal justice agencies.

These new professional, anti-racist networks attracted criticism from the Marxist, anti-racist left (Sivanandan 1990). This analysis echoed familiar Marxist analyses of the ways that indigenous leaders within the Labour movement had, for a long time, been effectively incorporated into the governing classes, seduced into privileged lifestyles, and hence their rebellious power neutered. From this view, the liberal versions of anti-racist narratives endorsed multiculturalism, the ideology of human rights, and tended to disconnect racism from an analysis of class inequality. The focus of this perspective shifted to symbolic and ameliorative concerns. These included, for example, struggles against racist language and barriers to professional employment. This was seen to be at the expense of the struggle for material redistribution and against overt violence and discrimination: those reforms that would improve the lives of those at the bottom of the labour and housing market barrels.

From this perspective, the new liberal narratives of anti-racism, and the new public grants and jobs that emerged in their wake, provided a rationale and an upward mobility route for an emerging liberal, black and minority ethnic middle class, with withering roots in the poorer communities that they claim to represent. They also attracted criticism from the political right. The *Daily Telegraph*, the *Spectator* and other right-wing publications describe these networks as the 'race relations industry', advocacy groups with a vested interest in 'cop-bashing', and highlighting statistical data and incidents that denigrate the police and other criminal justice agencies. This is viewed as advocacy for extra state resources to fund their causes and jobs. They are held to share the vices of the liberal elites in being unduly sensitive to human rights of the anti-social. They are held to be soft on criminals (unless offenders attack victims championed by liberal causes), 'free riders' taking advantage of the welfare state, and those perceived to constitute a threat to the interests and values of the nation, and some who are a terrorist threat (Hitchens 2004; Phillips 2006).

There have, over time, been moves to create more diverse, official ethnic classifications in the census and other government surveys and also in local police crime categories and statistics. However, when crime, policing and justice statistics are aggregated by the Home Office, as required in the annual publication of race, crime and justice statistics under section 95 of the Criminal Justice Act 1991, ethnic, class-based cultural variations are buried within the principal categories of white, black (those of – directly or indirectly – sub-Saharan African heritage), and Asian (those originating in the Indian subcontinent). A range of lobbies has resisted altering the official categories and statistics. Predictably, a recent review of the annual 'section 95' publication of race and crime statistics rejected any fundamental change (Institute of Criminal Policy Research 2004). Hence, for example, disproportionality in police stops data continues to focus principally on the white, black and Asian categorisations of the population and the census-based residential population data as the basic denominator used for measurement.

The power of iconic individual stories

Notwithstanding some critical commentary on state endorsed and produced race categories and collated statistics, these remain the dominant source of official authorisation for what is considered to be 'truth' about the links between race and crime in the circuits of power that count most (Stenson 1991). They also help to provide official endorsement for the generalisation of personal narratives in everyday life and in media accounts. This powerful narrative operates as a familiar frame for particular case stories. This has aligned a long cast list of victims of what is seen as institutionalised racism over many years. In recent years these have included, for example, black former paratrooper Christopher Alder, who died in police custody in Hull in 1998 after a fight outside a nightclub. He was the subject of a report by the Independent Police Complaints Commission, accusing the officers who dealt with Mr Alder of a 'most serious neglect of duty' and 'unwitting racism' (*Guardian*, 28 March 2006). Anthony Walker was the victim of racist attack by two young white men in Merseyside in December 2005, in a predominantly white working-class area, though the police were not accused in this instance of contributing to it nor of neglect in investigating the death. Here the problem of institutionalised racism is seen as deriving not so much from state agencies as from what is depicted as pervasive racism among sections of lower-class white populations.

The shooting to death by anti-terrorist officers of an innocent young Brazilian man, Jean Charles de Menezes in July 2005 in the wake of the London terrorist bombings is also, at the time of writing, the subject of an investigation by the Independent Police Complaints Commission, amid widespread claims that the shooting was the result of racist targeting of people who looked as if they may be south

Asian or Arab. This has since been accompanied by continuous, often polarised, public commentary. There is concern about the extent to which, on the one hand, the police avoid racism and Islamophobia, treating all citizens equally and fairly and protecting human rights. Commentators on the other side of the argument note that the London bombings, resulting in 52 innocent deaths and over 700 people injured, were the work of a group of young British-born Muslims involved in an extremist Islamist group. One of them had made a 'martyrdom tape', later broadcast, explaining and justifying their actions. This proven empirical reality is said to warrant selective profiling of this population category for police stops and airport security practices, in order to protect the public against further attacks. This argument grew more strident when a group of eight young British Muslims were charged in August 2006 with planning to blow up passenger planes.

Events and cases like these can have a powerful impact on national and local collective stories and consciousness about police-minority relations. Tony Jefferson, one of the authors of the seminal *Policing the Crisis*, has argued that among minority groups particularly, the source of claims about the nature of stop and search and other encounters with the police do not just derive from personal experience (Jefferson 1991). They are drawn from the stories told by friends, relatives and others and become woven into familiar story-lines that blur the boundaries between individual and shared experience. Among their functions is a warning to expect the worst from the police. We can add that this can involve stereotyping of the police, as if instances of racist malpractice are always the true face of the police in general. This operates with a similar logic to the racist stereotyping of minorities, based on spectacular examples of deviance by individuals, held to be icons of whole communities.

The continuity and power of this kind of narrative, which focuses on personal experiences, is revealed in current political, journalistic and academic commentary. For example, the London *Evening Standard* (3 April 2006) carried a report about a 41-year-old black female senior race adviser to the Metropolitan Police and London's Mayor, Ken Livingstone, and a Labour candidate in the May 2006 local elections. The following analysis draws on direct quotes from the race adviser, which appeared in the *Evening Standard* article. Note that the category of 'black' used here is the old political category that draws in the net all those who are not white and are united by the common experience of racism. Moreover, this is a discourse that plays down the significance of gender and class differences, dress codes or other indicators of chosen subcultural identity among black people so defined. The colour difference and the discrimination it attracts are presented as the most significant factors. The newspaper report noted that the annual 'section 95' figures on race and crime published a week before by the Home Office indicated that black people were six times more likely to be stopped than white people and showed a 14 per cent year on year increase in the number of black people being stopped and searched.

The race adviser said that, 'We have come to expect this as part of the life experience of being a black person in Britain.' She claimed that police had stopped her 39 times in her life (modest in relation to the experience of black males) and that being pulled over by the police was 'part of the life experience of being a black person in Britain'.

A Saab driver, she claimed that she was so familiar with being stopped she always carried a copy of her passport and police pass. Black people were said to face persecution in the wake of 9/11 and the introduction of the Terrorism Act, which increased police powers to stop and search. 'Why is it that everyone who is being stopped is black? In their eyes, a terrorist is not a white male. My crime was driving while black.'

Furthermore, middle-class status and respectable appearance seem not to offer protection: 'I dress smartly, but it doesn't seem to make any difference. It is all about racial stereotyping.'

An accompanying photograph of the well-coiffed and smartly attired race adviser reinforced this. It was claimed that there is a gulf between the language of racial equality uttered by senior police managers and front line policing: 'The reality on the ground is far different from what is being said in the boardroom.'

It was claimed that key change over time was a shift from overt, abusive to more covert forms of racism, and despite the recommendations following the Macpherson Report, after the murder of Stephen Lawrence, there had been scant discernible change since 1981:

The stop and search figures do not give the black community any confidence in the police ... We want to see more police on our streets, but this practice is building bad relations with them. Black people are being over-policed as potential criminals and under-policed as victims of crime.

We do not query the veracity of the race adviser's account of personal experience. It is accepted in good faith. Yet its power lies not simply in the veracity of the account, and the personal honesty of the author of the account. Rather, the power, meaning and significance of stories like this derive from their rhetorical, including emotive, form and their alignment with official statistics on police stops. Their floating within a long stream of such narratives over many years also bolsters these accounts. Hence the experiential account coexists with rhetorical forms within the narrative that attempt to generalise this personal experience to the status of a metaphor. This stands for the experience and fate of the generality of black people, as differentiated from that of white people.

Furthermore, the public credibility of the account is bolstered by the high status of the complainant and support by a leader article in the same issue of the newspaper endorsing the claims and calling for the police service to address these concerns. This accreditation is particularly striking given that it appeared not in a liberal newspaper like the *Guardian*, *Independent*, or *Observer*, but in the *Evening Standard*, a stable-mate within Associated Newspapers of the *Daily Mail*. The publications of Associated Newspapers have for generations been associated with the robust right wing of the Conservative Party. This account coexists uneasily with their more familiar line. They have consistently scourged the perceived shibboleths of political correctness, defended English nationalism and what is depicted as the white heartland of Middle England, been critical of the welfare state and those who exploit it, especially legal and illegal immigrants and their descendants, and promoted tough policies of immigration control and law and order. This was particularly evident in May 2006 when these newspapers powerfully criticised the Home Office for failing to deport large numbers of foreign serious offenders at the end of their sentences. Many photos of non-white offenders and lists of names accompanied the stories. This effectively emphasised their status as threateningly 'other' in relation the majority of citizens.

Conclusion: towards the paradigm of inter-ethnic relations

The dominant liberal race relations narrative is under attack now not just from the hard left and right. It is also criticised from the middle grounds of politics and academia, though as yet the critical ingredients have not been assembled into a powerful recognisable narrative frame. This needs further development. The litmus test of this will be the ability of a new narrative to insert personalised stories of particular signal offenders, victims and their circumstances, and styles of professional, non-discriminatory policing into public discourse. Nevertheless, we can begin to identify some of the elements out of which a new paradigmatic narrative, more relevant to the present, may begin to take shape.

First, it is in the nature of personalised accounts of what has happened to us, and people like us, that their evidential basis and general applicability is difficult to assess. How can we compare our experience with that of others, no matter how passionately or self-righteously we may advance our claims? Drawing on research in Leeds in the early 1990s, Tony Jefferson argued that race and ethnic categories used to identify offenders and those stopped by the police were misleading, and made it difficult to compare like with like (Jefferson 1991). For example, how meaningful is it to compare rates for officially recorded police stops of designated black and white people without controlling for social class and other key variables? Insofar as it was possible to judge, in that setting, young lower-class white men were as likely to be stopped as black young men, and then – unlike in the post 9/11 world – young Asian men were less likely to be stopped than other groups. This reminds us that stopping with or without searches has been a standard feature of the policing of young lower class men for generations (Brogden 1985). Weight is added to this argument by a small study of stop and search in Islington by Jock Young, which controlled for class and cultural ethnic categories within the broader racial categories. This showed that in the poorer parts of Islington young Irish men were most likely to be stopped and young middle-class African men were among those least likely to be stopped (Young 1994).

In addition, statistical claims about disproportionality in police stop and search, using census residential data as the denominator, are not matched by studies that use street populations as the denominator. Replicating Home Office studies in a range of sites, studies by the present authors of police stops in relation to available street populations in Slough and Reading did *not* show that Black and Asian young men were disproportionately stopped (Miller *et al.* 2000; Waddington *et al.* 2004). One of the main changes since the growth of immigration from the 1950s has been in the ethnic make-up of the young lower-class male population using the urban streets. As the present authors have argued (Waddington *et al.* 2004: 892–3), this demonstrates the need to go beyond 'Black, White and Asian' identifiers to categorise the bulk of the population. They reflect, at best, the old patterns of immigration from the British colonies of

Africa, the Caribbean and the Indian subcontinent. The new sources of immigration cast a broader global net. In this context we need to recognise the importance of 'ethnic' categories that denote culturally defined collective identities within all the main racial categories (Fitzgerald 1993; Gelsthorpe 1993).

There is a population of undocumented illegal immigrants whose numbers are, by definition, hard to estimate, but which most commentators admit is very considerable. Census returns are likely to have been least reliable in the poorer wards where illegal migrants are most likely to be concentrated. This further calls into question the validity of relying on census, rather than street population data, in assessing disproportionality, especially in relation to police stops. In addition, according to Office of National Statistical figures, officially known net immigration has been running to around 300,000 per annum over the last decade; increasingly this has included growing numbers of people from the Horn of Africa, Latin America, Eastern Europe and other countries with slender if any historical links with, or knowledge about, the British Empire. Recent government estimates claimed that from Poland alone around two million people had travelled to Britain between 2004 and 2006 (*Evening Standard*, 24 April 06).

These demographic movements have created awesome demographic complexity, and often incendiary intergroup relations in UK cities that spill beyond the moulds of the old Race Relations and Racism narrative. These often first become visible in school playgrounds (Asthana and Townsend 2006). They include tensions between longer and more recently settled minority groups, which are familiar to and present serious challenges to police managers and other authorities. They echo the increasing tensions between African-Americans and the new waves of migrants from Latin America into the USA. The serious disturbances in the Lozells area of Birmingham in 2005 between African-Caribbean and Asian groups are an indication of these trends. In these conditions, unsurprisingly, despite the ideological visions of liberal anti-racists, there is little evidence that many people designated as 'Asian' define themselves as black. Furthermore, it is worth investigating anecdotal claims that Sikhs, Hindus and other non-Muslims – in the face of prejudice against Islam since the terrorist attacks of 9/11 and the London bombings of July 2005 – are retreating from the catch-all category of 'Asian', especially if it is used as a synonym for Muslim.

The storylines of the emerging paradigm would prioritise the need for varied empirical research and recover some of the older, neglected theoretical and methodological tools of criminology, particularly the need for sensitivity to spatial differences. This would require narratives that would restore criminological tools and themes cast asunder by the previous dominant narrative. We should no longer assume, in an ideological default position, that whites are the oppressors and non-whites the victims in conflict situations. Instead of assumptions, we need careful and systematic empirical investigation. This is a particular lesson for those who describe themselves as radical criminologists but who rely mainly on the critique of others' work. Their critiques of power would carry more weight if accompanied by sustained empirical research into these phenomena.

Just as in Chicago in the 1930s, much of what is coded as racist violence and crime is located within the intense competitive struggles between ethnic and other groups trying to survive in the modern city. Recognising this will greatly enhance the capacity of criminology to make credible contributions to public policy debates. We need to foreground the investigation of links between police behaviour and that of the young men they try to control, the social, economic, political and cultural contexts, and intergroup struggles, which provide the backcloth for police–community interaction. Research for the Youth Justice Board in several London boroughs in 2002 points the way. This demonstrated striking spatial variations, emphasising the close interconnections in some areas between high levels of street volume crime, police stops, unemployment, and other indicators of social deprivation, together with significantly low levels of school attainment, especially by the government's Key Stage 3, among young ethnic minority males (Fitzgerald et al. 2003). Moreover, this framework needs to further explore the links between deprivation, spatial and cultural segregation, and vulnerability of young people to recruitment by terrorist networks.

The subtle and complex interplay between home, school, street, media culture, and other settings and influences, needs much closer investigation, for the purposes of policy-making, than the narrow narrative focus on racism will permit (Pitts 1993; Gunter 2004; Hallsworth 2005). Emphatically, this is not to deny the reality of racist victimisation, particularly in rural and predominantly white outer suburban areas where non-white people may be very vulnerable (Chakrabarti and Garland 2004). However, we cannot assume that the same racist dynamics operate everywhere from John O'Groats to Lands End. Power relations between ethnic groups can vary between locations and between age groups (Webster 1996). Hence, in many urban areas the framework of description and explanation highlighting racism, manifest in the Macpherson Report, is ill-equipped to analyse and narrate the complexities of modern urban life. Given the strong vested interests in retaining the existing dominant narratives, it would be surprising if the presentation of this argument does not evoke hostile reaction, including – as we have already experienced – *ad hominen* attacks. Such a reaction should not be allowed to foreclose open criminological debate. More profoundly, it betrays the interests of the populations it purports to serve.

References

Asthana, A. and Townsend, M. (2006) 'Knives Rule the Playgrounds as Inter-racial Violence Soars', *The Observer* 4 June.

Bowling, B. and Phillips, C. (2002) *Racism, Crime and Justice*. Harlow: Longman.

Brogden, M. (1985) 'Stopping the people – Crime Control versus Social Control', in J. Baxter and L. Koffman (eds) *Police: The Constitution and the Community*, Abingdon: Professional Books, pp. 91–110.

Chakrabarti, N. and Garland, J. (eds) (2004) *Rural Racism*, Cullompton: Willan Publishing.

Clancy, A., Hough, M., Aust, R. and Kershaw, C. (2001) *Crime, Policing and Justice: The Experience of Ethnic Minorities. Findings from the 2000 British Crime Survey*. Home Office Research Study 223, London: Home Office.

Cohen, P. and Bains, H. S. (eds) (1988) *Multi-Racist Britain*, Basingstoke: Macmillan.

Cook, D. and Hudson, B. (eds) (1993) *Racism and Criminology*, London: Sage.

Dench, G., Gavron, K. and Young, M. (2006) *The New East End, Kinship, Race and Conflict*, London: Profile Books.

Fitzgerald, M. (1993) ' "Racism": Establishing the Phenomenon', in D. Cook, and B. Hudson (eds) *Racism and Criminology*, London: Sage, pp. 45–63.

Fitzgerald, M. Stockdale, J. and Hale, C. (2003) *Young People and Street Crime*, London: Youth Justice Board for England and Wales.

Foster, J., Newburn, T. and Souhami, A. (2005) *Assessing the Impact of the Stephen Lawrence Inquiry*, Home Office Research Study 294, London: Home Office.

Gelsthorpe, L. (1993) 'Approaching the Topic of Racism: Transferable Research Strategies?', in D. Cook and B. Hudson, *Racism and Criminology*, London: Sage, pp. 77–95.

Gelsthorpe, L. and Sharpe, G. (2005) 'Criminological Research: Typologies Versus Hierarchies', *Criminal Justice Matters*, 62, Winter: 8–9.

Gunter, A. (2004) 'Can't Blame the Youth: An Ethnographic Study of a Black East London Neighbourhood', PhD thesis, Buckinghamshire Chilterns University College/Brunel University.

Hall, S., Chritcher, C., Jefferson, T., Clarke, J. and Roberts B. (1978) *Policing the Crisis, Mugging, the State, and Law and Order*, London: Macmillan.

Hallsworth, S. (2005) *Street Crime*, Cullompton: Willan Publishing.

Hitchens, P. (2004) *The Abolition of Liberty: The Decline of Order and Justice in England*, London: Atlantic Books.

Home Office (2001) *Community Cohesion: A Report of the Independent Review Chaired by Ted Cantle*, London: Home Office.

Innes, M. (2004) 'Reinventing Tradition? Reassurance, Neighbourhood Security and Policing', *Criminal Justice*, 4(2): 151–71.

Institute of Criminal Policy Research (2004) *Race and the Criminal Justice System: An Overview to the Complete Statistics 2002–2003*, Kings College, London: Institute of Criminal Policy Research.

Jefferson, T. (1991) 'Discrimination, Disadvantage and Police-work', in E. Cashmore and E. Mclaughlin (eds) *Out of Order: Policing Black People*, London: Routledge.

Jewkes, Y. (2004) *Media and Crime*, London: Sage.

Lakoff, G. and Johnson, M. (1980) *Metaphors We Live By*, Chicago: University of Chicago Press.

Macpherson, Sir W. (1999) *The Stephen Lawrence Inquiry: Report of an Inquiry by Sir William Macpherson of Cluny*, CM 4262–1, London: HMSO.

Miller, J., Quinton, P. and Bland, N. (2000) 'Police Stops and Searches: Lessons From a Programme of Research', Home Office Briefing Note 1–6, London: Home Office.

ODPM (2004) *Creating Sustainable Communities: The Community Plan*, London: Office of the Deputy Prime Minister.

Phillips, M. (2006) *Londonistan: How Britain is Creating a Terror State Within*, London: Gibson Square Books.

Pitts, J. (1993) 'Theoreotyping: Anti-racism, Criminology and Black Young People', in D. Cook and B. Hudson (eds) *Racism and Criminology*, London: Sage, pp. 96–117.

Rock, P. (2004) *Court Victims' Rights, The Home Office, New Labour, and Victims*, Oxford: Oxford University Press.

Shearing, C. D. and Ericson, R. V. (1991) 'Culture as Figurative Action', *British Journal of Sociology*, 42: 481–506.

Singh, G. (2000) 'The Concept and Context of Institutional Racism', in A. Marlow and B. Loveday (eds) *After Macpherson: Policing after the Stephen Lawrence Inquiry*, Lyme Regis: Russell House Publishing, pp. 29–40.

Sivanandan, A. (ed.) (1990) *Communities of Resistance*, London: Verso.

Smith, D. (1978) '"K Is Mentally Ill": The Anatomy of a Factual Account', *Sociology*, 12: 23–53.

Solomos, J. (1993) 'Constructions of Black Criminality: Racialisation and Criminalisation in Perspective', in D. Cook and B. Hudson (eds) *Racism and Criminology*, London: Sage, pp. 118–33.

Stenson, K. (1991) 'Making Sense of Crime Control', in K. Stenson and D. Cowell (eds) *The Politics of Crime Control*, London: Sage, pp. 1–32.

Stenson, K. (2005) 'Sovereignty, Biopolitics and the Local Government of Crime in Britain', *Theoretical Criminology*, 9 (3): 265–87.

Stenson, K. and Edwards, A. (2004) 'Policy Transfer in Local Crime Control: Beyond Naïve Emulation', in T. Newburn and R. Sparks (eds) *Criminal Justice and Political Cultures: National and International Dimensions of Crime Control*, Cullompton: Willan Publishing.

Stenson, K., Travers, M. and Crowther, C. (1999) *The Police and Inter-Ethnic Conflict*, Report commissioned by the Metropolitan Police Service, London.

Waddington, P. A. J., Stenson, K. and Don, D. (2004) 'In Proportion: Race, and Police Stop and Search', *British Journal of Criminology*, 44: 889–914.

Webster, C. (1996) 'Local Heroes: Violent Racism, Localism and Spacism amongst Asian and White Young People', *Youth and Policy*, 53: 15–27.

Wilkins, L. T. (1991) *Punishment, Crime and Market Forces*, Aldershot: Dartmouth.

Young, J. (1994) *Policing the Streets: Stops and Search in North London*, London: Centre for Criminology, Middlesex University.

Chapter 8

Reform by crisis: the murder of Stephen Lawrence and a socio-historical analysis of developments in the conduct of major crime investigations

Mark Roycroft, Jennifer Brown and Martin Innes

Introduction

> Social problems are not straightforwardly obvious in society. They must be identified, and those concerned with them must be persuaded that they are timely and urgent if anything is to be done about them.
>
> (Gubrium 2005: 527)

The Macpherson Report (1999) reframed the murder of Stephen Lawrence from a failed homicide investigation into an indictment of racial politics, injustice and victims' rights. Rock (2004) articulates the galvanising effect that Macpherson's findings had on the UK criminal justice system. The result of this reframing process was that the report effectively misdiagnosed the causes of many of the problems that it catalogued (Innes 1999). In locating the shortcomings of the police investigation into the Lawrence murder as 'institutional racism', there was a failure to appreciate that the observed errors, omissions and mistakes related to inadequacies of the systems and processes that are part of the standard operating procedures of police homicide investigations. The key to this misreading of the systemic problems lies in the isolation of Macpherson's focus on racial discrimination rather than considering a historic perspective whereby lessons could be learnt from previous problematic major crime investigations. We will argue that there is an iterative process revealed through such a longitudinal analysis, whereby first, certain features must be present before particular failed murder investigations are the subject of official enquiries, and second, there is a pattern to failings and remedies that lead to innovation in murder detection practices.

In this chapter we explore what happens when the failed Lawrence murder investigation is not treated in isolation, but is seen as being one among a number of major crime investigations carried out by the police where problems and difficulties have been identified. Drawing upon a number of sources, most notably the Social Amplification of Risk (SARF) framework (Pidgeon *et al.* 2003), we propose a theoretical model to explain why particular failed or problematic murder investigations excite public attention and how resultant enquiries seek to produce reforms in investigative practice as purported solutions. The model offers a formulation that takes into account the external contexts and triggers that amplify the public and political visibility of particular police investigations, and result in recommendations for procedural and technological change. We suggest there to be a cycle whereby pressures exerted *by* the police for innovation are reflected through investigative shortcomings and subsequent pressures *on* the police. Central to our thesis is the decline and restoration of trust in the institution of policing.

Problematic investigations and police reform

Reviewing the development trajectory of reform in police investigative procedures over the past three decades, it is immediately apparent that Lawrence was one of a sequence of cases where difficulties and problems with some aspect of police work have been publicly identified. Take, for example, the Challenor corruption case, the difficulties in identifying Peter Sutcliffe, the 'Yorkshire Ripper', the miscarriages of justice in the 1980s and early 1990s, the killing of Damilola Taylor, and the Soham murders of Holly Wells and Jessica Chapman. As is evident even from this edited list of problematic police investigations, the nature of the problems that have been made manifest is varied, including the fabrication of evidence, poor case management and difficulties in handling witnesses. Taking a time-span perspective, it does seem that at particular historical moments certain high-profile major crime investigations come to be seen as problematic in some fashion (i.e. achieve some measure of amplification). Then the conduct of the investigation itself is enquired into, either through a public or internal enquiry resulting in reform in some aspects of policing practice.

Loader and Mulcahy (2003) have recently suggested that policing can be conceptualised as a 'cultural lens', wherein shifts and changing currents in the constitution of the social and cultural orders are refracted through the institution of policing. In their analysis, developments in policing are cast as articulations and animations of wider social changes. Shifts in the disposition and practices of policing can be understood as responses to an array of social forces that impact upon and shape how policing is performed. But they maintain, in illuminating such changes, that policing is not a passive agent. Rather it animates alterations in the social environment. How policing is practised and conducted has wider implications in terms of structuring the constitution of social order.

Considering specifically the domain of crime investigation, in a revision to Loader and Mulcahy's thesis, we would argue that the introduction of significant reform is not a continuous progression and development; rather, it tends to occur in 'fits and starts'. There are comparatively long periods of stability in investigative practice that are set apart from other periods of intense turbulence, when more radical reconfiguration takes place. Punch's (2000) arguments about the timing of police corruption scandals are helpful in this regard. Corruption and police misconduct, he posits, are not accidental, individual aberrations, but they are persistent and constantly recurring hazards generated cyclically by the nature of the police organisation itself. Punch suggests that the time span is about ten years for the cycle to be completed. It starts with a crisis or *cause célèbre* being triggered by the discovery of potential corrupt practices. There then follows an inquiry that defines the nature of the corruption, and makes suitable recommendations, which are then implemented. Cultural adjustments to the proposed origins of the malpractices are made and routines modified. Eventually, however, a reinvention of the original problem occurs. In a subsequent elaboration of this basic thesis, Punch (2003) proposes that the solutions typically proposed as part of these cycles of crisis and reform tend to revolve around the same issues: management and supervision, working practices, training, awareness raising, and improved confidence in accountabilities. The fundamental problem, he suggests, lies in the diagnosis. In attributing blame for the problem the focus is often upon key, blameworthy individuals – the 'rotten apples'. But in so doing, the systemic causes (in the orchard) of failures are often avoided and omitted from consideration.

Bringing the arguments of Loader and Mulcahy (2003) and Punch

(2000, 2003) together, it is possible to construct a synthesis of their accounts of police reform to assist in understanding the timing, meaning and implications of inquiries into problematic major investigations. Central to such an account is the ongoing development of social order including the evolution of cultural mores, values, institutions and ways of life. These macro-structural changes can create tensions in that the social and cultural order comes out of alignment with the rules and standards for behaviour encoded in law. Particularly, for an institution such as the police that is centrally involved in translating the law 'in books' into 'action', misalignments can occur, creating a climate of increasing tension as the rules they are enforcing and the ways in which they are doing this have lessening legitimacy and moral authority among sections of the public. Any such tensions are brought into sharp relief by the occurrence of signal events: those incidents that are differentiated from the more routine and ongoing background noise of social life. This was the case with the Stephen Lawrence murder, which acquired public visibility set against a climate of increasing awareness of race discrimination.

Signal events are incidents that induce a notable change in terms of how people, think, feel or act (Innes 2004). This can involve anger, fear, or the generation of political campaigns. In the Lawrence case, the failure of the police to provide protection or justice to the victim massively amplified the public insecurity that was generated by the original crime, causing these sorts of cognitive, affective and behavioural reactions among the public, but in particular among black and minority ethnic communities.

Signal events that result from a perceived failure of the police or other authorities tend to exhibit a sense of gravitational pull around which coalesce public fears and concerns. In effect, the signal event becomes an empirical manifestation of a particular social problem and functions as a focus for mounting public, and consequently political, pressure for something to be done about this issue. One response to such circumstances is to mount some form of enquiry into the causes and to attempt to diffuse the tension by making recommendations for reform. The establishment of an inquiry into the specific event thus provides a vehicle where aspects of police practice or the rules codified in law that police enforce can be considered in detail and compared in light of wider, changing social values. In effect then, the recommendations arising from the inquiry seek to realign policy and/or practice.

The social amplification of risk

Risk researchers propose that particular events have different signal values (Slovic 2000). In effect, the notion of signal value is used to capture the differing capacities of hazards and potential hazards to exert influence over those people who are made aware of them. Thus it has been shown that rarer, more spectacular and high consequence risks typically evince more public concern than do more commonplace, 'low' impact risks.

SARF formulations thus seek to explain why certain hazards are attributed a higher signal value than others and an instructive analysis in this respect is provided by Gowda (2003) with reference to the child murders of Megan Kanka in the United States in 1994 and Sarah Payne in the UK in 2000. The Kanka case, it is argued, involved a deliberate process of risk amplification wherein the resulting 'Megan's Law', providing for disclosure of the whereabouts of released paedophiles, was the product of making connections between a specific case and a more abstract and yet seemingly pervasive threat of sexual licence. In contrast, the Sarah Payne case, although invoking similar campaigning strategies, is nevertheless cast as an instance of risk attenuation in that public pressure apparently failed to stimulate legislative or police procedural change. Central to Gowda's application of SARF to these cases is the presence of a stigmatised activity (paedophilia); vulnerable victims (children); the backdrop of a decline in trust in the criminal justice system; the deliberate creation of an agenda connecting the specific case and the general sense of malaise; and the presence of vociferous advocates.

Stigmatisation makes an important contribution to the social processes by which the sense of risk or harm attributed to an event is amplified. Stigma in this sense is taken to mean the posing of risks, which are often inequitably distributed and may disproportionately affect vulnerable groups. The presence of a sense of vulnerability adds to the vividness of the images associated with consequences of the risks that are posed. The combination of stigmatisation and 'imageability' contributes to the taint and/or discredit associated with the particular incident or episode. We extend some of these processes to the present analysis. We take stigma to mean a disadvantaged group (in the Stephen Lawrence case this would be the black and minority ethnic communities) where there is some background activity, such as political activation, which is animated by members of the group being harmed.[1]

In their account of responses to risk, Douglas and Wildavsky (1983) identify that an important aspect of dealing adequately with risk, is the ability to blame someone or something. The attribution of blame is a vital component in terms of rendering harm understandable, calculable and thus controllable. In relation to troublesome murder investigations, the setting up of some form of review, whether this be internal or external and public, as with the Macpherson Enquiry, can be cast as a mechanism for divining and attributing blame for any failures that can be detected.

Applying these theoretical resources to the specific issue of problematic police murder investigations, such as the Stephen Lawrence case, the instigation of subsequent enquiries into the conduct of the police's work can be cast as a form of symbolic contest wherein some aspect of police culture or practice is being challenged by wider social forces that are in play in society. As such, the setting up and conducting of a review or enquiry into the police investigation becomes a potentially pivotal point in the development of policing wherein the disposition of policing and its organisational routines is in tension with the development of morals, values and standards in society more generally. This tension is relieved by these pivotal cases wherein policing is reformed and thus brought up-to-date with wider current social norms and mores.

The nature of this process, that is essentially dialectical in its realisation, can be summarised in the schematic mapped out in Figure 8.1. The dynamics of the model operate around connections being established between a set of foreground and background factors. The foreground triggers are aspects of the incident that are used to warrant and support the need for reform. But in order for these incident-relevant issues to gain political traction and impetus they need to connect with several background agendas. These allow the case in question to function in a manner akin to what Edelman (1964) dubs a 'condensation symbol', that is, through a particular set of circumstances, illuminating more general concerns.

The process by which reform of investigative policy and/or practice is instigated depends upon the presence of what Innes (2003) labels a 'pure victim'. The 'pure' victim is one who has not engaged in deviant behaviour in the past and who cannot be blamed for their victimisation. It is important to note that not all victims will be essentially pure, but this can be compensated for to a degree by the magnitude of the injustice that is done to them. Thus, if their treatment by the criminal justice system is particularly grievous, then they may still become suitable subjects for successful reform campaigns.

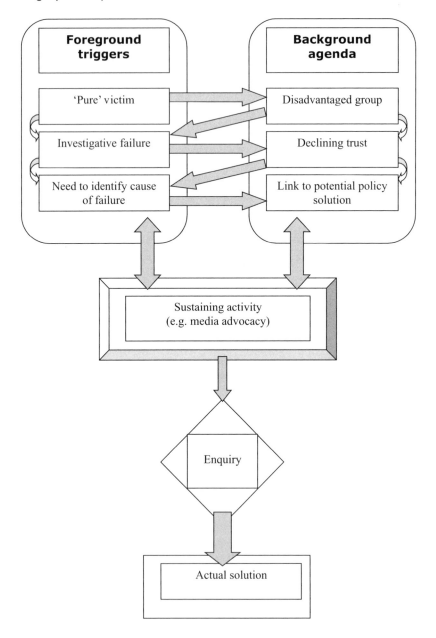

Figure 8.1 Dialectical investigative reform model

In order for the reform process to gain momentum the victim will have to be part of a disadvantaged group around whom concerns are already circulating. These concerns will focus both upon their position in society and also the response typically provided to them by agencies of the criminal justice process. The possible identification of an investigative failure in the specific case connects with the sense of disadvantage and stigma attached to this group, which in turn amplifies and reinforces a sense of declining trust among both the members of the group concerned and society more generally. It is important to note that any such sense of a decline in trust is not just a product of the specifics of the individual case, but that the circumstances of the case amplifies such perceptions. The final background agenda that comes into play is that there must be an existing recognition that in some way the causes of the failure of the specific case can be redressed by a particular policy solution that has already been recognised, albeit only by some people. As indicated by the smaller curved arrows in Figure 8.1, alongside the connections between the foreground triggers and background agendas, links will also exist between the factors that together make up the foreground and background to reform pressures.

In terms of converting these foreground and background factors into a campaign that generates some form of enquiry, the mass media play a key role in sustaining the impetus. In particular, media outlets can provide a voice to those who seek to contest the denials that are often initially registered by the police when confronted by accusations of failure. But media interventions are also effective when they focus upon various dimensions of the foreground triggers and background agendas and in the process sustain public and political interest in the case. In sustaining the momentum the necessary conditions are created where an inquiry is instigated. The inquiry will recommend some form of reforming solution to the specifics of the case in order to address the issues it raises. Importantly, though, the reform recommendations will have been foreshadowed by the potential policy solution that already exists as part of the background agenda. In an effort to trace the workings of this model more fully we shall examine the Yorkshire Ripper investigation (1969–1980) and Sir Lawrence Byford's report into its difficulties and problems.

The Yorkshire Ripper and the Byford Report

Peter Sutcliffe, whose crimes led to him being labelled the 'Yorkshire

Ripper', was eventually charged with 13 murders in 1981, following a police investigation that cost £4 million, involved 250 detectives and lasted five and a half years (Bland 1992). The first victims were prostitutes, but in June 1977 Jayne MacDonald was murdered, who according to Beattie (1981: 145) was 'an innocent, perfectly respectable woman'. This was important because 'at the time they were being slaughtered there seemed to be little sympathy for [the prostitute victims] ... not until Jayne MacDonald, the first of the innocent victims, was there any real public outcry' (Beattie 1981: 145). Thereafter, Beattie contends, media interest and criticism was sustained until the Ripper's arrest in 1981. Several of the victims' mothers (e.g. Irene MacDonald, Doreen Hill) mounted campaigns that stimulated further media attention. As is discussed in more detail below, there were also ongoing manoeuvres within the police service and the Home Office to develop computer applications to assist the police in their information management functions. The ingredients for the dialectical model to work were thus all present:

1 There were suitable vulnerable 'pure' victims.

2 They were members of an at risk and disadvantaged group (women).

3 The failures of the investigation were manifest in that the assailant was only caught after an extended period during which time additional victims were killed.

4 This failure of the police to provide appropriate levels of protective service contributed to a climate of fear and declining trust.

5 This amplified the need to find out why the police were unable to catch the perpetrator.

6 This was further stimulated by the presence of advocates (victims' mothers) who were provided a politically powerful voice via mass media coverage.

7 In addition there was a policy solution being actively promoted from within the police service – the better management and cross-referencing of information by means of computerisation of police data.

Interestingly, Ronald Gregory, the investigating force's chief constable, was quoted as saying, 'If we had known this investigation was going to reach such proportions we would have used a computer from the beginning' (Beattie 1981: 144).

Byford's (Home Office 1982) diagnosis of the problems pertaining to the investigation of the crimes committed included an explicit recommendation for the police to explore the potential for computer systems to assist in information management tasks on large-scale, complex investigations. It was a recommendation that contributed directly to the introduction of the Home Office Large Major Enquiry System – the computer system now routinely used for what Innes (2003) describes as 'investigation management' and 'information management' functions on more complex major crime investigations. But proposing such reform was not as radical as it might first appear, in that work to develop computer applications for policing had been ongoing for some time prior to the Byford Report.

In 1959 the Home Office set up the Joint Automatic Data Processing Unit, whose function was to introduce computers into British policing (Pounder 1985). Nothing much happened until the late 1960s when Roy Jenkins, then Home Secretary, visited the United States of America and was impressed by the role computers were playing in Police Departments there. He duly charged the Police Scientific and Development Branch to develop operational computer systems for the UK (Charlesworth and Hellawell 1979). In 1968 a national computer system was proposed and in 1972 the Police National Computer (PNC) was installed. Two trial projects were also initiated, a command and control application in Birmingham and a criminal intelligence system in Slough, in 1972 and 1977 respectively (Fraser 1978). By the early 1980s, 30 police forces had and were anticipating developing computer systems. Interestingly it was Special Branch who saw and made use of the intelligence capability, being four times more likely to access the PNC (Pounder 1985). Pounder also describes the Newman plan based upon the Metropolitan C computer, which was to be used as part of a strategy to contain crime based data on large scale surveillance of selected populations combined with rapid deployment to incidents in specific areas. Charlesworth and Hellawell (1979) noted the patchy take-up by forces and severe fiscal restraint by local and central government that frustrated further national developments. A succession of senior police officers wrote position papers advocating the introduction of national and integrated computer systems (e.g. Edwards 1971; Meadus 1973; Fraser 1978). The development of computer applications to assist in aspects of police work was ongoing then, but the Byford Inquiry provided a vehicle via which such claims could be advanced, perhaps more rapidly than they would otherwise have done.

If not wholly radical, then, Byford's focusing in upon this issue is nonetheless interesting because it foreshadowed subsequent wider societal debates about how public service organisations and institutions function in information-rich environments. The Home Office summary report in the Ripper investigation (the original full report remains unpublished) commented on the serious handicap created for the investigative process by unprocessed information and the lack of collation of connected information. Having identified an 'information overload' problem as central to the difficulties that were experienced, a number of Byford's key reform recommendations gravitated around this theme. Effectively, then, this represents an explicit and early linking of policing with the sorts of 'information age' themes that have come to be far more prevalent in recent years (cf. Castells 1997; Ericson and Haggerty 1997). The prescient insight that policing can and should seek to harness computer processing power to assist with processing large volumes of intelligence and information needs to be contextualised in terms of how information was being managed at the time, on massive index card systems. In certain aspects, then, the implementation of this aspect of Byford's recommendations is part and parcel of what Ericson and Shearing (1986) identify as a trend towards the 'scientification of policing'.

Byford's proposal to make better use of computer technology was also envisaged as a solution to the problems beginning to be encountered by policing resulting from greater geographical mobility in the population at large. One of the problems illuminated by the failings of the Ripper investigation was how police respond to crimes that cross jurisdictional borders (Egger 1990). The fact that Peter Sutcliffe was a travelling criminal, whose offending was not constrained to particular local areas, meant that the exchange of intelligence and evidence between several forces became an important factor in police being able to assemble an overarching understanding of the offences in question. This was a particular weakness identified by Byford, indeed there was a systemic condition of 'linkage blindness' evident in the police enquiries being split between several forces and agencies (Egger 1990). The identification of this problem provided an important signal to policing agencies about some of the problems they would face in the future should they not update and improve their information management storage and retrieval systems. Computers not only enabled more data to be stored and searched more effectively, they also embodied a potential for better information communication channels between agencies.

In accordance with the comments made at the start of this chapter, some of these themes about the conduct of policing have been revisited and revived more recently in the Bichard Report (2004) into the failings of police and other public agencies identified in the aftermath of the killings of Holly Wells and Jessica Chapman at Soham. Bichard identified a number of systemic failings in terms of the standard operating procedures underpinning police intelligence databases and how they store and exchange data. There are distinct echoes here of some of the findings associated with Byford some quarter of a century previously, but the change in context in which any such concerns are articulated is important. Byford was writing at a time when notions of computerisation and the capacities to process large amounts of data that computers provide were just beginning to manifest their consequences for organisational life. In effect, Byford was urging the police to take some tentative steps towards harnessing such information processing power and to integrate it into their working practices. In contrast, Bichard was writing at a time when computers have become a ubiquitous component of policing and part of how formal social control efforts are routinely enacted. Set against a period when concerns with and uses of intelligence have become more pronounced (Innes *et al.* 2005), and indeed the definition of police intelligence is in the process of being revised and widened (Ratcliffe forthcoming; Innes and Sheptycki 2004), Bichard's identification of a need for improvement in how intelligence data is handled and processed by policing organisations captures and refracts a potentially important shift in police practice.

Harnessing computer technologies was thus the solution proffered to the causes of investigative failure identified in the Yorkshire Ripper case. However, the definition of the problem was framed by a second background social agenda concerning gender politics and particularly second-wave feminism culminating in the 1975 Sex Discrimination Act (Heidensohn 1992). As women gained increasing rights to equality, so their treatment by public services and the quality of services provided to them came under increasing scrutiny. The police service had resisted the inclusion of female officers within the legislation and this case had resurfaced debates about the role of women in police and in society more generally (Brown and Heidensohn 2000).

Having outlined the key facets of the dialectics of investigative reform model, we will now apply it to a focus upon the Lawrence investigation in an effort to detail what insights it provides.

Investigative reform and the Stephen Lawrence case

Ben Bowling (cited in Rock 2004: 413) argues that in many ways Stephen Lawrence was an 'ideal' victim for the police, in that he was from a good family and had not himself been in trouble with the police. And yet, it is fairly conspicuous that in investigating his murder the police did not provide an adequate level of service. In terms of how events unfolded subsequently, Stephen's ethnicity was important because the failings in his particular case condensed and were emblematic of much wider failings in the police's treatment of black and minority ethnic people as victims of crime. As noted by both Bowling (1998) and Rock (2004), the political context surrounding the multiple disadvantages experienced by non-white people in Britain, both in terms of interactions with the criminal justice system and more widely, play an important part in framing how reactions to Stephen Lawrence's murder played out over time. Such issues were set against conditions in which there was a general decline in public trust in the police among the population, a trend particularly marked among young people from minority ethnic backgrounds (Bowling and Phillips 2002; Reiner 2000). Moreover, the advocacy of Stephen's mother Doreen was a key element in the amplification of the investigative failings. So again we can see the ingredients for this murder include:

1 A vulnerable and 'pure' victim.
2 He was a member of an at-risk and disadvantaged group (black youth).
3 The failures of the investigation were manifest in that the case against the assailants was woefully inadequate.
4 This failure of the police to provide appropriate levels of protective service contributed to a climate of fear and declining trust.
5 This amplified the need to find out why the police were unable to catch the perpetrators.
6 This was further stimulated by the presence of advocates (Doreen Lawrence – the victim's mother) who were provided with a politically powerful voice via mass media interest.
7 In addition there was a policy solution being actively promoted from within the police service – better training for investigating officers, improved management of investigations and development of the family liaison officer role.

The race component of the unfolding story was significant in further ways in that the attribution of the investigative failings by the Macpherson Report to processes of institutional racism established a connection to existing thoughts about the need to reform aspects of police practice and how police interact with minority ethnic communities. This aspect of the dialectical process of reform was not just about race, though; it also connected with a wider secondary agenda concerning the treatment of victims in the criminal justice process. This is reflected in the Macpherson Report's advocation of a more victim-centred approach to investigation that treats dealing with the concerns of those harmed by the crime as a matter on a par with identifying any suspects. One particular dimension to the solution proposed to this issue was the increased use of family liaison officers (FLOs) to support and help bereaved persons following a crime. But in keeping with the key facets of the reform model outlined, this was not necessarily a new development. Some forces had been using FLOs as part of their responses to major crimes for some time preceding Macpherson's intervention.

Conclusion

By their very nature, the inquiries that are launched into problematic major crime investigations, whether they be publicly or internally conducted, tend to have their horizons delimited by the need to identify the cause of and remedy to the immediate problems that are the focus of their remit. In so doing, though, there is a danger that their wider purpose and function is not illuminated. In this chapter we have argued that while inquiries into problematic major crime investigations do invoke reform in the pragmatics of detective work, they also perform a cultural role, inasmuch as they provide a vehicle for realigning the inherently conservative institution of policing with the social mores, values and norms of wider society.

According to this analysis, the political repercussions of the identified failings of the police investigation into Stephen Lawrence's murder were less significant in terms of understanding some of the difficulties associated with responding to contemporary major crime incidents, than with addressing how the standards and values of the police had effectively failed to adjust to the development of a multicultural society.

Subsequent to the publication of the Macpherson Inquiry's findings issues of race have been played out in two further recent inquiries into major investigations that have been publicly labelled as problematic.

But in the cases of Damilola Taylor and Victoria Climbié, the theme of race intermingles with concerns about the security of young people. In the Damilola Taylor case we see the murder of a young black boy that in terms of how it was reported in the mass media brings together, in a single narrative, cultural themes of insecurity to do with young people and the dangers of life in major urban areas. Similar themes resonate through the Victoria Climbié case, but an additional layer of complexity is evident and the public inquiry launched into it. The long-term abuse that she suffered at the hands of her aunt and her aunt's boyfriend bring to the fore concerns about the constitution of the family. But in the failure of the local social services to protect Victoria from this abuse, issues about the effectiveness of state agencies is once again evident. Harm to and the killing of children and the media narratives manufactured in respect of such cases often resonate with themes of 'innocence betrayed', and this is certainly the case in both the Taylor and Climbié cases. An important factor here, though, is how implicit cultural connections are developed over time, between what are otherwise unconnected cases. The Harper/ Maxwell/Hogg series of murders in the 1980s and the murders of Lin and Megan Russell in Kent in 1996 are both cases where this theme of innocence betrayed is encapsulated. They are also cases where concerns about the efficacy of the police investigations were voiced. These did not, however, gain traction because the perpetrators were eventually identified. However, by their presence, these precedent cases framed the production of narratives for the Taylor and Climbié cases. This is in accordance with the general thrust of the dialectical reform model outlined that suggests that a new permutation of the original crisis is likely to recur periodically.

A second thread to our argument has been that given this predisposition of inquiries into problematic investigations to focus upon single cases, the systemic nature of some of the problems pertaining to the conduct of major crime investigations remain unilluminated. If one compares and contrasts some of the issues that have been identified across a number of troublesome police investigations over the years there are a number of common themes present. The dialectical model developed in this chapter provides some insight into why some cases gain political traction and momentum leading to reform of policy and practice. Equally importantly, it predicts that the failure to enquire into the nature of the systemic tensions and stresses that bedevil how police investigate major crimes means that the Stephen Lawrence case will not be the last time when a victim is badly let down by the police investigation into their murder.

Note

1   See Rock (2004) for an analysis of the political campaign.

References

Beattie, J. (1981) *The Yorkshire Ripper Story*, London: Quartet Books/Daily Star.

Bichard, M. (2004) *The Bichard Inquiry Report*, London: HMSO.

Bowling, B. (1998) *Violent Racism: Victimization, Policing and Social Context*, Oxford: Clarendon Press.

Bowling, B. and Phillips, C. (2002) *Racism, Crime and Justice*, London: Longman.

Brown, J. and Heidensohn, F. (2000) *Gender and Policing*, London: Macmillan.

Castells, M. (1997) *The Network Society*, Oxford: Blackwells.

Charlesworth, A. and Hellawell, K. (1979) 'Police Technology in the 21st Century,' a paper presented to the 26th Annual Conference of the Police Superintendents' Association of England and Wales, Torquay 25th–26th September.

Douglas, M. and Wildavsky, A. (1983) *Risk and Culture*, Berkeley: University of California Press.

Edelman, M. (1964) *Symbolic Uses of Politics*, Urbana, IL: University of Illinois Press.

Edwards, T. (1971) 'Use of Computers in Operational Police Work', Bramshill papers from the 8th Intermediate Command Course.

Egger, S. (1990) 'Linkage Blindness: A Systemic Myopia', in S. Egger (ed.) *Serial Murder: An Elusive Phenomenon*. Westport, CT: Praeger.

Ericson, R. and Shearing, C. (1986) 'The Scientification of Police Work', in G. Bohme and N. Stehr (eds) *The Knowledge Society: The Growing Impact of Scientific Knowledge on Social Relations*, Dordrecht: D. Riedel, pp. 129–59.

Ericson, R. and Haggerty, K. (1997) *Policing the Risk Society*. Oxford: Clarendon Press.

Fraser, G. (1978) 'National Police Computer Plan', *Interface Quarterly*: 200–1.

Gowda, R. (2003) 'Integrating Politics with Social Amplification of Risk Framework; Insights from an Exploration in the Criminal Justice Context', in N. Pidgeon, R. Kasperson and P. Slovic (eds.) *The Social Amplification of Risk*, Cambridge: Cambridge University Press.

Gubrium, J. (2005) 'Introduction: Narrative Environments and Social Problems', *Social Problems* 52 (4): 525–28.

Heidensohn, F. (1992) *Women in Control*, Oxford: Clarendon.

Home Office (1982) *Yorkshire Ripper Case: Review of the Police Investigation by Sir Lawrence Byford*, London: Home Office.

Innes, M. (1999) 'Beyond Macpherson: Managing Murder Enquiries in Context', *Sociological Research Online*, 4 (1): http://socresonline.org.uk/4/1.

Innes, M. (2003) *Investigating Murder: Detective Work and the Police Response to Criminal Homicide*, Oxford: Clarendon Press.

Innes, M. (2004) 'Signal Crimes and Signal Disorders: Notes on Deviance as Communicative Action', *British Journal of Sociology*, 55 (3): 335–55.

Innes, M. and Sheptycki, J. (2004) 'From Detection to Disruption: Some Consequences of Intelligence-led Crime Control in the UK', *International Criminal Justice Review* 14: 1–14.

Innes, M., Fielding, N. and Cope N. (2005) 'The Appliance of Science: The Theory and Practice of Crime Intelligence Analysis', *British Journal of Criminology*, 45 (1): 39–57.

Loader, I. and Mulcahy, A. (2003) *Policing and the Condition of England*, Oxford: Clarendon Press.

Macpherson, W. (1999) *The Stephen Lawrence Inquiry: Report of an Inquiry Led by Sir William Macpherson of Cluny*, CM 4262-1, London: HMSO.

Meadus, D. (1973) 'The Developing Use of Computers in the Police Service,' Bramshill Papers from 19th Intermediate Command Course.

Pidgeon, N., Kasperson, R., and Slovic, P. (eds) (2003) *The Social Amplification of Risk*, Cambridge: Cambridge University Press.

Pounder, C. (1985) *Police Computers and the Metropolitan Police*, London: Greater London Council.

Punch, M. (2000) 'Police Corruption and its Prevention', *European Journal on Criminal Policy and Research*, 8 (3): 301–24.

Punch, M. (2003) 'Rotten Orchards: "Pestilence", Police Misconduct and System Failure', *Policing and Society*, 13 (2): 171–96.

Ratcliffe, J. (forthcoming) Intelligence Led Policing, in Williamson, T. (ed.) *The Handbook of Knowledge Based Policing*, Chichester: Wiley.

Reiner, R. (2000) *The Politics of the Police*, 3rd edn, Oxford: Oxford University Press.

Rock, P. (2004) *Constructing Victim's Rights*, Oxford: Clarendon Press.

Slovic, P. (2000) *The Perception of Risk*, New York: Earthscan Books.

Chapter 9

View from within: the realities of promoting race and diversity inside the police service

Brian Holland

There is no doubt that the police service has made significant progress in the area of race equality in recent years. However, there is still a long way to go ... Willingness to change at the top is not translating into action lower down, particularly in middle management where you find the ice in the heart of the police service ... (Commission for Racial Equality press statement, 8 March 2005)

This perceptive 'ice in the heart' observation from the Commission for Racial Equality (CRE), coming as it did at the end of its 12-month investigation into the police service, perfectly summarises the author's feelings as to the progress of the police service post-Lawrence. It is also an appropriate starting point for a chapter which reflects on the turbulent five-year career of a 'race equality' specialist working with Greater Manchester Police (GMP), and hopefully provides both encouragement and direction for 'diversity' specialists and police personnel alike. However, before doing so, it is necessary to go back to the 'heady days' of the Lawrence Inquiry itself and, in particular, the day David Wilmot, the former GMP Chief Constable, made his famous (though some would say infamous) comments about racism. Those remarks made in October 1998 – accepting the concept of 'institutional racism' in the police – were of truly 'seismic' proportions in the context of the Lawrence Inquiry; this is how one police magazine summarised the occasion at the time:

> David Wilmot, Chief Constable of GMP, provoked much
> comment with his statement that the police ... has institutional
> racism ... [but] ... local Police Federation chairman Mike Huby
> said 'Many officers are hurt that their chief constable is saying
> that racism is institutionalised in the force, because by that he is
> implying that everybody in the force is a racist.' (*Police Review*,
> October 1998, p. 2)

This extract sums up the mood of the period and encapsulates the
strains that existed between the GMP hierarchy and the Federation at
the time. Indeed, such tensions were to remain in this delicate area
for the remainder of David Wilmot's leadership up to his retirement
in September 2002. It was an occasion that would also prove a
landmark in my own career. In 1998 I was working for the CRE in
Leeds and recall vividly the reaction of colleagues as they perused
the newspaper headlines at the time. Everyone was amazed – and
impressed – that the chief constable of England's second largest
police force would go public in that way. Less than two years later I
was appointed as 'race advisor' to GMP.

This chapter therefore attempts to capture the experiences of a
'diversity' specialist taking the plunge into the world of policing;
a world that was quite alien after almost 20 years with the CRE.
However, it was the prospect of working for a progressive
constabulary that proved crucial and the opportunity to work for a
police leader who was brave enough to publicly dissent from most
of his Association of Chief Police Officers (ACPO) colleagues on
the most controversial issue post-Lawrence – 'institutional racism'.
Moreover, what better opportunity for an old CRE 'campaigner' to
promote liberal CRE thinking and good practice within the inner
sanctum of senior police management?

There were to be few regrets. Indeed, it proved an eventful
five years punctuated with moments of high drama – notably
Mark Daly's revelations in *The Secret Policeman* BBC documentary,
discussed at greater length later in this chapter – but all eventually
culminating in positive fashion with the creation of a permanent
corporate Diversity Command Unit, which was clearly lacking for
most of my time with GMP. The reader will therefore be taken on
a five-year journey identifying the challenges facing a newcomer to
the police culture and the struggles to get race and diversity centre
stage in an environment where such issues were often pushed to the
periphery. The chapter further considers the lessons to be drawn from
a 'short-termist' culture that has historically resisted the allocation of

sustainable resources in this crucial area of business for the police. The chapter considers in some detail not only GMPs specific response to the Macpherson Report, Operation Catalyst, but also a significant later initiative, the Respect Programme, both of which played their part in finally positioning 'diversity' issues as core business within GMP. Finally, it will be argued that a key feature of GMP's modest success has been the adoption of 'action plans' that are not only practical and meaningful in policing terms but also overtly harnessed to the commitments of chief officers. It is suggested that the strategy adopted by GMP in this regard offers some chance of success for a police culture historically dogged by cynicism, indifference and poor organisational memory.

History, culture and memory loss

What does seem indisputable is that ... an attitude of suspicion and mistrust has grown up between the police and the immigrant communities – this ironically at a time when the police are trying to bring about a better understanding between themselves and immigrant groups.

This *Guardian* newspaper extract dated 10 July 1969 refers to a report published that year by the Institute of Race Relations and reminds us that the public debate about the poor relationship between the police and the minority ethnic communities surfaced in Britain well before the Macpherson Report in 1999 and, indeed, the earlier report by Lord Scarman in 1981, both of which are recognised as seminal landmarks in this debate. Moreover, this reference perfectly encapsulates what has become a tired (some might say tiresome) observation that the police are forever trying to bring about improvements but seem forever dogged by failure.

The Institute's 1969 research, published as *Colour, Citizenship and British Society* (Deakin 1970), captured the experiences of those early migrants living in Britain who were identified as struggling against discrimination in many aspects of their daily lives including housing, employment, health, public services; and where a poor relationship with the police was already being cited as a significant factor in that experience (Deakin 1970: 251–8). The report's references to police training are particularly revealing and could so easily have appeared in the covers of the Macpherson Report a generation later. The outdated terminology is a give-away but that aside, the issues are all too familiar. Significantly, the report makes an explicit link with racism by citing Hunte's 1965 polemic, *Nigger Hunting in England?*, which alleged overt police brutality inside the police service at that time (Deakin 1970: 244). It also referred to the 1958 disturbances in Notting Hill, London (1970: 248) where inaction by the police to combat racial attacks by 'teddy boys' was an issue at the time (Hiro 1973: 55; Hall 1978: 23; Gilroy 1982: 143; Fryer 1984: 391).

Given these historical references, it therefore appears that this poor relationship has persisted for over 40 years (Jefferson and Walker 1993; Lambert 1970; Lea 1986; McLaughlin and Cashmore 1991); moreover, as Benyon observed back in the 1980s, even then this relationship was being dubbed a 'tale of failure' (Benyon 1986). This is all sobering stuff and judging by more recent examinations it is a 'gulf' still to be bridged (Rowe 2004: 1).

At the time of David Wilmot's speech in 1998, I was working in the CRE's legal department, and also completing a part-time doctorate with Bradford University around the issue of racial harassment in football (Holland 1995 1997 1999); but career-wise a new challenge beckoned. At that time, an opportunity arose to move away from litigation and transfer across to work on implementing the Macpherson Report. In doing so, this involved delving back into the history of the relationship between the police and ethnic minority communities. From this research it became clear that, historically, three themes recur when examining the link between racism and the police (Benyon 1986; Foot 1965; IRR 1979; Macpherson 1999; Scarman 1981). First, there was a perception among the minority ethnic communities that they have been (and remain?) over-policed – with the use of stop and search powers doubtless most notable; second, the belief that the service under-police minority communities – particularly in terms of their investigation of race hate crime; and third, the extent to which there exists an underlying racist culture inside the police service which, ideologically, sustains the other two elements and which, between them, thereby both discourages minorities from joining the police and makes life difficult for those that do. Thus, collectively, these three elements have historically led to a breakdown in the 'trust and confidence' that ethnic minority communities have in the police service; and thus a key tenet of British policing – 'consensus policing' (Scarman 1981: 62–3) is totally undermined. These three elements, expressed as a pictorial 'three-piece puzzle', have thus sustained and guided my approach and direction to these issues ever since.

Much has been written about police culture (Adlam and Villiers 2002; Coleman and Gorman 1982; Gilroy 1982; Reiner 2000; Rowe 2004;

Sanders and Young 2000; Waddington 1999a) and some specifically in the context of tackling racism. As Rowe (2004: 43) has rightly pointed out, 'police culture ... needs to be understood in broader and more complex terms if efforts to overcome racism within the service are to succeed'. One aspect of that culture, often neglected in the literature, is the endemic 'short-termist' approach in the service which leads to what will be termed organisational 'memory loss'. This feature of its culture obviously reflects its function as an emergency service that, by its very nature has to cope with crises on a daily basis, whether it is road accidents, murder scenes or terrorist attacks, and every police officer is trained to instinctively know what to do and how to cope in such situations. However, such admirable skills unfortunately have a downside. They inevitably encourage a *modus operandi* preoccupied with the now and the immediate; once a crisis or incident is over, the culture encourages everyone to move on to the next 'job' – to use policing parlance. This explains why the police so often seem to revisit issues in cyclical fashion. Therefore, the way the police have handled the relationship between itself and the ethnic minority communities has followed this pattern. The police service has seemingly never grasped the simple lesson that dealing with relationships and issues around trust and confidence are qualitatively not the same as dealing with road accidents, terrorist attacks or public order disturbances. Thus, what is being suggested is that such failings are inherent to a culture that easily 'forgets' the issues and lessons of yesterday.

What follows is an account of how one police force – Greater Manchester Police – boldly faced up to the challenge of race and diversity issues, then embarked on a series of predictably short-term projects and operations that falsely treated reports such as that from the Lawrence Inquiry as 'critical incidents', with all the attending crisis management techniques. As a consequence there is evidence that in this regard the police appear unable to grasp the long-term logic that flows from such reports, particularly in terms of sustained resources and consistent expertise.

The rise and fall of Operation Catalyst

On 24 February 1999, on the publication of the Macpherson Report, David Wilmot followed up his famous 1998 speech by going public again, but this time to announce the launch of Operation Catalyst – an internal project to follow up the report's 70 recommendations. The word 'catalyst' had been chosen because it had been used by

Jack Straw, the Home Secretary at the time, as he presented the Macpherson Report to Parliament and expressed the hope that the report would act as a 'catalyst for change'. The chief constable re-emphasised his commitment, declaring in devotional terms: 'I will do all in my power to carry through what needs to be done to limit and eradicate racism within GMP.' David Wilmot had clearly 'nailed his colours to the mast' and seemed determined to make this issue a defining feature of his remaining leadership of GMP.

Operation Catalyst consisted of a dedicated project team of five under the day-to-day management of a superintendent. Overall, the project team was answerable to a Project Board chaired by the deputy chief constable and consisted of representatives from key departments across GMP, the Police Authority, all the staff associations including the Black and Asian Police Association, and two lay members chosen by an existing long-standing community-based advisory group – the Policy Advisory Committee on Race Issues (PAC). Key to Operation Catalyst was the creation of 23 sub-projects which between them embraced all 70 recommendations contained in Macpherson. On being launched, the Operation Catalyst project team embarked on a 'scoping study' of the Macpherson Report plus additional recommendations from the HMIC report published around the same time, *Winning the Race – Revisited* (HMIC 1999). Having scoped all these recommendations, it was the Catalyst project team's role to liaise with the appropriate departments to negotiate respective responsibilities for each sub-project activity and agree appropriate terms of reference. This exercise seemingly created tensions between the Catalyst project team, as the 'driving' element in the process, and individual departments, which were expected to take appropriate action and allocate resources to 'deliver' tangible outcomes. All the indications are that some departments perceived this as 'extra' work for which they had insufficient resources, time and expertise. Within a 'diversity' environment, this was an early attempt to mainstream equality across the organisation and it was met with significant resistance.

The Project Board met once a month, when departmental representatives were required to provide updates on their respective sub-projects assisted by the project team. The system adopted was known as 'exception reporting'. This involved providing written reports prepared by the project team in liaison with departments on each of the 23 sub-projects, and these were intended to provide updates on progress. However, this methodology ultimately proved problematic and for some departments, a convenient means of masking progress. However, in their defence, some departments were genuinely left struggling to cope with minimum in-house expertise and inconsistent support from a Catalyst team itself struggling at times to cope with the demands of dozens of departments eagerly seeking guidance and support.

During this period I was a lay member of the Catalyst Project Board, at that time representing the CRE, though chosen by a vote of the community consultation group (the PAC); the other lay member on the Board was the TUC representative on the group. The amount of paperwork that flowed through that Project Board was considerable even on the basis of an 'exception reporting' method and it was clear that real difficulties were surfacing about the progress of some of the sub-projects. One difficulty was that there was little regard as to which sub-projects were of most importance. In truth, some sub-projects were implicitly more important than others – for example, race hate crime, stop and search and HR issues around recruitment and retention as well as discipline and complaints. However, this was never made explicit; for it seemed important to the Project Board to retain pressure on all sub-projects to avoid 'slippage' by some sub-projects becoming labelled as less important. In any event, the end result was that Catalyst had created a juggernaut of a project, that was ideologically sound but one that had an inherent long-term logic that would never be properly recognised and/or acknowledged.

One of the sub-projects had the remit to appoint a force race advisor at assistant director level. The rationale behind this appointment was two-fold. First, this senior advisor would be a key member of the Catalyst project team, as long as it was operating; and second, the post would thereafter be the focus for future race equality work. I successfully applied for this post and commenced on 1 June 2000. On being appointed, I became an integral part of the Catalyst project team. A key part of the role was not to 'sell' the Catalyst 'product' but rather to promote the individual role of force race advisor itself. The significance of this emphasis did not become apparent until later. Throughout the summer of 2000 I designed and delivered a series of presentations and briefings across the organisation. This included departments with responsibility for the Catalyst sub-projects and the territorial divisions in localities including Bolton, Oldham and Stockport, and liaising with locally-based community and race relations officers. Such appointments had existed since the mid-1990s and were innovative for their time. However, their status and role was often ill-defined though they were at least a permanent specialist local divisional resource.

These briefings, entitled 'Towards a New Policing Culture', were designed to explicitly connect with the Lawrence Report and to implicitly incorporate the analysis described earlier. These briefing sessions inevitably touched upon some potentially sensitive issues – not least of these was 'institutional racism' – but all the areas covered were intended to show a pathway towards greater credibility for the police service and gaining the trust and confidence of minority ethnic communities. The sessions covered police culture (and therefore 'institutional racism'), the handling of race hate crime, stop and search, diversity training, minority ethnic recruitment, retention and progression, 'complaints and discipline', and community consultation as the key elements. There were many challenges along the way – some openly questioned the validity and usefulness of the concept of 'institutional racism' and the wisdom of the chief constable's remarks in this regard. For the most part, the presentations were met with polite applause at their conclusion, but there was a distinct lack of genuine enthusiasm. Worryingly, there was a good deal of negativity about Operation Catalyst and much suspicion as to the role and motives of their newly appointed force race advisor from the CRE. However, the post had the personal blessing of the chief constable as he regularly reinforced both privately and publicly. That support was perhaps most explicit on 22 August 2000 when a community consultation conference was held entitled 'Operation Catalyst – One Year On'. On this occasion David Wilmot openly endorsed the new race advisor appointment and described it as one of the 'successes' of the Catalyst initiative. It was at this point that it became apparent that much (indeed too much) was being invested in the force race advisor role. However, during his 'one year on' speech, the chief constable significantly highlighted those sub-projects that interestingly reflected my 'three-piece puzzle' and confirmed the extent to which David Wilmot was clearly tuned in to the 'big issues'. His speech thus referred to a new race hate crime 'investigation model', increased diversity training, setting up a new stop and search project board, enhanced status of community beat officers and the creation of a new 'positive action team' within the HR domain to push issues concerning ethnic minority recruitment, retention and progression. However, significantly, the speech made no explicit reference to 'institutional racism' but instead couched racism within a more orthodox and predictable context, as follows:

> I know it will be your fervent wish, as it is mine, that we continue to work together to rid our society of race and hate

crime. For my part, I make no apology for repeating what I said last year, and will continue to say, that I will do all in my power to ... limit and eradicate racism within GMP. (*Manchester Evening News*, 23 August 2000)

A subtle change of emphasis was thus detected with further references to 'institutional racism' by the chief constable becoming less frequent thereafter. Between the August 2000 community conference and the following November, there would also be a significant shift in the respective profiles of Operation Catalyst and the force race advisor with the centre of gravity clearly shifting from the former to the latter as the decision to wind up the Catalyst project team took effect.

Clearly, within police parlance, the word 'operation' within Operation Catalyst was always going to imply something short-term and temporary. Therefore, within six months of David Wilmot addressing his community audience, Operation Catalyst, as a key corporate resource, would cease, with the exception of the race advisor. Moreover, to reinforce the 'memory loss' thesis, all the Catalyst project team members – by then very knowledgeable and fully up to speed on all aspects of the Lawrence issues – were moved on to other work. One officer went to the traffic section, another to become a detective PC, yet another to head up the domestic violence team. But this is the way of things in the police service: a crisis is identified, temporary resources are allocated and then, having done the 'job', everyone 'moves on'. It is no wonder that some members of the Black and Asian Police Association (BAPA) at GMP were sceptical of the Catalyst initiative. As the former BAPA chair later observed:

Although no formal audit of the Catalyst [project] outcome has been conducted to date, it is [my] view that the reviews and studies carried out by the sub-project teams are more rhetoric than real. (Harding 2003: 84)

By the time the Catalyst team was fully dispersed in November 2000, I was still naively confident that the 23 sub-projects, created as part of the overall Catalyst project, could continue and ultimately deliver reforms on a mainstreaming basis. Instead, however, the overall Catalyst enterprise subsequently faded with only a limited amount achieved. There were some traces left from the Catalyst landscape, notably a progressive race hate crime investigative model, a separately resourced positive action team in the HR domain and a revitalised Equal Opportunities Unit. However, notwithstanding these features, the force race advisor was thereafter to be the main 'torchbearer' for the Catalyst 'spirit' within GMP senior management. The Catalyst sub-projects continued in name only with *ad hoc* reporting to the Policy Advisory Committee on Race Issues. In reality, however, with the dismantling of the Catalyst Project Board the accountability aspect had all but gone and no formal audit would take place until 2003 when the ghost of Catalyst would reappear in the aftermath of the next crisis – *The Secret Policeman* documentary.

Riots, reforms and regime change

With the Operation Catalyst team ending its work, the overall project remained thereafter like the spectre at the feast, with the author becoming the main driver for race equality and diversity at senior management level. Notwithstanding the resource situation, a series of key initiatives were set in motion, not least of which would focus on the reforms arising from the 2000 Race Relations (Amendment) Act. It was judged that work around this Act could become a major opportunity to sell the race equality 'product' to senior and middle management and 2001 was therefore anticipated to be an important year in that regard. However, unforeseen events across the Atlantic and on the western edges of the Pennine Hills, between them scuppered all plans in this regard. The Oldham riots of May 2001 and the September 11 attacks in New York both, in their different ways, raised yet new issues to add to the 'diversity' agenda for the police service. In this case it was the implications of policing fragmented, segregated communities and the relationship with Muslim communities that was to become the big national debate; all of which would yet again bring resources and expertise back into focus.

In spring 2001, two big legislative reforms were in the pipeline. First, there was the proposal to make chief constables vicariously liable for the behaviour of their officers, and second, the introduction of race equality schemes for the whole of the public sector, including the police service. These reforms were embodied in the Race Relations (Amendment) Act 2000 and between them the Home Office and CRE were determined to maximise their impact (Home Office 2001; CRE 2001a, 2001b, 2001c). Indeed, it was to be a constant strand of activity right through to 2005, though the extent to which this would be so could not have been predicted in 2001. The 2000 Act introduced a battery of new legal commitments for the public sector, including a demand to publish race equality schemes from 1 June 2002. Few had had any experience of such schemes, which according to CRE briefings in February 2001 were a product of the Northern Ireland equalities experience (CRE 2001d; McNaney 2001). The force race advisor took responsibility to lead on this, and by March 2001 a series of road-show appearances were being delivered on the implications of the 2000 Act for key departmental managers along with press articles (Holland 2001a, 2001b).

However, this process was abruptly interrupted and temporarily abandoned in May 2001 with the eruption of disturbances in Oldham. I was dispatched to the town on a trouble-shooting mission to try to uncover the underlying causes of the riots and to make recommendations for GMP. This was given increased urgency when the government announced a publicly funded review of the disorders (Ritchie 2001). My three-month research in Oldham was effectively a revisit to a town where two CRE investigations in the early 1990s had already detected fragmentation and segregation. One inquiry involved Oldham Council (CRE 1993) and the other a private estate agent company (CRE 1990); both of these focused on the allocation of housing in the town that was serving to separate communities. To return to Oldham after ten years was to rediscover this process of separation and dislocation, which had intensified in the intervening decade. The report produced for GMP attempted to put the disturbances and community policing in a socio-economic and cultural context and it was submitted to the Ritchie Independent Review panel as an independent paper separate from that prepared on behalf of the chief constable (Holland 2001c). The paper referred to the CRE's earlier investigations and developed a spatial analysis of race hate crime in the town using analytical tools developed by Webster (2001a, 2001b). Overall, the paper concluded that each public agency had to take responsibility for each aspect of the town's governance and socio-economic well-being; thus, just because social fractures become manifest through public order disturbances, this did not make the police service overwhelmingly and/or automatically culpable for what happened. In short, I concluded that Oldham's experience was not mirroring the disturbances of the early 1980s in Brixton, Toxteth, Moss Side and elsewhere when policing methods were overtly connected with public ill-feeling (Holland 2001c, 2001e, 2002b).

At the end of this period – in October 2002 – a new regime was ushered in and the Wilmot era of leadership came to an end. Michael Todd's arrival as Chief Constable marked an important and significant moment with respect to GMP's direction and style in the race and diversity sphere. Mr Todd had been with the Metropolitan Police and had therefore observed the Lawrence Inquiry from close quarters. He had no apparent previous connection with GMP and, inevitably within the culture of the police, the new leader was going to inject new thinking and ideas; i.e. the previous regime was now history and a new reign had begun. One of the key questions that seemed to be on everyone's lips when Michael Todd began was whether he subscribed to the concept of 'institutional racism'. All the indications were that Mr Todd wanted to talk in different terms from David Wilmot – his preoccupation was with fairness and discrimination rather than racism or sexism, and so on, whether that be internal to GMP or in terms of policing methods on the street. Michael Todd was clearly more interested in the overall concept of 'institutional discrimination' and encouraged work towards developing an overarching Diversity/Equalities Scheme to eventually incorporate the current Race Equality Scheme.

This initiative would eventually lead to a draft Diversity Scheme being published for public consultation and evaluated at a community seminar on 21 October 2003. Coincidentally, this would be the day the BBC broadcast *The Secret Policeman* documentary. In the meantime, the new Chief Constable was clearly under heavy pressure, which was reflected in public reports at the time (HMIC 2003b) and very obviously his preoccupation was with performance-related indicators around crime and detection. This heralded the creation of a 'GRIP' (Greater Manchester Review to Improve Performance) process to drive managerial reforms and structural changes within GMP. GRIP is a regime where all senior managers – particularly commanders on division – are held to account on a monthly basis on all aspects of their performance in fighting crime in their localities. On the face of it, this overtly quantitatively driven approach appears adrift from the qualitative tendencies of 'diversity', but there are some connections and this approach was instrumental in the creation of the Diversity Command unit in April 2005, which boldly would attempt to inject performance-related concepts as part of the new unit's approach.

However, much was going to happen in the intervening two years that no one could have predicted – except perhaps the producers at the BBC in London! For as the year of 2003 dawned, few were aware that a previously obscure journalist, Mark Daly, was secretly preparing to join the ranks of probationer constables with Greater Manchester Police and things would never quite be the same again.

The year 2003 began quietly enough in diversity terms; the GMP

Race Equality Scheme (RES) was up and running and I was still touring the force with a presentation about the 2000 Act and GMP's RES; a new RES monitoring officer had been appointed, a working group was drafting an overarching Diversity Scheme and, in addition, a new computer-based Diversity Knowledge Bank was being designed to replace a conventional customs and culture booklet. However, by May 2003 rumblings were beginning to be heard in South Manchester as the HMIC completed a local divisional or Basic Command Unit (BCU) inspection and suddenly police culture was back on the agenda. Paragraph 1.55 of the report pulled few punches:

> The inspection team encountered a male dominated culture within the BCU. This was manifest by sexist jokes, sexual innuendo and banter, and exclusionary language. This was compounded by, on occasions, a lack of sensitivity in relation to respecting dignity of others specifically with reference to rank/ grade, race and culture. (HMIC 2003a: 14)

This was serious stuff and the repercussions were to go well beyond the South Manchester BCU, not least because the same paragraph went on to refer specifically to the 2000 Act, stating, 'Knowledge and awareness of the Race Relations (Amendment) Act and its practical application was low' (HMIC 2003a: 14). This was HQ territory and it appeared that the RES briefings designed and delivered by the force race advisor had not adequately influenced middle management and the HMIC were clearly dissatisfied that the 2000 Act reforms were not being taken seriously. By the summer of 2003, it became clear that the *ad hoc* reactive culture within GMP was beginning to become exposed publicly. By this time I had been given a permanent contract but the race advisor brief had been extended to embrace the wider spectrum of diversity beyond race – it was now 'race and diversity' advisor.

At this point – summer 2003 – the vision of a dedicated Diversity Unit of some kind being created to properly drive all these crucial issues still seemed remote, but this HMIC BCU report into South Manchester, with hindsight, represents a significant juncture.

The Secret Policeman: the new catalyst?

Rumours about an undercover journalist infiltrating GMP began circulating in August 2003 and, as a consequence, the crisis management apparatus swung into action to manage what was regarded as a 'critical incident'. This included setting up a Gold Group to run the process, which is standard procedure inside the police service to handle major incidents. A Gold Group is very much the inner sanctum and, for example, it is very rare for there to be any outside lay involvement. However, on this occasion an exception was made and the Director of the Manchester Community Relations Council participated in the group meetings to provide external advice and counsel. Key to the discussions were the impact on the community, GMP's overall credibility and the way GMP was to control information in the wake of an inevitable media frenzy.

This chapter does not attempt to retrace in any detail the complex build-up to the eventual broadcast of the *The Secret Policeman* television documentary on 21st October 2003, except to suggest that two camps had quickly formed as to the rights and wrongs of what the BBC had done. There were those who clearly felt morally outraged by the BBC's tactics; while others felt that it was part of the BBC's public service broadcasting remit to expose any racism in the culture of the police. The date of the broadcast was known in advance and GMP's attempts to get the broadcast shelved proved fruitless. Indeed, I did not support such attempts, believing that it would prove counterproductive. It was clearly more important to focus on the substance of the revelations rather than questioning the BBC's motives and tactics in making the documentary. Ultimately, the revelations were dramatic and overt racism was displayed, not least the antics of the probationer from North Wales police wearing the infamous improvised Ku Klux Klan pillowcase hood. As cited earlier, on the day of the broadcast – 21 October – GMP had already arranged a community consultation day to consider a draft Diversity Scheme for GMP; but the day's events were unsurprisingly overshadowed by intense apprehension as to what would be revealed in the programme and what it could mean for GMP's reputation.

The mood in GMP in the aftermath of the TV broadcast was decidedly gloomy and there was some speculation as to why the BBC had chosen GMP as its target. It was widely accepted that the remarks by David Wilmot in 1998 about 'institutional racism' had been key; and thus the ghost of Catalyst once again appeared. Within days of the 21 October broadcast, Operation Catalyst files were being re-evaluated and sub-projects reports reassessed. By November 2003, I was advising on the creation of a Catalyst Revisited project (Holland 2003), and by December this had been reformulated as the Respect Programme, with the words 'operation' and 'project' being deliberately avoided; the word 'programme' had been preferred as a means of encouraging longevity to the life of any new team. In many ways the Respect Programme team and the Respect Board to which it was accountable, was reminiscent of Operation Catalyst and the Catalyst Board and this could so easily have become the usual short-term project with a limited lifespan of a couple of years. However, the force race and diversity advisor was determined that history would not repeat itself. In the event, the Respect Programme genuinely turned out to be a very different type of project from Catalyst. The word 'respect' was chosen to connect directly with the behaviour displayed in the BBC documentary, which provided ample evidence of 'disrespect' (Holland 2003 2004). The significance of the 'respect' was not lost on an organisation that was very conscious of GMP's direct connection with these very public events – it had not happened at the Met but on GMP's own doorstep and that was very significant.

The Respect Programme's aims were 'to value and promote diversity in GMP; actively tackle exclusionary behaviour; and respect and respond appropriately to the needs of all our communities' (Holland 2003). In addition, however, the new initiative introduced a new dimension that was missing within Operation Catalyst – a personal commitment which stated that 'it is the responsibility of every member of GMP's staff to (1) respect and respond to each person's needs; and (2) identify and actively challenge exclusionary behaviour' (Holland 2003 2004). As will be suggested, although many of the substantive activities carried out by the Respect Programme team were not dissimilar to those carried out by the original Catalyst team some four years earlier, significantly the tone and language of the Respect Programme would prove more appealing, more relevant and had a greater ability to capture the imagination of a team of chief officers moving very gradually towards accepting the need to put the 'diversity dimension' within its core business. Ironically, it was the race element that would again prove controversial and a vehicle that this GMP regime would not have naturally chosen; but to its great credit, GMP grasped the nettle on this occasion.

As the Respect Programme was being assembled in November 2003, the Commission for Racial Equality (CRE) was preparing to investigate related matters. The Commission had noted the posture of ACPO and the HMIC at the national level and appeared to have concluded that there would never be a better opportunity to conduct an investigation into the police service. And this was reinforced by a national debate that was beginning to take hold post-*Secret Policeman* around the theme: how can we stop racists joining the police? It was a theme that was to preoccupy a key element of the CRE's 2004 investigation and, once again, it is the nature of police culture that reappears.

The CRE investigation was to be in two parts, with the interim report being produced in June 2004 and a final draft by March 2005. In terms of headlines it was the earlier interim version that captured the media's attention, focusing as it did on the CRE's analysis of a sample of police and police authority 'race equality schemes'. Not surprisingly, GMP was in the sample, and under new powers given to the Commission under the 2000 Act, GMP's scheme (and that of others) was deemed partially 'non-compliant'. Moreover, along with other forces in the sample, a 90-day deadline was set to rewrite RES documents to make them legally compliant under the 2000 Act. It was a demanding deadline but one that was met by GMP. On this occasion, resources were available within the Respect Programme team to assist in the rewrite and this was significant. This was further aided by the Respect Team assisting on other important areas of work, not least of which was the ACPO Race Equality Action Plan (ACPO 2004) drafted by a nationally co-ordinated team. All of this gradually built up pressure for permanent resources to be made available once the Respect Programme had run its course. Some chief officers were still pushing for a minimalist approach; others in the command were pushing for a more substantive team. Significantly the label 'diversity' was to be introduced to replace 'respect' and the word 'command' to provide the new unit with status and an overt connection with chief officers.

Diversity Command emerges

Between January and April 2005, interdepartmental negotiations took place to determine the resources and structure of a new entity to drive race and diversity issues at HQ level. It was clearly going to absorb most of the existing Respect Programme team plus additional staff from related departments, all to be headed by a Director of Diversity directly managed and accountable to an assistant chief constable. This would be crucial in terms of the credibility of the new unit and its ability to influence and promote change across the organisation. Hence there was clearly a 'symbolic' aspect to the role of this new entity: its very existence and attachment to chief officers was sending out a clear and unambiguous signal that diversity issues were now part of GMP's core business. Indeed, this is what was lacking when the post of force race advisor was created under the Catalyst regime in 2000: that post had the right symbolism but it lacked proper support and resources to go with it.

However, the allocation of permanent resources and their connection with command level would only fulfil one aspect of its status and credibility. Additionally, any new unit would need to sell itself as something that was practical and supportive as well as being expert in its field. This aspect became apparent during a series of briefings sessions for senior managers organised in the period between January and March 2005 in the wake of the CRE investigation (CRE 2004 2005) and the Morris Inquiry Report (Morris 2004). The briefings also ran parallel to the distribution of a *Race Equality Scheme Workbook* (GMP 2005b) distributed and completed by every member of GMP's staff in that period and with time officially allocated to complete the task. The briefings to senior staff and the workbook were opportunities to sell the moral, business and legal context of diversity. However, in doing so it became apparent as to what makes police middle management sit up and listen; it is certainly not any hint of morality nor, surprisingly, so much the legal dimension. Rather, it is the 'business' case that was most appealing; in policing terms, this translates as operational policing or performance-related activities (Holland 2005b). Thus it was clear that any new resources allocated, no matter how large or small, would need to have a supportive and practical role *vis-à-vis* 'real' policing work, if diversity was ever going to connect and sell itself within the organisational culture.

With these important considerations in mind, the structure of the Diversity Command unit had to be appropriately structured to appeal to a middle management culture sceptical of such initiatives, as was highlighted by the CRE (CRE 2005). Learning the lessons from the Operation Catalyst experience, it was important that while promoting the concept of mainstreaming and local ownership, departments and local BCU divisions would need direct assistance to review their own domains in diversity and equality terms; and this would prove to be a key role for the Diversity Command Unit. To promote diversity locally every BCU division and department would appoint a Diversity Champion to liaise with HQ's unit and set up local Diversity Action Groups (DAGs) to drive and monitor local work. Therefore, each local area or individual department would retain ownership and control of their diversity work carried out, but with the back-up of expertise and practical help from the Diversity Command Unit. Within the unit itself this function would be undertaken by a Field

Action and Support Team (FAST) working to a Local Diversity Work Template: Minimum Standards (Holland 2005a). A key feature of the template is its attempt to enhance the credibility and status of the exercise and to put diversity work in policing language by stating that tasks contribute to: 'aiding the delivery of improved performance and operational effectiveness'. This proved to be well received and a simple breakthrough in making diversity issues real, understandable and acceptable to middle management culture. The template's suggested areas of activity were not overtly prescriptive, nor overtly political in their direction or tone. For example, the BCU divisional version made specific reference to the need to monitor both hate crime and stop and search figures, but this was couched in operational and performance terms with the perceived political dimension of trust and confidence deliberately left as implicit rather than explicit.

Finally, within the Diversity Command Unit structure itself, it was crucial to have a 'fieldwork' side underpinned by sound policy and development expertise keeping abreast of current developments within all six strands of diversity, i.e. race, faith, gender, sexual orientation, disability, and age, and whether it is in the context of employment, training, service delivery or operational policing. With this in mind, the post of force race and diversity advisor was 'converted' into a managerial position to become head of a Policy and Development section wholly dedicated to advising and offering a 'knowledge bank' facility. The total complement of staff being considered for this unit at the time of writing was 18 and there were plans to have a mixture of both uniformed staff and police staff in all sections. The Diversity Command is currently being headed by a chief superintendent, but in 2006 a non-uniformed Director of Diversity was appointed.

Catalyst for change: programmes and practicalities

> In the absence of a fundamental programme of reform that addresses the institutional role of the police and confronts racism in all its guises, it is clear that the agenda outlined in the Macpherson Report and the significant efforts that many in the police service have made will not rewrite the 'tale of failure'. (Rowe 2004: 168–9)

This chapter has attempted to provide some insight into the realities and practical difficulties of promoting the 'fundamental programmes' that Rowe refers to above. A key argument has been that any programmes created to bring about organisational change need to be well considered, sustained and fully resourced for the long term. In the wake of the Macpherson Report's publication in February 1999 the police service was under tremendous pressure to 'do something' and GMP was no exception in that regard. GMP had already been modestly innovative in the early 1990s with the appointment of locally-based community and race relations officers and the creation of a personnel-based Equal Opportunities Unit. Clearly, the former Chief Constable, David Wilmot, wanted to build on those earlier initiatives. Operation Catalyst was the result and it was a classic short-term project to 'get through' the perceived crisis – the 'critical incident'. However, the problem was that the very structure of Operation Catalyst had an inherent long-term logic that would never be properly recognised and/or acknowledged. Those 23 sub-projects were too elaborate and clearly demanded sustainable well-managed resources to complete. Such resources were never likely to be available and instead there was an expectation that the force race advisor, with limited internal credibility among middle management peers, would miraculously 'deliver' what a whole project team had struggled to implement over 18 months.

Thereafter, there would be a two-year period, prior to *The Secret Policeman* episode, when race and diversity issues would be kept alive by a series of events and mini-crises: notably the Oldham riots and the momentum of the government's legislative reform programme around the 2000 Race Relations (Amendment) Act, which would all combine to become *ad hoc* vehicles to keep such issues on the internal agenda.

Without doubt, *The Secret Policeman* television documentary was to become the true 'catalyst for change' within GMP. The BBC documentary clearly had a direct impact on GMP and proved better able to penetrate the organisation's culture than the Lawrence Report. The Stephen Lawrence murder was about the Metropolitan Police in London; the revelations in *The Secret Policeman* were much closer to home and that made a great deal of difference. However, despite the documentary's direct impact on GMP, in the two years that followed the momentum was almost lost and organisational 'memory loss' again began to reappear; but the mistakes of Operation Catalyst were not repeated. Lessons had been learnt and the Respect Programme subsequently became the foundation of a tangible organisational shift within GMP. Thus, the Respect Programme seamlessly became the Diversity Command Unit in April 2005 and the ideological battle over the importance of resources was finally won. The word 'Command' became crucial in giving the new unit credibility and status with a direct managerial connection with chief officers.

But apart from the resources battle, there was a further crucial element to be negotiated and that was the way in which diversity and equality work was to be mainstreamed within the various parts of the organisation – whether that be BCUs or individual HQ departments. While it is important for all public sector organisations and agencies to find suitable means of spreading ownership in this regard, it is particularly important in the context of the police culture where short-termism is rife.

All parts of the public sector have been bombarded with reports and recommendations from a variety of sources, and the police have faced dozens relating to diversity. While most attention is often directed at the ability of organisations to understand the issues and shift their ideological stances, less attention is given to the simple practicalities of 'driving' change and acting appropriately on the wealth of recommendations on offer.

GMP has modestly begun to acknowledge the importance of these practical elements in the process of organisational change. A key start has been to ensure that equalities and diversity have legitimacy and are fully incorporated into the very fabric of police core business. I believe that GMP has finally acknowledged this, and in the context of the prevailing culture of the police, that is significant progress. Thus, in GMP, diversity issues now have status, recognition and are underpinned by permanent resources: middle management can no longer run away from these issues. There is therefore been some 'melting of the ice' and the Greater Manchester Police experience has important lessons to be heeded by practitioners and academics alike.

References

Adlam, R. and Villiers, P. (eds) (2002) *Police Leadership in the 21st Century: Philosophy, Doctrine and Developments*, Winchester: Waterside Press.

Association of Chief Police Officers (2004) *Race Equality Action Plan for the Police Service*, London: ACPO.

Benyon, J. (1986) *A Tale of Failure: Race and Policing*, Policy Papers in Ethnic Relations 3, Centre for Research in Ethnic Relations, Warwick: University of Warwick.

BBC (2003) *The Secret Policeman*, BBC1, 21 October.

Coleman, A. and Gorman, L. (1982) 'Conservatism, Dogmatism and Authoritarianism in British Police Officers', *Sociology*, February.

Commission for Racial Equality (1990) *Racial Discrimination in an Oldham Estate Agency: Report of a Formal Investigation*, London: CRE.

Commission for Racial Equality (1993) *Housing Allocation in Oldham: Report of a Formal Investigation*, London: CRE.

Commission for Racial Equality (2001a) *Statutory Code of Practice on the Duty to Promote Race Equality – Consultation Draft*, London: CRE.

Commission for Racial Equality (2001b) *Statutory Code of Practice on the Duty to Promote Race Equality: A Guide for Public Authorities – Consultation Draft*, London: CRE.

Commission for Racial Equality (2001c) *Ethnic Monitoring: A Guide for Public Authorities – Consultation Draft*, London: CRE.

Commission for Racial Equality (2001d) 'Beyond Rhetoric: CRE Seminar on the Implications of the 2000 Race Relations (Amendment) Act', Manchester, 28 February.

Commission for Racial Equality (2002) *A Place for Us All: Learning from Bradford, Oldham and Burnley*, London: CRE.

Commission for Racial Equality (2004) *Formal Investigation into the Police Service: Interim Report*, London: CRE.

Commission for Racial Equality (2005) *Formal Investigation into the Police Service: Final Report*, London: CRE.

Deakin, N. (1970) *Colour, Citizenship and British Society*, abridged version of the Institute of Race Relations Report, London: Panther Modern Society.

Foot, P. (1965) *Immigration and Race in British Politics*, London: Penguin.

Fryer, P. (1984) *Staying Power: The History of Black People in Britain*, London: Pluto Press.

Gilroy, P. (1982) 'Police and Thieves', in Centre for Contemporary Cultural Studies (1982) *The Empire Strikes Back: Race and Racism in 70s Britain*, London: Hutchinson University Press, pp. 143–82.

Greater Manchester Police (1998) *Customs and Culture Pack*, Manchester: GMP.

Greater Manchester Police (1999) *The Power of Language: A Guide to Inappropriate Language*, Manchester: GMP.

Greater Manchester Police (2002) *The Race Equality Scheme 2002–2005*, Manchester: GMP.

Greater Manchester Police (2004) *Race and Diversity Monitoring Report: A Report to the Community 2003/2004*, Manchester: GMP.

Greater Manchester Police (2005a) *The Race Equality Scheme 2002–2005 (Revised)*, Manchester: GMP.

Greater Manchester Police (2005b) *The Race Equality Scheme Workbook*, Manchester: GMP.

Hall, S. (1978) 'Racism and Reaction', in Commission for Racial Equality (1978) *Five Views of Multi-Racial Britain*, London: CRE, pp. 23–35.

Harding, W. R. (2003) 'Has Greater Manchester Police Subscribed to the Race Equality Agenda Post Stephen Lawrence 1999?' Dissertation submitted for the award of Master of Business Administration, Manchester Metropolitan University Business School, March (unpublished).

Her Majesty's Inspectorate of Constabulary (1997) *Winning the Race: Policing Plural Communities*, London: Home Office.

Her Majesty's Inspectorate of Constabulary (1999) *Winning the Race: Policing Plural Communities – Revisited*, London: Home Office.

Her Majesty's Inspectorate of Constabulary (2000) *Winning the Race: Embracing Diversity*, London: Home Office.

Her Majesty's Inspectorate of Constabulary (2003a) *BCU Inspection of South Manchester*, London: Home Office, May.

Her Majesty's Inspectorate of Constabulary (2003b) *Inspection of the Greater Manchester Police*, London: Home Office, June.

Her Majesty's Inspectorate of Constabulary (2003c) *Diversity Matters*, London: Home Office.

Hiro, D. (1973) *Black British, White British*, London: Monthly Review Press.

Holland, B. (1995) 'Kicking Racism out of Football: An Assessment of Racial Harassment in and Around Football Grounds', *New Community*, 21 (4): 567–86.

Holland, B. (1997) 'Racial Harassment in and around Football Grounds: The Implications for Policing and Crowd Management' Foundation Course Seminar in Stadium Management, School of Social and International Studies, University of Sunderland.

Holland, B. (1999) 'Across the Lines: Racial Harassment in and Around Football Grounds', PhD Thesis, Bradford: University of Bradford.

Holland, B. (2001a) The Implication of the Race Relations (Amendment) Act 2000: Briefings to Managers and Commanders.

Holland, B. (2001b) 'New Act – New Challenges: The New Race Relations Amendment Act', *Brief*, Greater Manchester Police Newspaper, March.

Holland, B. (2001c) *Oldham in Context: Submission to the Ritchie Inquiry*, Manchester: Greater Manchester Police.

Holland, B. (2001d) *Diversity Training: Future Scope, Development and Direction*, discussion paper, Manchester: GMP.

Holland, B. (2001e) 'Oldham: Grasping the Challenges', *Brief*, Greater Manchester Police Newspaper.

Holland, B. (2002a) 'Future Structure of the Policy Advisory Committee on Race Issues: Striving for Accountability and Effectiveness', Paper to PAC Meeting, Greater Manchester Police, 7 March.

Holland, B. (2002b) 'Policing Oldham', *Connections*, Spring: 12–13.

Holland, B. (2003) 'The Future of Race and Diversity work in GMP: A Discussion Paper', Manchester: GMP.

Holland, B. (2004) 'Racists Will Join the Police!' paper to Infolog Conference, 'Why Do Racists Join the Police – Can We Stop Them?', 22 January London.

Holland, B. (2005a) 'RES means Respect, Responsibility and Results', Presentation to GMP BCU Commanders and Departmental Heads, Race Equality Scheme Briefing Series, December 2004 to March 2005, Greater Manchester Police.

Holland, B. (2005b) 'Leading Cultural Change: Breaking the Ice in the Heart of the Police Service,' paper to Infolog Conference, Developing Good Practice, London, 6 April.

Home Office (2001) *Race Relations (Amendment) Act 2000: New Laws for a Successful Multi-Racial Britain*, London: Home Office.

Hunte, J. A. (1965) *Nigger Hunting in England?*, London: West Indian Standing Conference.

Institute of Race Relations (IRR) (1979) *Police Against Black People: Evidence Submitted to the Royal Commission on Criminal Procedure*, Race and Class Pamphlet No. 6, London: Institute of Race Relations.

Jefferson, T. and Walker, M. (1993) 'Attitudes to the Police of Ethnic Minorities in a Provincial City,' *British Journal of Criminology*, 33 (2): 251–66.

Lambert, J. (1970) *Crime, Police and Race Relations*, London: Oxford University Press.

Lea, J. (1986) 'Police Racism: Some Theories and their Policy Implications', in R. Mathews and J. Young (eds) *Confronting Crime*, London: Sage.

Macpherson, Sir W. (1999) *The Stephen Lawrence Inquiry: Report of an Inquiry by Sir William Macpherson of Cluny*, CM 4262–1, London: HMSO.

McLaughlin, E. and Cashmore, E. (eds) (1991) *Out of Order: The Policing of Black People*, London: Routledge.

McNaney, P. (2001) 'Public Sector Experience from Northern Ireland', presentation to CRE Seminar, *Beyond Rhetoric*, 28 February, Manchester.

Morris, W. (2004) *The Case for Change: People in the Metropolitan Police Service*, London: Metropolitan Police Authority.

Reiner, R. (2000) *The Politics of the Police*, 3rd edn, Oxford: Oxford University Press.

Ritchie, D. (2001) *One Oldham, One Future: The Oldham Independent Review Panel Report*, Manchester: Government Office North West.

Rowe, M. (2004) *Policing, Race and Racism*, Cullompton: Willan Publishing.

Sanders, A. and Young, R. (2000) *Criminal Justice*, 2nd edn, London: Butterworth.

Scarman, Lord (1981) The *Brixton Disorders: 10–12 April 1981 – Report of an Inquiry by the Rt. Hon Lord Scarman OBE*, November 1981, Cmnd 8427, London: HMSO.

Waddington, P. A. J. (1999a) 'Police Canteen Sub-culture: An Appreciation', *British Journal of Criminology*, 39(2): 287–309.

Webster, C. (2001a) 'Young People, Racism and Racist Violence: Racialising Space and Temporising Race', paper to British Sociological Association Conference, Manchester Metropolitan University.

Webster, C. (2001b) 'Race, Space and Fear: Imagined Geographies of Racist Violence', paper to workshop, The Geography and Politics of Fear, University of London Union.

Index

'Undercover Copper' (documentary)
xvi–xvii
Unit Beat System 9
unwitting racism
in Lawrence Report 70, 71, 78,
84, 132
in Scarman Report 69
urban disturbances 2001 114, 119

victims 153–5
Virdi, Gurpal 24–5, 33

Waddington, P.A.J. xxi
Waldron, John 6–7, 10
Walker, Anthony xiii, 138
Walker, C. 116, 117
Wells, Holly 159

Werbner, P. 113
West Indian Standing Conference
(WISC) 10
West Indies Federation 8
'whiteness' 38
Whitfield, James xvii
Wildavsky, A. 153
Wilmot, David 27–8, 165–6, 169–70,
172–3
Wilson, Harold 10
Winning the Race – Revisited (HMIC)
170
Wolfendale, Clive 30
Working Party on Police Training in
Race Relations 13

Yorkshire Ripper case 155–9
Young, J. 142